Reflections on Literature for Children

Reflections on Literature for Children

Edited by
Francelia Butler *and* Richard Rotert

With a foreword by
Leland B. Jacobs

Library Professional Publications
1984

Copyright 1984 Francelia Butler. All rights reserved.
First published 1984 as a Library Professional Publication,
an imprint of The Shoe String Press, Inc., Hamden,
Connecticut 06514
Printed in the United States of America

Library of Congress Cataloging in Publication Data

The paper in this book meets the guidelines for permanence and
durability of the Committee on Production Guidelines
for Book Longevity of the Council on Library Resources.

Library of Congress Cataloging in Publication Data
Main entry under title:

Reflections on literature for children.

"Compiled of selections from various volumes of the
Children's literature annual"—
Includes index.
1.   Children's literature—History and criticism—
Addresses, essays, lectures. I. Butler, Francelia,
1913– . II. Rotert, Richard, 1948– .
PN1009.AIR43   1984   809'.89282   84–12554
ISBN 0-208-02054-3 (alk. paper) (cloth edition)
ISBN 0-208-02075-6 (alk. paper) (paperback edition)

This book is dedicated to
"Robbie"
Robert Douglas Wright
with best wishes.

RR

Contents

Foreword by   *Leland B. Jacobs*   ix
Acknowledgments   xiii
Introduction   1

A NOTE ON STORY...
AND A FEW STORIES FOR THE VERY YOUNG

1. A Note on Story   *James Hillman*   7
2. Some Remarks on Raggedy Ann and
   Johnny Gruelle   *Martin Williams*   11
3. Child Reading and Man Reading:
   Oz, Babar and Pooh   *Roger Sale*   19
4. Back to Pooh Corner   *Alison Lurie*   32
5. Prickles under the Frock:
   The Art of Beatrix Potter   *Seth Sicroff*   39

SOME MEANINGS IN CHILDREN'S LITERATURE

6. Notes on the Waist-High Culture   *John Seelye*   46
7. On Writing for Children   *Isaac Bashevis Singer*   51
8. On Not Writing for Children   *P. L. Travers*   58
9. Webs of Concern: *The Little Prince*
   and *Charlotte's Web*   *Laurence Gagnon*   66
10. Death in Children's Literature   *Francelia Butler*   72

POETRY CAN SAY IT BEST

11. The Evolution of the Pied Piper   *Bernard Queenan*   92
12. The Sane, the Mad, the Good, the Bad: T. S. Eliot's
    Old Possum's Book of Practical Cats   *Marion C. Hodge*   99
13. "Over the Garden Wall/I Let the Baby Fall":
    The Poetry of Rope-Skipping   *Francelia Butler*   113
14. Breaking Chains: Brother Blue, Storyteller   *John Cech*   125

SOME EXTRAORDINARY WRITERS
AND THEIR CHARACTERS

15. Aesop as Litmus: The Acid Test of
    Children's Literature   *Robert G. Miner, Jr.*   148
16. Pinocchio: Archetype of
    the Motherless Child   *James W. Heisig*   155
17. An Unpublished Children's Story
    by George MacDonald   *Glenn Edward Sadler*   171
18. Mr. Ruskin and Miss Greenaway   *Michael Patrick Hearn*   182
19. Reflections on *Little Women*   *Anne Hollander*   191
20. Tradition and the Talent of
    Frances Hodgson Burnett: *Little Lord Fauntleroy*,
    A Little Princess and *The Secret Garden*   *Phyllis Bixler Koppes*   201
21. The Sea Dream: *Peter Pan* and
    Treasure Island   *Kathleen Blake*   215
22. E. Nesbit's Well Hall, 1915-1921:
    A Memoir   *Joan Evans de Alonso*   229
23. An Epic in Arcadia: The Pastoral World of
    The Wind in the Willows   *Geraldine D. Poss*   237
24. Narnia: The Author, the Critics,
    and the Tale   *Walter Hooper*   247
25. Maurice Sendak and the
    Blakean Vision of Childhood   *Jennifer R. Waller*   260
26. Harriet the Spy:
    Milestone, Masterpiece?   *Virginia L. Wolf*   269

Index   276

Foreword

How far the study of literature for children has come since the publication of *Children's Literature* (Rand McNally and Company) by Charles Madison Curry and Erle Elsworth Clippinger in 1920! Even a cursory examination of the contents of this book leads one to note how limited was the quantity of books of quality for children available in the English language at that time; how narrow was the scope of the prose fiction and poetry; how few picture story books, biographies, and works of realistic fiction for older children there were to recommend; and how meager was the criticism of children's literature that Curry and Clippinger were able to cite.

This is not to say that there were no superior writings for children in the early part of the twentieth century. Fairy tales, myths, and legends were in ample supply. And such names as Louisa May Alcott, L. Leslie Brooke, Mary Mapes Dodge, Eugene Field, Kate Greenaway, Howard Pyle, Frances Hodgson Burnett, Kate Douglas Wiggin, Ernest Thompson Seton, E. Nesbit, Jules Verne, and Frank R. Stockton were among the recognizable writers of the times. Too, some substance in criticism could be noted in Walter Barnes's *Types of Children's Literature*, Orton Lowe's *Literature for Children*, and Anne Carroll Moore's *Roads to Childhood*.

From such roots there has been a rather steady development in the scholarly look into literature for children. Not only has the literature itself blossomed; it is also more widely recognized that what was once thought to be a separate "juvenile" literature is now seen as an integral part of what is known as the field of literature, which includes what is for adults as well as for boys and girls. This means that Peter Rabbit, Homer Price, Alice, and Long John Silver, for example, live in the same domain as David Copperfield, Madame Bovary, and Captain Ahab. Such thinking has undoubtedly been a factor in leading both to broader reviewing of children's books and to a more substantial criticism of literature for children.

That more substantial critical consideration of children's books was given insightful underpinnings by Anne Carroll Moore in *The Three Owls* (The Macmillan Company), and *My Roads to Childhood* (Doubleday, Doran and Company, Inc.); by Emelyn Gardner and Eloise Ramsey in *A Handbook of Children's Literature* (Scott, Foresman and Co.) in 1927; and by Annie E. Moore in *Literature Old and New for Children* (Houghton Mifflin Company), published in 1934.

In *A Handbook of Children's Literature*, Gardner and Ramsey, like Anne Carroll Moore, go well beyond the anthology approach used by Curry and Clippinger. While not foregoing a critical consideration of the traditional literature available from the past, these writers recognized that what was currently being written for children was not merely ephemeral. It deserved to be viewed as a new literature that could "open vistas to children," that is not "commonplace," and as such worthy of critical commentary. They point to the writings of Lewis Carroll, Rudyard Kipling, Mark Twain, Walter De La Mare, A. A. Milne, and Charles J. Finger to make their point. While the number of books Gardner and Ramsey would recommend highly seems quite limited compared with what is available today, one does note a movement toward a more extensive modern literature than Curry and Clippinger were able to report.

In *Literature Old and New for Children*, Annie Moore takes a critical stance, as do Gardner and Ramsey and Anne Carroll Moore. Her discussion of the various genres centers on a critical assessment of what she finds of import in what was available for children at the time of her writing. She also noted enthusiastically that in a relatively short period of time there had been a remarkable growth in the availability of books for children designed "wholly for pleasure reading," and that there was greater selectivity in the collecting and editing of the traditional literature. Moore believed firmly that a very significant new literature for children was in the making, including some writings that were "classics to be."

In 1947 May Hill Arbuthnot's *Children and Books* (Scott, Foresman and Company) made its appearance, and once again the criticism of literature for children was advanced. By the time Arbuthnot's book was published, the number of books for the young was enormous. The matter of what to discuss had become a prodigious task, calling for critical insights thought less urgent in previous times. Arbuthnot also had studies in psychological and other social sciences as well as historical and literary scholarship on which to draw that had been only recently available. By using such scholarly aids, Arbuthnot set a fresh direction for a substantial consideration of various genres for her contemporaries and even for those who today wrestle with critical thinking about children's literature.

In 1953 *A Critical History of Children's Literature* (The Macmillan Company) was published. In it its writer—Cornelia Meigs, Anne Eaton, Elizabeth Nesbett, and Ruth Hill Viguers—traced the literary offerings available to children from the beginnings of recorded time to the time of publication, with critical commentary as to what has endured and why. They also observed how time and cultural circumstances had affected the development of a literature for children. As these authors gave consideration to their own times, these writers, like Arbuthnot, recognized the immense surge in the publication of literature for children and attempted to delineate "threads of influence" and thrusts toward what was just emerging in the full flowering of a literature for girls and boys.

Now that it is recognized that writings for children truly are literature and that there is extensive, significant literature for children, children's books are being widely reviewed and scholarly criticism is growing markedly. Such criticism is being significantly aided by the work of such eminent scholars as Paul Hazard, Suzanne Langer, Louise Rosenblatt, Marjorie Fischer, Isabelle Jan, and Northrop Frye, whose thinking affects the critical judgments made by those currently writing about children's literature.

This volume of essays is indicative of the dimensions and directions criticism in the field of children's literature is taking today. Some of these essays critically put traditional literature into historical perspective. Some indicate the staying power of individual writers or individual works. Some cast a critical eye on the literary dimensions of popular culture. Some explore the creation of literature from the writer's viewpoint. But all the writers of these essays make clear that, as critics, they respect what is written for children. All these writers' explorations of aspects of children's literature makes their unique contributions to a serious body of criticism, so necessary if the field is to be as productive in aesthetic inventiveness, experimentation, variation, creation, enrichment, and pleasure as children deserve.

Leland B. Jacobs
Professor Emeritus of Education
Teachers College, Columbia University

Acknowledgments

This text has been compiled of selections from various volumes of the *Children's Literature* annual. We acknowledge with appreciation the permissions that have been granted by individuals and institutions to use copyrighted or otherwise controlled materials.

The Children's Literature Foundation for the following articles from Volume VII: "The Evolution of the Pied Piper" by Bernard Queenan; "The Sane, the Mad, the Good, the Bad: T.S. Eliot's *Old Possum's Book of Practical Cats*" by M. C. Hodge, Jr.; "Tradition and the Individual Talent of Frances Hodgson Burnett: A Generic Analysis of *Little Lord Fauntleroy*, *A Little Princess*, and *The Secret Garden*" by Phyllis Bixler Koppes.

Harvard University for "The Little Girl that Had No Tongue" by George MacDonald, by permission of the Houghton Library, published as 'The Little Girl that Had No Tongue': An Unpublished Short Story by George MacDonald" by Glenn Sadler from Volume II.

Yale University Press for the following articles from Volume IX: "Reflections on Little Women" by Anne Hollander; "Breaking Chains: Brother Blue, Storyteller" by John Cech; "Notes on the Waist-High Culture" by John Seelye.

The New York Times Company © 1973, reprinted by permission " 'Over the Garden Wall/I Let the Baby Fall': The Poetry of Rope-Skipping" by Francelia Butler from Volume III.

Michael Patrick Hearn © 1980 for "Mr. Ruskin and Miss Greenaway" from Volume VIII.

P. L. Travers © 1975 for "On Not Writing for Children" from Volume IV.

Karen Wright Rohr for photographs of Brother Blue used in this book.

The following selections appeared originally in the first six volumes, published by Temple University Press.

de Alonso, Joan Evans. "E. Nesbit's Well Hall, 1915–1921: A Memoir" Volume III.

Blake, Kathleen. "The Sea-Dream: Peter Pan and Treasure Island" Volume VI.

Butler, Francelia. "Death in Children's Literature" Volume I.

Gagnon, Laurence. "Webs of Concern: Heidegger, The Little Prince, and Charlotte's Web" Volume II.

Heisig, Father James. "Pinocchio: Archetype of the Motherless Child" Volume III.

Hillman, James. "A Note on Story" Volume III.

Hooper, Father Walter. "Narnia: The Author, the Critics, and the Tale" Volume III.

Lurie, Alison. "Back to Pooh Corner" Volume II.

Miner, Robert G., Jr. "Aesop as Litmus: The Acid Test of Children's Literature" Volume I.

Poss, Geraldine D. "An Epic in Arcadia: The Pastoral World of The Wind in the Willows" Volume IV.

Sale, Roger. "Child Reading and Man Reading: Oz, Babar, and Pooh" Volume I.

Sicroff, Seth. "Prickles under the Frock" Volume II.

Singer, Isaac Bashevis. "Isaac Bashevis Singer on Writing for Children" Volume VI.

Waller, Jennifer R. "Maurice Sendak and the Blakean Vision of Childhood" Volume IV.

Williams, Martin. "Some Remarks on Raggedy Ann and Johnny Gruelle" Volume III.

Wolf, Virginia L. "Harriet the Spy: Milestone, Masterpiece?" Volume IV.

Introduction

To explore in detail all forms of the field of children's literature in one volume would be virtually impossible. One must use a billy goat approach—and leap from peak to peak. Fortunately, there are some unifying principles, one the nature of Story itself: the telling rather than the content is of first importance to children. For this reason, this collection of reflections on children's literature begins with an essay by James Hillman, who gave the Terry lectures at Yale, following such notables as Dewey, Fromm, and Jung himself.

All of the writers included here have shown in one way or another a commitment to stories and books for children. They have much to say, and insights to share with parents, librarians, teachers, and students. The literature they write about comes from many periods and places, from ancient to contemporary times.

The essays are clustered in four groups. In the first, Raggedy Ann is taken up by one of her fans, Martin Williams, head of Jazz and Popular Culture at the Smithsonian Institution. Critic Roger Sale muses on the role of some beloved children's book characters as they influence the child who becomes father to the man. Such essays underscore the growing interest in "baby" literature such as that created by May Cutler of Tundra Books in Montreal. As many keen observers have told us over many years, the joy of books, of handling them and listening to voices and to words that soon become stories—these responses can be developed from birth.

The second group of reflections, on meaning, begins with the thoughts of John Seelye and continues with the concepts and words of Isaac Bashevis Singer, the Nobel prizewinning author who has written many beautiful stories for children. P. L. Travers, author of *Mary Poppins*, asserts whimsically that she does not write for children, and Laurence Gagnon applies

Heidegerrian philosophy to his analysis of *The Little Prince* and *Charlotte's Web*.

Poetry is next considered. Bernard Queenan researched Browning's *Pied Piper* in Hamelin in order to produce an animated film of the poem, narrated by Peter Ustinov, and his essay here is based on his research. T. S. Eliot's cats—which have also frolicked in a prizewinning Broadway musical—are examined by Marion Hodge, Jr. In "Breaking Chains," John Cech makes the black soul chants and the magic of Dr. Hugh Morgan Hill (Brother Blue) come alive.

A large group of pieces in our collection are about the works of some extraordinary writers for children: those of Aesop, black ambassador from Lydia to Greece; George MacDonald, literary father of Carroll, C. S. Lewis and J. R. R. Tolkien; the extraordinary author-editor Frances Hodgson Burnett; playwright Scotsman James Barrie; and poet/blood-and-thunder-adventure writer, Robert Louis Stevenson. E. Nesbit's Well Hall is visited, and other characters explored include those in Kenneth Grahame's *Wind in the Willows*, Lewis's Narnia series and Sendak's pictured dream worlds, Alcott's *Little Women* and *Harriet the Spy*.

The nature of that most famous of all puppets, Pinocchio, examined by the Jungian, Father James W. Heisig. The role of puppets in children's literature is more extensive than is immediately apparent. They are closely related to the ancient art of storytelling up to the present use of successive puppet figures in animated cartoons. Such figures are still used in many parts of the world, as for instance in the all-night shadow plays in Indonesia and the puppet shows of Turkey and Greece. Translated to cardboard, they are used by Japanese storytellers who flash successive cards to tell the story of Kintaro (Strong Boy) or Momotaro (Peach Boy). On silk or canvas, Ethiopians use them to tell the story of Solomon and the Queen of Sheba. In India, storytellers display huge tapestries with rows of figures that make more vivid their narration of the adventures of the Hindu gods. They bring to mind some of Sendak's picture books influenced by comic illustrator Windsor McCay, creator of *Little Nemo*.

For those who wish to use this book as a textbook, an index is provided. A plan of study may be based on selections from the various groupings. For instance, *Raggedy Ann* and *Winnie-the-Pooh* would be followed by the study of *The Little Prince* and *Charlotte's Web*. Then Browning's *The Pied Piper* and T. S. Eliot's cats would be fun to listen to and think about. To add to the reading of the unpublished tale here reproduced from the research of Glenn Sadler, who has devoted a scholarly lifetime to the study of MacDonald, one of MacDonald's other books might be read: *At the Back of the North Wind*, *The Golden Key*, or *The Princess and the Goblin*. The treatment of death in children's literature could be explored in connection with these works. The social implications of Ruskin's *King of the Golden River* would make an interesting base for class discussion, which could be extended through a study of E. Nesbit's *Phoenix and the Carpet* or *The Railway Children*. A class or an individual could study the psychological implications of *The Secret Garden* or *Peter Pan*. Excellent films of many of these books are available, and an analysis of film techniques—what must be cut or added to make a good film from a book—would help students to prepare to write their own scenarios.* Language in stories should be studied, too, as many of the older stories have archaic constructions and even words that are difficult for children to understand.

Fables or stories can be converted into live play or puppet presentations, or portions of them can be videotaped with the help of library media specialists. New collections of local folklore can be made.

Above all, reading these essays will encourage many to return to or to read for the first time, perhaps, the stories upon which they are based. As the riches of children's literature unfold, librarians, teachers, and parents will find new resources to share with children.

---

*See *200 Selected Film Classics for Children of All Ages*. Springfield, ILL.: Charles C. Thomas, Publishers, 1984, for descriptions and addresses of distributors.

A Note on Story . . . and a Few Stories For the Very Young

1

A Note on Story

JAMES HILLMAN

From my perspective as depth psychologist, I see that those who have a connection with story are in better shape and have a better prognosis than those to whom story must be introduced. This is a large statement and I would like to take it apart in several ways. But I do not want to diminish its apodictic claim: to have "story-awareness" is *per se* psychologically therapeutic. It is good for the soul.

1) To have had story of any sort in childhood—and here I mean oral story, those told or read (for reading has an oral aspect even if one reads to oneself) rather than watching story on screen—puts a person into a basic recognition of and familiarity with the legitimate reality of story *per se*. It is given with life, with speech and communication, and not something later that comes with learning and literature. Coming early with life, it is already a perspective to life. One integrates life as story because one has stories in the back of the mind (unconscious) as containers for organizing events into meaningful experiences. The stories are means of telling oneself into events that might not otherwise make psychological sense at all. (Economic, scientific, and historical explanations are sorts of "stories" that often fail to give the soul the kind of imaginative meaning it seeks for understanding its psychological life.)

2) Having had story built in with childhood, a person is usually in better relations with the pathologized material of obscene, grotesque, or cruel images which appear spontaneously in dream and fantasy. Those who hold to the rationalist and associationist theory of mind, who put reason against and superior to imagination, argue that if we did not put in such grim tales in early impressionable years, we would have less pathology and more rationality in later years. My practice shows me rather that the more attuned and experienced is the imaginative side of personality

the less threatening the irrational, the less necessity for repression, and therefore the less actual pathology acted out in literal, daily events. In other words, through story the symbolic quality of pathological images and themes finds a place, so that these images and themes are less likely to be viewed naturalistically, with clinical literalism, as signs of sickness. These images find places in story as legitimate. They *belong* to myths, legends, and fairy tales where, just as in dreams, all sorts of peculiar figures and twisted behaviors appear. After all, "The Greatest Story Ever Told," as some are fond of calling Easter, is replete with gruesome imagery in great pathologized detail.

3) Story-awareness provides a better way than clinical-awareness for coming to terms with one's own case history. Case history too, as I have pointed out in *The Myth of Analysis* (Northwestern Univ. Press) and in *Suicide and the Soul* (Harper's Colophon), is a fictional form written up by thousands of hands in thousands of clinics and consulting rooms, stored away in archives and rarely published. This fictional form called "case history" follows the genre of social realism; it believes in facts and events, and takes all tales told with excessive literalism. In deep analysis, the analyst and the patient together re-write the case history into a new story, creating the "fiction" in the collaborative work of the analysis. Some of the healing that goes on, maybe even the essence of it, is this collaborative fiction, this putting all the chaotic and traumatic events of a life into a new story. Jung said that patients need "healing fictions," but we have trouble coming to this perspective unless there is already a predilection for story-awareness.

4) Jungian therapy, at least as I practice it, brings about an awareness that fantasy is the dominant force in a life. One learns in therapy that fantasy is a creative activity which is continually telling a person into now this story, now that one. When we examine these fantasies we discover that they reflect the great impersonal themes of mankind as represented in tragedy, epic, folktale, legend, and myth. Fantasy in our view is the attempt of the psyche itself to re-mythologize consciousness; we try to further this activity by encouraging familiarity with myth and folktale. Soul-making goes hand in hand with deliteralizing consciousness and restoring its connection to mythic and metaphorical thought patterns. Rather than interpret the stories into concepts and rational explanations, we prefer to see conceptual explanations as secondary elaborations upon basic stories which are containers and givers of vitality. As Owen Barfield and Norman Brown have written: "Literalism is the enemy." I would add: "Literalism is sickness." Whenever we are caught in a literal view, a literal belief, a literal statement, we have lost the imaginative metaphorical perspective to ourselves and our world. Story is prophylactic in that it presents itself

always as "once upon a time," as an "as if," "make-believe" reality. It is the only mode of accounting or telling about that does not posit itself as real, true, factual, revealed, i.e. literal.

5) This brings us to the question of content. Which stories need to be told? Here I am a classic, holding for the old, the traditional, the ones of our own culture: Greek, Roman, Celtic, and Nordic myths; the Bible; legends and folk-tales. And these with the least modern marketing (updating, cleaning up, editing, etc.), i.e. with the least interference by contemporary rationalism which is subject to the very narrowing of consciousness which the stories themselves would expand. Even if we be not Celtic or Nordic or Greek in ancestry, these collections are the fundamentals of our Western culture and work in our psyches whether we like it or not. We may consider them distorted in their pro-Aryan or pro-male or pro-warrior slant, but unless we understand that these tales depict the basic motifs of the Western psyche, we remain unaware of the basic motives in our psychological dynamics. Our ego psychology still resounds with the motif and motivation of the hero, just as much psychology of what we call "the feminine" today reflects the patterns of the goddesses and nymphs in Greek myth. These basic tales channel fantasy. Platonists long ago and Jung more recently pointed out the therapeutic value of the great myths for bringing order to the chaotic, fragmented aspect of fantasy. The main body of biblical and classical tales direct fantasy into organized, deeply life-giving psychological patterns; these stories present the archetypal modes of experiencing.

6) I think children need less convincing of the importance of story than do adults. To be adult has come to mean to be adulterated with rationalist explanations, and to shun such childishness as we find in fairy stories. I have tried to show in detail how adult and child have come to be set against each other: childhood tends to mean wonder, imagination, creative spontaneity, while adulthood, the loss of these perspectives ("Abandoning the Child," *Eranos Jahrbuch*, 40 ([1971]). So the first task, as I see it, is restorying the adult—the teacher and the parent and the grandparent—in order to restore the imagination to a primary place in consciousness in each of us, regardless of age.

I have come at this from a psychological viewpoint, partly because I wish to remove story from its too close association with both education and literature—something taught and something studied. My interest in story is as something lived in and lived through, a way in which the soul finds itself in life.[1]

Note

1. Some short works relevant for the point of view presented in this note: J. Hillman, "'Pathologizing' and 'Personifying'" (Yale University Terry Lectures, 1972), in *Art International*, 17, nos. 6 and 8 (Summer and Oct., 1973); M.L. von Franz, *Creation Myths* (Zurich: Spring Publications, 1972) and J. Hillman, *Pan and the Nightmare* (Zurich: Spring Publications, 1973).

2

Some Remarks on
Raggedy Ann and Johnny Gruelle

MARTIN WILLIAMS

Raggedy Ann is found everywhere: in card shops, doll shops, dime stores, bookstores. There are some twenty titles from the original Raggedy Ann series in print. Yet, if you look in any standard reference volume, you will find no entry on her or her author, Johnny Gruelle, dead since 1938. He was not even in *Who's Who*.

Johnny Gruelle was a hack. Or, to put it more politely, he was a prolific author and illustrator. He turned out a mound of children's stories, illustrated books, comic strips, drawings. He even illustrated an ambitious edition of the Grimm Brothers, very handsome stuff considering it was done by a self-taught illustrator.

Now if a man is that prolific, if he writes so many books in a series, and other material as well, one is apt to view his work with suspicion. His writing couldn't be very good if there's that much of it. And generally speaking, much of Gruelle's writing isn't good. But the interesting thing to me is that the best of Gruelle is very good indeed, and unique, as far as I know, in children's literature.

Probably I do not need to say that some hacks write well on occasion. Robert Greene, the Elizabethan playwright, might be considered a hack, but he is still read, and some of his plays are very good. Daniel Defoe is the standard example of a hack whose best work is still read. Here in America, we have the example of another children's author, the man who wrote *The Wizard of Oz*. L. Frank Baum wrote an incredible amount of material, under various pseudonyms, some male and some female, in addition to some fourteen books about Oz. We are only beginning to acknowledge that Baum was a very good writer and that some of his books are really excellent—say, *The Patchwork Girl of Oz*, or *Tik Tok of Oz*, or even better, a non-Oz book called *Queen Zixi of Ix*, which I sometimes think is the best American children's story ever written.

The problem with people who are prolific is that one has to read all in order to find the good works. One has to sift, examine, and that's not necessarily easy. I don't mean to say that I've done something terribly hard in reading Gruelle, but I have read a great deal of him, including all the Raggedy Ann books, and I have come to certain conclusions about him.

Biographically, from what I can discover from talking to a few people, and from looking Gruelle up in the few places where one can look him up, this very talented man was a born innocent. It seems that he went through most of his life, almost until the end, without a moral problem to his name. He was kind to everybody simply because it didn't occur to him to be any other way. He was never tempted to be rude or mean. And it is that kind of moral innocence which is both the virtue and the limitation of his writing.

Johnny Gruelle was born in Arcalo, Illinois, in 1880, but he was raised in Indianapolis. His father, Richard B. Gruelle, was a self-taught painter, well-known in the Middlewest for his landscapes. I think the American Middlewest, its ways, and its language are very much present in the Raggedy Ann books, a reflection of the attitudes and speech patterns of people of that time.

Gruelle and his brother Justin and sister Prudence apparently had healthy, somewhat casual upbringings. They were all brought up with the idea of the importance of art with a little "a," rather than of a refined, somewhat snobbish thing called Art, with a capital "A." If one drew and painted, one produced art—whether it was editorial cartoons, comic strips, portraits of the wealthy or landscapes or whatever. Quality wasn't what made it art or not art. One did his best and didn't worry about Art.

While still in his late teens, Johnny Gruelle had become the cartoonist on *The Indianapolis Star*, and then a few years later, on *The Cleveland Press*. He did every kind of drawing that a newspaper might require of a staff cartoonist. He drew weather cartoons, political cartoons, and he illustrated stories for which there weren't photographs. He got through his work so fast and so well that he had time on his hands. He used that time writing and illustrating original children's tales. It turned out that the editor liked these, so he published them in the paper too.

Then in 1910, Johnny went to visit his father, who had by then moved to Norwalk, Connecticut. While he was there, the New York paper which was then called the *Herald* held a contest to see who could come up with the best idea for a Sunday comic feature. Johnny Gruelle entered the contest twice, under two different names, and he won the first prize and the second prize. The first prize went to the adventures of an imaginary little elf named Mr. Twee Deedle, which continued for several years in the *Tribune* and the *Herald Tribune*, and was syndicated to other papers as well.

Johnny, married by then, had moved his family up to a town in Connecticut near Norwalk, called Silvermine, an artists' colony. He began turning out an incredible quantity of material for everything from *Physical Culture* magazine to joke magazines like *Judge*, and he wrote and illustrated children's stories for *Good Housekeeping*, and *Woman's World*.

Gruelle was a not uncommon combination of laziness and industry. Behind a man like that there is often a driving woman. Gruelle's wife Myrtle was apparently just that. She used to stop him if he felt like going fishing or like playing with the neighborhood children. She might drag him in to his studio and sit him down and say, "You've got some drawing to finish for *Life* magazine." And while he drew—this man-child Johnny Gruelle—she would sit and read him fairy tales.

The Gruelles had a daughter named Marcella whom they loved much. (At that point they had no other children; there were subsequently two sons, Worth and John Junior). Marcella died unexpectedly when she was fourteen years old. She had had a rag doll that had belonged to Prudence, her aunt. It was called Raggedy Ann, and in memory of Marcella, Gruelle wrote and illustrated a series of stories about the doll, and Marcella's other dolls, little short tales of imaginary about-the-house adventures. These became *Raggedy Ann Stories*, published in 1914. They were so popular that they were followed by sequels. Indeed, there was a sequel almost every year, and sometimes two a year, until 1937, the year before Gruelle died.

In the meantime, of course, the popularity of the Raggedy Ann books had meant other uses of the character. In the mid-1930's, for instance, Gruelle used to do a single newspaper panel drawing each day for a small distributing syndicate. Daily, there was a little drawing of Raggedy Ann with a verse, or a bit of advice, always very cheerful and happy and sun-shiny, as the stories usually are. Also in the '30's, partly for reasons of health and perhaps other reasons that I'm not quite sure of yet, Gruelle moved his family to Miami. There this adult innocent met his first real temptations and, it seems, succumbed to them. People in Silvermine tell me that when he would return north for a visit, he would be overweight, bloated, puffy-eyed, and talking away about the fact that he was busy every afternoon attending cocktail parties. Within a few years, Gruelle was dead. There was very little attention paid to his death, although his books were still selling then, as they still are now.

The first group of *Raggedy Ann Stories* is based on the idea, not a new one, that dolls have a secret life. They come to life when people are asleep or when people go away on a trip. They can walk and talk and have all kinds of adventures on their own. The dolls find a puppy and adopt it and have to make arrangements for the puppy when "the real-for-sure folks," as Gruelle calls them return. Or, Raggedy Ann falls in a bucket of paint and has to be scraped and washed and have another face painted on. There one gets a double perspective of the way the real people are thinking about all this—the way Marcella particularly is thinking about it—and the way Raggedy Ann (without ever admitting it to the real people, of course) is thinking about it herself.

These first stories were followed almost immediately by a collection of *Raggedy Andy Stories*. Raggedy Andy is of course the brother doll to Raggedy Ann. Some of these tales, I think, are charming. One of them tells how all the dolls sneak down into the kitchen one evening while the real-for-sure people are away and have a wild taffy pull. There's a last minute escape, when the dolls get everything cleaned up and everything exactly the way it was. Before the adults come through the front door, they all scatter up to the nursery and back into bed and get back in the same position as they were when they had been left.

Many of the stories in these early books are trivial. But children often like them. They like the premise of the secret life of the dolls and they don't mind the repetitiousness. There are other, later, collections of short Raggedy Ann tales. One is called *Marcella Stories*, and another is called *Beloved Belindy*. Now, Beloved Belindy was a black "Mammy" doll of a kind that would never be written about now. She's just a nice matriarchal being in the midst of the other dolls, who happens to be black. I do think that some of the black servants in Gruelle's books are patronized but I don't think Belindy was. Anyway, *Beloved Belindy* was the fourth collection of short domestic tales about the dolls.

To go back a little bit, however, the third Raggedy Ann book, meanwhile, had been of a different sort. It is not a collection of short stories but a long tale called *Raggedy Ann and Andy and the Camel with the Wrinkled Knees*. (Long titles, and long phrases like that, charmed Johnny Gruelle, and he used them all the time.) In this story, Gruelle took us into his own version of fairyland, which he called the Deep Deep Woods, a wooded area behind Marcella's backyard.

Gruelle's Deep Deep Woods is a very American enchanted place, by which I mean it is a singular combination of European elements and the products of his own very American imagination. There are witches but they aren't really very evil; unkind maybe, but that's the worst you could say about them. And there are wizards and magicians, some of whom are a little mean, and put spells on you but they aren't really very bad spells. And sometimes they hide people away. But that's about it.

Then there are princesses and princes: they are all handsome or beautiful and sometimes they're disguised as other people or other things, and reveal themselves in the end. And there are kings, some of whom are grouches of course. There are little magical beings with names like Sniznoddle, Snarleyboddle, Little Weekie the Goblin, the Bollivar, the Snopwiggy, and his friend, the Wiggysnoop, and Mr. Hokus, who of course is a magician. And there are magic spells that can be broken with riddles like "why does a snickersnaper snap snikers?" That's not very European, is it?

The Deep Deep Woods is—again like Gruelle himself—an innocent kind of world, mostly full of niceness and kindliness and some naughtiness. Raggedy Ann herself early acquires a heart that is sewn inside her, a candy heart on which is written, "I love you." Well, if you've got "I love you" written all over your heart, you don't have many moral decisions to make. They come easy.

There is one device in these stories that comes up over and over again, one which is typical of the popular children's writing of the time—it also shows up in British children's literature—and that is the almost endless feast of sweets: donuts, creampuffs, ice cream sodas, ice cream. Book after book has mud puddles which turn out to be chocolate ice cream rather than mud, or fountains in the middle of the woods, enchanted fountains, which spout sodas, or bushes on which grow cookies or cream puffs or donuts. Everyone stops and eats his head off. It's enough to make a diet-conscious adult sick to his stomach.

There's another aspect of Raggedy Ann's kindliness that I find a little disturbing. On occasion, Raggedy Ann behaves like a real busybody in the Deep Deep Woods. She finds out that owls eat mice and she doesn't like that, so she converts the owls to cream puffs. She has a wonderfully uncomplicated idea of what's best for everybody else. (Sometimes it reminds me of American foreign policy.)

But then there are marvelous small touches. For instance, in the book called *Raggedy Ann in the Deep Deep Woods*, the two dolls are wandering along, looking at the sights and saying hello to the animals, and they run into two old owls who live in a tree top. Mama Owl, who's old, and Papa Owl, who's also old and tired from having worked for years in a buttonhole factory. It's typical of Gruelle's inventiveness to make up that kind of thing.

But in reading these books, one may decide that this man is just pouring out words, and pouring out plots and ideas and incidents, and one may wonder: does he have any writing *style*? Or is he just pushing the plot along?

I think he did have a writing style, and I think it was distinctly American. The hint comes from those words like the Snarlyboodle, and the Snoopwiggy, and Little Weekie. That's the kind of word-making that little children indulge in, making words and names out of bits and pieces of other words and sounds they've heard adults use. Johnny Gruelle succeeded in several ways in writing stories by using the methods of a child, not an adult. For another example, there are the little repetitions he uses. Hookey the Goblin is always Hookey the Goblin. That's his name, the whole thing:

"Mary Jane Adams lives down the street."
"Oh, Mary Jane?"
"No! Mary Jane Adams."

We've all heard children do this kind of thing, particularly small children. They're just learning to talk, perhaps, and just learning names, just learning the fact that most of us have three names, (and some of us four and five) and they like to say it all. It's a verbal game with them, and Gruelle used it in his books.

In *Raggedy Ann and Andy and the Camel with the Wrinkled Knees*, there's a character named the Tired Old Horse, but sometimes he's the Old Tired Horse, sometimes he might be the Tired Horse or the Old Horse but usually he's the Tired Old Horse or the Old Tired Horse, and he is never, never just the Horse. Also, there are princesses and princes, and there is a Loony King and a witch, as well as the Old Tired Horse. But soon we meet a group of pirates who have a great big pirate ship that navigates on the land by virtue of the fact that it has four wooden legs which walk the ship along like a great horse. These pirates run around doing pirate things to the dolls and the people. But very early, Gruelle's charming drawings begin to reveal something to us: the great big red nose on the pirate leader is a false nose, and the bandanna on the mean looking pirate covers up the curly hair of a little girl. This assemblage is really a group of Marcella's friends who are playing a game, pretending they are pirates. Soon we realize that the whole story is a game being played by the children about the dolls, and that they're making it up as they go along. We have all done that as children, surely, making up a story and acting it out with a group of playmates. And it rambles and goes in every direction it can go in until mother calls us for lunch or supper.

Johnny Gruelle put these tales together with the same kind of easy whimsy, the same kind of casualness, which children use when improvising a story-game for themselves. And he's the only writer that I've ever read (I may be ignorant of others) who consciously imitates the way children make up stories in writing a book for children.

Did Gruelle write any *great* books? I think he did write one great book: the book which was originally called *The Paper Dragon: A Raggedy*

Ann Adventure, and is now published as *Raggedy Ann and the Paper Dragon*. It's about a little girl named Marggy who has lost her father. Well, he's sort of misplaced actually; it isn't a very bad situation. There's a naughty magician involved, and there's Marggy's mother in the story. And Raggedy Ann and Raggedy Andy are typically helping them in finding Marggy's father, or Marggy's Daddy as Gruelle would put it, in the Deep Deep Woods. The dragon of the title is a very Oriental dragon until it gets a hole punched in his side and is patched with a Sunday comic section stuck on with some filling from a cream puff. That Americanizes him.

The dragon is completely hollow inside and at one point the bad guy of the story props his mouth open with a stick because he wants to use him for a chicken coop. But that doesn't work very well because if the chickens can run in easily, they can also run out easily. The dragon is also full of dry leaves, fallen leaves that blew in while he was yawning. Raggedy Andy gets put inside him at one point. He wanders around for a little while, and, as I remember, he can't find anything or anybody. All he finds are these dry leaves which make the dragon cough from time to time, and eventually cough Raggedy Andy out. It's that kind of rambling, meandering narrative which Gruelle does very charmingly, and particularly in this book.

The book also has good characterizations. Of course they are brief, almost blunt. Raggedy Andy loves to get into boxing and wrestling matches. They never really amount to much, but he likes to box and wrestle. The villains and the bad magicians are always irascible and usually rather foolish—propping the dragon's mouth open so that the chicken's could get in, but also get out. At one point, the villain says something like, "If you want to find Marggy's Daddy, you must do something for me first. That's the way it always is in fairy tales." And Raggedy Ann says, "But this isn't a fairy tale." "Of course it's a fairy tale!" he answers. "How else could you two rag dolls be walking around and talking if it wasn't a fairy tale?" That's blunt, and that's probably a child's way of looking at it.

There is one other Gruelle book which I'd like to recommend especially. As I said earlier, there's a whole collection of dolls in Marcella's doll nursery, and one of them is Uncle Clem the Scotch Doll. There's a book built around him called *Wooden Willie*, in which the Scotch Doll and the doll called Beloved Belindy have an adventure. Incidentally, this story originally appeared as a newspaper serial in 1922, and in that version it is a Raggedy Ann and Andy adventure.

I haven't said very much about Gruelle's illustrations, but anyone who has ever seen Gruelle's drawings, in that soft line of his, knows he has seen something special. To know how good they are, simply compare them to those in the books published after Johnny's death that have illustrations done by others, chiefly by Justin Gruelle, his brother, or by Worth Gruelle, his son.

I think there's no question that Johnny Gruelle's reputation would be much higher, and that he would be in the history of children's literature, if he hadn't written so much. But he did write some very good books. And he had his own way of depicting a child's mind and a child's outlook. So I would like to think that before my life is over, we could read about Johnny Gruelle in volumes on American writers and in volumes on American artists.

3

Child Reading and Man Reading

Oz, Babar, and Pooh

ROGER SALE

This essay began some years ago when I reread the Oz books in order to write an appreciation of them. I had read them fairly often since childhood, but found that the prospect of trying to say something paralyzed me; I was, I discovered, being haunted by my own experience as a child reading these books. I could, it seemed, live with that experience only as long as I was silent and asked few questions; it became haunting when I imagined writing for an audience that of course had not had my experience. As long as I tried to speak simply as a man, as a literary critic, I could perhaps say a great deal, but I would be running from the ghost that haunted me, and I did not want to do that and was not sure I could. The present essay is an effort to turn my difficulty into my subject: child reading as a fact in man reading, the differences it makes in the way the man reads that the child was reading those books before him. Inevitably I was thrown back on my own experience, though I can hope that the kind of thing that happened to me happened to others, with the same or different books from those I am going to discuss. Oz, Babar, and Pooh are my subjects because I read them all and loved them as a child, because they are quite different from each other, because they were written for children and so avoid the problems and difficulties raised by fairy tales, folk stories, or adult classics adapted for children, where the original or natural audience is not children exclusively. Each of those reasons will, I hope, begin to seem relevant as I go along. I want to start by taking up the books in the order listed, with passages and episodes, and working up my generalizations from them.

At the opening of Ozma of Oz, the third of L. Frank Baum's series, Dorothy Gale and her Uncle Henry are on a ship bound for Australia, and a storm comes up. The captain is not alarmed but advises everyone to stay below, but Dorothy has been dozing while this message is being delivered, and so, when she wakes and does not find her uncle, she goes on deck. She sees there, clinging to a mast, a man that might be Uncle Henry, and she rushes toward him but gets no closer than a chicken coop lying on the deck when the storm doubles its force and she is hurled from the boat, holding on to the coop:

> Dorothy had a good ducking, you may be sure, but she didn't lose her presence of mind even for a second. She kept tight hold of the stout slats and as soon as she could get the water out of her eyes she saw that the wind had ripped the cover from the coop, and the poor chickens were fluttering away in every direction, being blown by the wind until they looked like feather dusters without handles. L. Frank Baum, *Ozma of Oz* (Chicago, 1907), p. 19.

The storm is not so much a storm as it is an event that creates situations and problems. A moment later, Dorothy climbs into the coop:

> "Well, I declare," she exclaimed with a laugh. "You're in a pretty fix, Dorothy Gale, I can tell you! and I haven't the least idea how you're going to get out of it." (p. 20)

Both Baum and Dorothy are surprised, but unexcited. If you go off for Australia you can get caught in a storm, and if you get caught in a storm you are liable to be blown overboard and be in a pretty fix.

When the wind dies Dorothy sleeps on the floor of the coop, and in the morning she discovers one remaining hen at the far end. The hen has just laid an egg, and she and Dorothy start a conversation. Dorothy said to herself after a minute or two:

> "If we were in the Land of Oz, I wouldn't think it so queer, because many of the animals can talk in that fairy country. But out here in the ocean must be a good long way from Oz." (p. 26)

Indeed, the ocean is a long way from Oz, and a long way from Kansas, too. Just as one expects animals to talk in Oz and not to talk in Kansas, so one isn't sure what to expect on the ocean. So the two find themselves discussing the hen's grammar, which turns out to be rather like Dorothy's.

After a while the coop lands on a sandy beach. They find a key, and an admonitory inscription in the sand. Both are hungry, and this leads to a long conversation about whether it is better to eat live things, like bugs, or cooked dead things, like chickens who have eaten bugs. The hen gets her bugs, and Dorothy finds a grove of trees on which grow lunch pails, filled with food. Later Dorothy discovers a door with a keyhole, so she tries the key she found on the beach, that being the only one she has, and it works. Inside is a mechanical man named Tik-Tok, and though he turns out to be "magic," his makers, nonetheless, are Smith and Tinker, American mechanical geniuses. Baum's instinctive rightness about tone and detail allows us to move from a real world to an improbable world to a magic world without any fanfare. The sentences come easily, and imply they were no harder to write than it would be to take the journey they describe. His way is to fix himself in the present, and to have Dorothy respond to each new detail with the same unshakable acceptance and curiosity with which she faced the one before it. Our problem is not to classify each detail according to how realistic or likely it seems, but to do as Dorothy does and take each one as it comes, because that, as we have always known, is the way to get out of pretty fixes.

At night people go to sleep, in the morning they search for food. In the face of a disused mechanical man you look for a key to wind him up. It is precisely the atmosphere of Baum's writing not to be atmospheric, or faerie, or invoking, mysterious, gripping. The one false note in all the early chapters is the sentence about Dorothy's not losing her presence of mind when thrown overboard by the storm; for the rest, Baum does nothing to separate himself as a narrator from his heroine. It is her story, her acceptance, her curiosity and inventiveness, and he implies he could do no better than she does at taking a journey to a magic country. In the next passage it is quite striking the way everything is unselfconsciously merged into the dramatic present, with no sense of Baum considering or calculating the past, the future, or the possibilities of magic. Princess Langwidere of the land of Ev, who has a collection of thirty heads she can put on and take off as she pleases, is assessing Dorothy's head:

> "You are rather attractive," said the lady presently. "Not at all beautiful, you understand, but you have a certain style of prettiness that is different from any of my thirty heads. So I believe I'll take your head and give you No. 26 for it."
> "Well, I believe you won't!" exclaimed Dorothy.
> "It will do you no good to refuse," continued the Princess, "for I need your head for my collection, and in the land of Ev my will is law. I have never cared much for No. 26, and you will find that it is very little worn. Besides, it will do you just as well as the one you're wearing, for all practical purposes."
> "I don't know anything about your No. 26, and I don't want to," said Dorothy firmly. "I'm not used to taking cast-off things, so I'll just keep my own head." (pp. 97-98)

What Dorothy is so grandly accepting here is much more important than Langwidere's No. 26 head, and that is the fact that she has such a head.

Dorothy is totally inside the situation, the moment, and not the least bit interested in how heads might get off and on, or even in how best to deal with this imperious princess. She wants only to make clear her indignity, and what she is or isn't used to—in Kansas, or in Ev.

All this seems to me marvelous; I reread these pages with undiminished admiration for Baum's assurance with Dorothy and Dorothy's acceptance of herself and her present tense. I say "undiminished" admiration because it has always been one of my favorite sequences in the Oz books. This, and others similar to it where Dorothy or Tip or Trot or Betsy Bobbin takes a journey to a magic country, filled me, when young, as I remember it, with a powerful if undefined sense that the world is fresh and possible. To be able to go, unintentionally, into a strange world and to accept each moment there—somehow, for me, that was and is morningtime, and I am sure that the value I placed on this possibility, and the value I thereby placed on the Oz books, is something that other children reading these books, to say nothing of adults coming to them for the first time, simply do not feel. When, for instance, the six-year-old son of a friend of mine says he doesn't much care for the Oz books because they are too cinchy, I know what he means, and in many ways I agree with him. But the child I was who read those beginning magical journeys to magic countries insists to the man who reads them now that he never be caught saying the Oz books are too cinchy, because that, for child and man, is not the point. When I was six it did not matter to me that the journey I liked best, in *The Road to Oz*, ended up at Ozma's long and boring birthday party; the book was my favorite anyway. Nor did the insipid satire and wit that mar so much of the middle sections of *The Land of Oz* keep me from loving the book because of its wonderful opening, with Tip, Mombi, Jack Pumpkinhead, and the trip to the Emerald City with the Sawhorse. Whenever I go back to these I feel their enchantment all over again, feel the delighted and exhilarated sense of its being morning and on a road that is magical not because its end is the Emerald City but because the heroine or hero at each step along the way is totally and unselfconsciously inside the situations that are taking them farther and farther from home. If I once read these sequences and did not feel this, then I would have lost part of myself.

But it is not the vividness of any particular memory concerning the Oz books that keeps me tied to the child that read them; I don't think that distinctness of memory is all that important. I have no single memory of Oz as clear as that of being frightened by a picture of a cat in a book called *Little Sandy Mandy*, but the vividness of the memory and the fear does not make the book an important one for me. The experience was of the sort that every child knows, and could have been provoked by any one of hundreds of pictures or stories where an animal looms up in a frightening way. Neither the book nor the fear nor the memory of either is particularly interesting, whereas the opening sequences of a number of the Oz books, though my memory of them is less distinct, gave me something that nothing else could give.

I want to return to this point later, after looking at Babar and Pooh, and try to see it again in the context created by all three groups of books. The sequence from Jean De Brunhoff I have chosen, from the second Babar book, *The Travels*, is not, like that from *Ozma of Oz*, distinctively good, but instead characteristic of all of De Brunhoff's books. Near the middle of *The Travels*, Babar and Celeste are rescued from a tiny reef by a huge ocean liner, but their relief soon gives way to frustration and anger when they discover the captain of the ship will not let them go ashore and instead puts them in the stables:

> "They have given us straw to sleep on," cried Babar in a rage. "And hay to eat as if we were donkeys! We are locked in! I won't have it; I'll smash everything to bits!" Jean De Brunhoff, *The Travels of Babar* (London, 1935), p. 23.

Celeste then offers the advice we usually associate with the name of Uncle Tom: "It is the captain. Let us be good, and he may set us free." Babar acquiesces, and on the next page we see only their large and seemingly defiant posteriors facing the captain who is selling the elephants to an animal tamer for his circus. Even though Babar and Celeste have gotten for her advice what others called Uncle Tom have often gotten, on the next page she is still counseling patience: "We won't stay in the circus long; we will get back to our own country and see Cornelius and little Arthur again." We then switch back to the elephant country where little Arthur is exploding a firecracker on the tail of an old rhinoceros named Rataxes, and Cornelius is unable to calm down the old rhino who is threatening war.

It is a sequence different from anything in Baum, destructive and apparently cynical. The false sense of security raised by the original rescue, the avarice of the ship's captain, the arrogance of the animal tamer who imagines it is he who trains animals already highly civilized, the folly of Celeste for trusting the captain and then for imagining that seeing Arthur and Cornelius will set everything to rights—every move that does not seem to instruct us in cynicism is rudely undercut. And throughout the Babar books we see that De Brunhoff does despair that life is ever more than momentarily free of trouble, or that hoping does much good, or that we can make rules for whom to trust or what to expect. He shows us misfortunes and disasters of a kind not usually found in children's books: betrayal, desertion, cruelty, adventurousness and curiosity rewarded with danger and punishment, poisonous snakes and mushrooms, house fires, nightmares, capricious weather, homesickness. But this list falsifies. De Brunhoff does relentlessly deal with these facts of life, but his total effect is nowhere near as Gothic or as gloomy as my descriptions imply.

The major reason for this is that there is no register inside the story to carry the burden of the pains and sorrow, and we are thus not asked to imagine ourselves inside these terrible situations. When the savages attack Celeste while she is taking a nap, we are given no sense of surprise or danger, no sense that the savages are doing anything extraordinary; when, shortly thereafter, the whale who has befriended Babar and Celeste leaves them on a reef while she goes in search of food and then never returns, we are not allowed to think the elephants have been sorely betrayed. De Brunhoff exhibits great assurance in all this, and offers therefore great reassurance. Instead of dwelling on the disasters, De Brunhoff is always moving on, thereby mitigating the possibilities for both hope and despair. The rhinoceroses do go to war with the elephants, but Babar and Celeste escape from the circus, too, and return home in time for Babar to devise a ruse that routs the enemy. De Brunhoff then says, "King Babar was a great general," and in exactly the same tone with which he says "It was a great misfortune" when, in *The Story of Babar*, the original king of the elephants dies from eating a bad mushroom. Nothing is allowed to be taken at its highest or most emotional pitch; in De Brunhoff's hands words like "cruel," "happy," "great," "fled," "choke," "poison," "play," and "help" are all defused, robbed of their capacity to excite or alarm. For him equilibrium is the great goal and achievement, and it is gained not so much by finding a single tone or an implied state of rest as by constantly juxtaposing and thereby reconciling disparate attitudes and possibilities.

If I ask myself how much of this did I see as a child, my answer is, Enough. I saw it, of course, in the pictures, which I loved, stared at, and returned to as I did to no others. De Brunhoff puts two Vs in the brow of an elephant chef to show anger, and I would stare, but not in fear; he takes the tusks off the nurse of Babar's children to show how frightened she is that Alexander might be killed, and I would stare, but without anxiety for Alexander; he makes whole murals of elephants at work or play, and I would stare, though not with any sense of their exertion or pleasure. It may seem that the pictures are at odds with the text, that the child is absorbed mostly with what is piquant or odd in the illustrations while the adult is mostly aware of De Brunhoff's superbly French acceptance of misfortune and disaster. Yet they do not work at cross purposes, nor does De Brunhoff bring them together by turning the dreadful into the piquant. When I stared at the Vs in the brows of the elephant chef I could afford to be fascinated because I knew, without knowing how I knew, that there was no reason to be scared. The chef is angry because Zephir has fallen into his vanilla cream, but in the picture no one is frightened or alarmed—Zephir himself is just forlorn—and the text assures us the moment will pass. The last sentence of the episode is "Celeste took Zephir away to wash him," and on the next page we are at a garden party on the grounds of the Palace of Pleasure (*Babar the King*, pp. 19ff). The absence of any strong or consistent register, plus the way the story loosely juxtaposes events rather than push deeply into one set of complications, plus the impassive tone of the narrator—these are De Brunhoff's techniques, and I had absorbed enough of their effects to know even as a very small child that I could stare at any one picture as long as I liked. De Brunhoff himself is similarly released into playing in his pictures, to delight in showing elephants using their trunks to hold glasses and pencils and chalk and to take baths and eat cakes and swing tennis racquets. The reassurance offered by the sequences is strong enough to withstand De Brunhoff's insistence on showing us a great many of the natural shocks to which flesh is heir, and the child can even be fascinated by the pictures showing disasters—the king of the elephants turning green with poison, the gargoyles and goblins of Babar's nightmare—because everything is working to convince him that this moment, though real, is transitory, something to be accepted as a part of life.

The child cannot say anywhere near as well as the man how all this is done, but he can receive the essential message of the text without being much interested in it; if for him the message is, "Look at the pictures," that is not the wrong message at all. It is not an accident that my happiest memories of reading aloud to my children are all of the Babar books. The effect of the relation De Brunhoff creates between his text and his pictures is to make a kind of alliance between child and man reading that allows each to do what he does in his own way without there being any necessity of either interfering or overlapping much with the other. If I cannot now stare at the pictures as my children could, as I could as a child, I can receive their witty truths my own way.

This point about Jean De Brunhoff's allying child and man so they can arrive at the same place by different routes, can help us see what is good and bad about the Pooh books of A.A. Milne. In reading the Babar books the child and the man operate independently, and the child need never feel that the man doing the reading is trying to guide or instruct him. Milne, on the other hand, openly and self-consciously tries to make an alliance between child and man. Not only do Milne and his son appear in the story as "you" and "I," but everything else is arranged so the child reader will agree to pursue those goals of good manners, good spelling, and obedience Milne is nudging him towards. There are many reasons why children do not read the Pooh books, as a rule, after they are old enough to read to themselves, but one reason is that the books depend on being read aloud in the spirit of a cozy relation between reader and read to.

Let me start with a passage that shows Milne pretty much at his worst:

> "We are all going on an expedition," said Christopher Robin, as he got up and brushed himself. "Thank you, Pooh."
> "Going on an Expotition?" said Pooh eagerly. "I don't think I've ever been on one of these. Where are we going on this Expotition?"
> "Expedition, silly old bear. It's got an 'x' in it."
> "Oh," said Pooh. "I know." But he didn't really.
> "We're going to discover the North Pole."
> "Oh," said Pooh again. "What *is* the North Pole?" he asked.
> "It's just a thing you discover," said Christopher Robin, not being quite sure himself. A. A. Milne, *Winnie-the-Pooh* (New York, 1926), pp. 112-113.

People and things are always being put in ranks; you calculate your superiority to someone and then worry about who is superior to you. Milne makes Christopher Robin feel superior to Pooh because Pooh can't say or spell "expedition"; then he wants Christopher Robin, or any child being read to, to feel inferior because they don't know how to get to the North Pole. Milne assumes it is important to know how to spell as well as he and I can, which it isn't, and that we would know how to get to the North Pole, which we don't. Milne is constantly vulnerable to the charge that the fun of his stories is based on a very shallow snobbery.

But Milne is more interesting than that, and we can perhaps get at it by noting the popularity of the Pooh books among adolescents. So many people in high school and college have told me they liked Pooh that I started asking what they liked, and invariably they would name something from this list: Pooh's hums, especially "The more it snows, tiddely pom" and "I could spend a happy morning Seeing Roo"; the spotted and herbaceous backson, Trespassers William, Piglet, Eeyore's gloominess, Poohsticks. All are part of that aspect of the book that is relaxed, lazy, cozy, nonsensical, and therefore, so the argument seems to go, really right about life. This is the Forest seen as Utopia.

What the adolescent sees is really there, but the Forest is no Utopia. The two books are essentially about the fact that Christopher Robin is now too old to play with toy bears. First he is given a world over which he has complete power, and if he is not very attractive as a deus ex machina in story after story, if he seldom is as interesting as the Pooh and Piglet to whom he condescends, the pleasures of his power are perfectly clear. But, secondly, he is now going to school, doing sums, spelling words, worrying about not getting things right, about being ridiculed, and all he can do, in effect, is to take his fear of embarrassment and his need to rank and his schoolboy facts, and impose them on the animals in the Forest. Pooh in fact is not a bear of very little brain, but Christopher Robin puts Pooh in situations where he will think he is because that is just what others are doing to Christopher Robin in his hours away from the Forest. Seen this way, Milne is a good deal shrewder and harder-headed than the adolescents' view of him. If he has none of Lewis Carroll's power and wisdom and resembles him only in his social prejudices, nonetheless most children do not like the Alice books because they are about the fear of growing up, and many children do like the Pooh books because they alter the focus slightly and are about how it is sad, but all right, that we grow beyond our early childhood.

I speak here as an adult, but suspect I was aware of a good deal of this when I was young. I can remember the strong effect that the most explicit statement of Milne's theme, in the closing sentences of *The House at Pooh Corner*, had on me:

> So they went off together. But wherever they go, and whatever happens to them on the way, in that enchanted place on the top of the Forest, a little boy and his bear will always be playing. *The House at Pooh Corner* (New York, 1928), pp. 177-178.

I find it hard to read that without something like tears beginning to move toward the surface of my eyes. Nor do I think this is sentimental of me, though I am quite aware that my tears are not so much for what is in the book as for my having read these sentences and wept over them as a boy. The lies they tell are known to be lies, which saves everything. Pooh and Christopher Robin do not go away together, and we know it. The Forest is now forever closed except in memory, and that is not a sentimental fact.

But Milne does not work this way most of the time. What I never saw as a child but see everywhere now is the way the Forest is becoming tainted long before the end by the alien values of Christopher Robin's and Milne's world. The primary activity of the animals is deferring, often bordering on sycophancy. As Pooh and Piglet in their clumsy ways, and as Rabbit and Owl in their more knowing but stupider ways, attempt to manage and control things, they constantly imitate Christopher Robin, or wish they could. Christopher Robin always wins because he can be lazy and mindless with Pooh and Piglet, or knowing and organizing with Owl and Rabbit, and his presence is felt everywhere, except by Kanga, herself

a mother, and Tigger, the outsider. What is worse, Milne's view of schoolboy and adult life is limited, empty, formalistic. It can be seen at its worst
in Rabbit's efforts to unbounce Tigger, at its most pathetic in Eeyore's
triumphant making of the letter A, its best in Christopher Robin's an-
nouncement that the stick in Pooh's hands is the North Pole. Even there,
though, where Christoper Robin is finding a neat way out of his problem
and is also making Pooh feel splendid, the idea is still that you keep control
over others by hiding your ignorance from them. Candor is seldom found
in the Forest, and a man reading the Pooh books to a child is bound to
worry that the child who really seems to like them is or will become a
little monster.

But, interestingly, that seldom happens, because the alliance Milne
seeks between adult and beginning schoolboy is just not that interesting.
The wit is surface wit, verbal playing, fun to hear but forgettable. The
child reading wants the adult reading in some relation other than the one
Milne offers, and a child who really knew what he liked might well turn
from the Pooh books and seek as antidote something like the Norse legends
or the grimmer of the Grimm tales or something else he will be able to
read with pleasure for the rest of his life.

If at this point I were going to try to draw some single conclusion
about the effects of child reading on man reading, then I should either
have chosen different examples or argued them differently. In the case of
Oz the child guides the adult, in the case of Babar the child and the man
seem to get to the same place by different routes, in the case of Pooh the
child and man see different things and only part of what the man sees is
the result of the child's having seen it before him. Other books give me
quite different relationships with myself as child reader. For instance, I
find Dr. Seuss' *And to Think that I Saw It on Mulberry Street* very pleasant,
but barely read it as a man at all and lapse into remembered childhood
reading with it, while, at the opposite extreme, my experience as a man
with the stories of Beatrix Potter has been so enthralling that it has blotted
out the much fainter experiences I had with them as a child. And so it
goes. There seems to be no way to calculate or predict the relation of child
to man with any given book.

But more can be said. The obvious fact to an adult is that all three
of my examples are very different from each other and one way to express
that difference is to label them American, French, and English. Baum's
belief in the bouyancy and practicality and simple dignity of his heroines
and heroes, his fascination with machines, some of which, like Ozma's
magic picture and Glinda's book of records, he thought of as magical but
which we call television and computer, his insistence that evil is only
grown-up people acting like naughty children—all these are characteristics

we think of as American. Jean De Brunhoff is distinctively French, much more knowing than Baum, more impassive, more civilized. In my more extravagant moments I have wanted to contend that those qualities for which Flaubert and Proust are best known they share with De Brunoff and if they are better they are not any purer than he. All this is not only different from Baum, but from Milne, too. De Brunhoff is witty but never funny, and with Milne it is just the other way around; De Brunhoff is very much a grown man and Milne is an arrested child; De Brunhoff seems able to take in almost anything for his subjects while Milne's world is excluding, enclosed, snug, and whimsical.

Each author gives so purely that the child by reading them must learn a great deal about what it is to be American, French, and English: Baum with his faith in the American child left on his own to cope with things; De Brunhoff with his faith only in his intelligence; Milne with his faith that if one learns how things are named and done then everything turns out for the best. Put that way we have almost parodies of national types, but the authors don't really put themselves that way, though when we start contrasting them it is the purity and completeness of each that is striking. I know that one of my pleasures with the Oz books was that each one started off with a different situation and often a different set of characters, such that it seemed a totally distinct book, and then each became an Oz book, and shared with the others Baum's essential tone and manner. In other words, at the beginning of each book it was still and always morning. So too with Babar and Pooh, because their authors need only a page or two to evoke their worlds in their completeness. It is like learning the difference between the taste of milk, water, and orange juice, and the tastes, once learned, are not forgotten or felt to be unimportant, and as long as one goes on reading these books and tasting those tastes, there will be a distinctiveness to each every time he returns, and one which also can become a way to know or recognize other things not obviously similar. The opening sentence of *The Road to Oz* is "Please, miss," said the shaggy man, "can you tell me the road to Butterfield?" Within fifteen pages the road to Butterfield leads out of Kansas into no place, then into a country recognizably magical, then into the city of the foxes, then to the discovery that we have somehow been on the road to Oz all along. It seems to me the most enchanting thing in all the Oz books, and whenever I hear or am reminded of any one detail in the sequence the whole thing comes back to me, so completely and purely does Baum make his details adhere one to another. Almost inevitably the relation of roads to Butterfield to roads to Oz has become my way of knowing all sorts of roads. Baum's magic journeys to magic countries came into my life when it was relatively unpopulated, nowhere near as varied or shifting in its values as it was to become, so the roots planted by these stories went deep and are always potentially in my experience, able to become consciously a part of it at a moment's notice.

But this fact about the purity of the experiences offered the child reading can also lead us to a converse fact, not about the distinctness of Oz, Babar, and Pooh, but about their commonality. For the effects of this early reading not only need not be but probably cannot be single. One word I used in writing about each author is "acceptance," because each in his different way is offering a kind of imaginative dogma about accepting. Baum, De Brunhoff, and Milne all are assurers, consolers, celebrating the actual and the possible in the midst of magic, confusion, loss, and lostness. Though I did not know this as a child, the more I think about it now the more it seems that I was ready to hear the different versions of the imaginative dogma each offered. Reduced to a single statement, the dogmas would be: for Baum, accept the present as being crucial, for the ability to deal well with each immediate circumstance is a kind of magic; for De Brunhoff, accept misfortune and the indifference and even the cruelty of others, not only because they are part of our condition but because their pains and sorrows are as transitory as the joys and peace that will follow; for Milne, accept the play of early childhood, for it is precious, accept that it is lost, accept the schoolboy and adult worlds that replace it. That which makes each writer pure, distinct, complete, is thus only part of the story; that which binds them together is at least as important.

What these writers taught me was not, I presume, to accept. The desire and the beginnings of the capacity to do that must have been present in me even before I knew them. But they could give me the terms of acceptance, the tone, manner and importance of so doing. I envied Dorothy Gale greatly, not so much because she could go to Oz as because she did so beautifully every step of the way, not by being strong or brave but by accepting and living inside each new situation. By comparison legendary figures like Arthur, or the boy David or Prometheus touched me less because they seemed fantastic. They were strong or brave enough to fight through or even to ignore their situations, and the appeal of that kind of figure had been pre-empted for me by the earlier and more appealing truths told me by Baum, De Brunhoff, and Milne; the more exceptional some feat was the less important it seemed. I read Superman desultorily. I created fantasies myself—as a rubberarmed pitcher, a winner of the World Series, a king of the sky—but I never invested much energy in them because in fantasies you do not have to accept.

I was, thus, a daylight reader, living in a daylight world. Those qualities about the Oz, Babar, and Pooh books which make them seem thin or tinny to others did not make them seem that way to me, and conversely, though I was fascinated by many fairy tales, I read them as something of a stranger, and their mysterious routes down to our deepest wishes and fears have never been as open and unclogged for me as they have been for many. All this I began to realize and put together only comparatively recently when I understood who were, for me, the irreplaceable authors: Spenser, Fielding, George Eliot, William Empson, all large and wise writers, all seeking our possibilities in consideration and acceptance of our condition. These are for me the writers who count most. Others, more daring and exciting, like Shakespeare and Lawrence, taught me how to speak, but Spenser, Fielding, George Eliot, and Empson seem to have had a deeper effect even than that, and on parts of me that are silent and would be, but for them, dumb. When I realized that fact, it was not difficult to see that they began to become irreplaceable for me long before I had heard of any of them, when I first read Baum, De Brunhoff, and Milne. My knowing and caring for them as a child made them capable of coloring everything that followed, and those who did not read about Oz, Babar, and Pooh as children or, even more, those who did but did not like them, those people are in some important respects very different from me.

The child reader defines not only the man reader, but the man, and on this score I doubt that I am alone. In going back to the books of our childhood and to the experiences we had with them, we discover a great deal; not that it was bliss in that dawn to be alive, but what most matters to us, even why. This truth is in itself similar to those told us by my particular authors, Baum, De Brunhoff, and Milne, and can lead us back with renewed awareness of one of the really permanent truths, that we are fathers, but not masters, of ourselves.

4

Back to Pooh Corner

ALISON LURIE

Help me if you can, I've got to get
Back to the House at Pooh Corner . . .
Back to the days of Christopher Robin and Pooh.
                    —*contemporary rock lyric*[1]

I was surprised when I heard these words sung to the accompaniment of electronic instruments, and also when, in the same week, I saw on the cover of *Rolling Stone* an advertisement of another rock group called "Edward Bear." But inquiry among my students confirms it—Pooh is still a big culture hero. He means as much to the Now Generation as he did to us Back When.

My friends and I not only read Milne's books over and over as children; all through high school and college we went on speaking his language, seeing people and events in his terms. My husband lived his first term at Middlesex as Piglet, with friends who were Pooh and Eeyore, and the school grounds and surrounding country were remapped accordingly; at college, I knew girls who went by the names of Tigger and Roo. Even today, occasionally, I will go back and reread a favorite passage.

Writing about the Pooh books, on the other hand, has been awkward (if not impossible) since 1963, when Frederick C. Crews published *The Pooh Perplex*.[2] It is not often that a satirical work achieves such success that it effectively destroys its object, but Crews almost managed it. He was not able to laugh into silence any of the dozen varieties of current literary criticism he so brilliantly parodied; but he did manage to stifle almost all critical comment on Winnie-the-Pooh for a decade.[3] No one likes to imitate an imitation, and anyhow Crews had said most of what could be said about Pooh in one disguise or another; his best insights occur in the essay by "Harvey C. Window," which appears to be self-parody. Even now, I begin this piece with some embarrassment, aware that I am in part only following one of the suggestions for further "responsible criticism" made by Crews's

"Smedley Force," a prominent member of the MLA who was "struck by the paucity of biographical connections between Winnie-the-Pooh and the [life] of A. A. Milne."

At first glance, Milne appears to be writing about his son, Christopher Robin, who was six when *Winnie-the-Pooh*[4] appeared in 1926, and about his son's toys. But there are indications in the books that Milne was also thinking of his own childhood, and the people that surrounded him in the past.

Born in 1882, Alan Arthur Milne was the youngest of three sons of John Vine Milne, the headmaster of a small suburban London School for boys. At Henley House the three Milne children lived a half-private, half-public life, playing and eating with their father's pupils, and joining the classes as soon as they were old enough. The world of Pooh repeats this in many respects. It is a very old-fashioned, limited society, without economic competition or professional ambition. There are no cars, planes, radios, or telephones; war, crime, and serious violence are unknown. Aggression is limited to the mildest form of practical joke, and even that generally backfires. Except for Kanga and Roo, there are no family relationships. The principal occupations of the inhabitants are eating, exploration, visiting, and sports. The greatest excitement centers around the capture of strange animals or the rescue of friends in danger; but the danger is always from natural causes; accidents, floods, storms. Apart from occasional bad weather, it is a perfectly safe world.

The setting seems to suggest pre-1900 Essex and Kent, where Milne spent his holidays as a child, rather than the milder and more thickly-settled countryside of Sussex where he lived as an adult. The landscape is fairly bare and uncultivated, consisting mostly of heath and woods and marsh. There are many pine trees, and the most common plants seem to be gorse and thistles. Rain, wind, fog, and even snow are common.

Milne claimed in his *Autobiography*[5] that he did not invent most of the characters in the Pooh books, but merely took over the toys which Christopher Robin happened to possess:

> . . . their owner by constant affection had given them the twist in their features which denoted character. . . . They were what they are for anyone to see; I described rather than invented. Only Rabbit and Owl were my own unaided work.

Nevertheless, there seem to be some echoes from Milne's own past in the dramatis personae. Milne's father, whom he describes in his *Autobiography* as "the best man I have ever known," was a serious, kindly schoolmaster, devoted to all his sons, as well as to the boys whose temporary guardian he was. Yet everyone recognized that Alan was his favorite child. The same situation occurs in the books, where Winnie-the-Pooh is the undisputed favorite of Christopher Robin. As a child Milne believed that his father "knew everything there was to know"; but in fact he was pedantic rather than wise. ("Later on . . . I formed the opinion that, even if father knew everything, he knew most of it wrong"). In this aspect, Milne senior may appear as Owl, the pompous schoolmaster ("If anyone knows anything about anything, it's Owl who knows something about something") who turns out to be nearly illiterate.

Milne's happy childhood centered round his father. As for his mother, he remarks:

> I don't think I ever really knew her . . . I neither experienced, nor
> felt the need of, that mother-love of which one reads so much . . .
> I gave my heart to my father.

He remembers his mother chiefly as a sensible, very efficient housekeeper ("She could do everything better than the people whom so reluctantly she came to employ: cook better than the cook, dust better than the parlour-maid . . . "). Like Rabbit, she lived in a state of preoccupations with small responsibilities and bossy concern for the duties of others. It is interesting that Rabbit, the officious organizer, and Owl, the solemn pedant, the characters most like caricatures of Milne's own parents, are also the only ones he claims to have invented himself, the live animals among the toys.

Next to his father, Milne's greatest attachment as a child was to his brother Ken, sixteen months older. Ken, he writes, was "kinder,. . . more lovable, more tolerant;" but Alan was brighter and quicker, though more timid. Like Pooh and Piglet, they were inseparable, so much so that they had hardly any use for other people:

> We had two day-dreams. The first was of a life on the sea . . . Our
> other dream . . . was, quite simply, that we should wake up one
> morning and find that everybody else in the world was dead.

Or, as Pooh puts it:

> I could spend a happy morning
>   Seeing Piglet
> And I couldn't spend a happy morning
>   Not seeing Piglet
> And it doesn't seem to matter
> If I don't see Owl or Eeyore (or any of the others)
> And I'm not going to see Owl or Eeyore (or any of the others)

Some of these others may also have real-life prototypes, either in Milne's childhood or that of his son. There is Kanga, the kind, fussy mother or nanny, with her continual "We'll see, dear," and lack of interest in anything except children and counting "how many pieces of soap there were left and the two clean spots in Tigger's feeder." Bouncy Tigger and little Roo are like many younger siblings, always pushing themselves forward in a noisy, simple-minded way, but no use in serious matters. Their arrival in the Forest, like the appearance of a younger brother or sister in early childhood, is sudden and unexplained:

> "Here—we—are— ... And then, suddenly, we wake up one morning, and what do we find? We find a Strange Animal among us. An animal of whom we had never even heard before!"

Rabbit, Pooh, and Piglet form a plot to get rid of Roo, but as might be expected, it fails—like Tigger in the sequel, he must be accepted in the Forest.

Finally there is Eeyore, the complete pessimist ("I shouldn't be surprised if it hailed a good deal tomorrow") who is depressive with delusions of persecution where Tigger is manic with delusions of grandeur. ("Somebody must have taken it," he remarks when his tail is lost. "How Like Them.") Eeyore may date from a later period of Milne's life, the years 1906-14 when he worked on *Punch*. The Editor at that time was Owen Seaman, "a strange, unlucky man," always dissatisfied and suspicious, given to blaming his errors on extraneous circumstances: upon losing a golf match, Milne relates, "he threw down his putter and said 'That settles it. I'll never play in knickerbockers again.' "

Among all these characters seen from a child's viewpoint, Pooh is the child himself. The rest have virtues and faults particular to some adults and some children; Pooh, the hero, has the virtues and faults common to all children. He is simple, natural, and affectionate. But he is also a Bear of Very Little Brain, continually falling into ludicrous errors of judgment and comprehension; he is so greedy that he eats Eeyore's birthday jar of honey on his way to deliver it. But these faults are also endearing; all of us at birth were stupid and greedy, but no less lovable for that. As Milne himself has remarked, children combine endearing natural innocence and grace with a "brutal egotism."

> "Oh, Bear!" said Christopher Robin. "How I do love you!"
> "So do I," said Pooh.

But slow though he is, Pooh always comes through in an emergency. When Roo falls into the river, everyone behaves in a typical way:

> "Look at me swimming," squeaked Roo from the middle of his pool, and was hurried down a waterfall into the next pool... Everybody was doing something to help. Piglet ... was jumping up and down and making "Oo, I say" noises; Owl was explaining that in a case of Sudden and Temporary Immersion the Important Thing was to keep the Head Above Water; Kanga was jumping

along the bank, saying "Are you *sure* you're all right, Roo dear?"
... Eeyore had turned round and hung his tail over the first pool
into which Roo fell, and with his back to the accident was grum-
bling quietly to himself... "Get something across the stream lower
down, some of you fellows," called Rabbit.

But it is Pooh who rescues Roo, as he later rescues Piglet; it is Pooh who
discovers the "North Pole."

If Pooh is the child as hero, Christopher Robin is the child as God. He
is also the ideal parent. He is both creator and judge—the two divine functions
shared by mortal parents. He does not participate in most of the adventures,
but usually appears at the end of the chapter, sometimes descending with a
machine (an umbrella, a popgun, etc.) to save the situation. In a way the
positions of child and adult have been reversed—the people around Christopher Robin are merely animals and his old toys. (So Alice exclaims "Why,
they're only a pack of cards!")

But the ironic view of the adult world and its pretensions is undercut
by another sort of irony addressed to adults who might be reading the book
aloud. These passages, which appear mostly at the beginning of *Winnie-the-
Pooh* (there are none in the sequel) take the form of condescending conversations between the author and Christopher Robin.

> "Was that me?" said Christopher Robin in an awed voice,
> hardly daring to believe it.
> "That was you."
> Christopher Robin said nothing, but his eyes got larger and
> larger, and his face got pinker and pinker.

Behind the godlike child is another and more powerful deity: A. A. Milne,
who has created both Christopher Robin and Pooh.

There are other hidden messages from the author to the adult or
adolescent reader. The verbal hypocrisies of greed are mocked in Tigger,
those of cowardice in Piglet, and those of polite etiquette in Rabbit. The
most straightforward anti-establishment remarks, however, are reserved
for Eeyore:

> "Clever!" said Eeyore scornfully ... "Education!" said Ee-
> yore bitterly ... "What *is* Learning? ... A thing *Rabbit* knows!"

A similar criticism may lie behind the frequent attempts of the characters
to elaborate some error or misunderstanding into a system, as with Pooh's
and Piglet's hunt for the Woozle. As soon as a real fact or observation is
introduced, the system collapses, and the Woozle vanishes.

Milne's language, too, contains hidden messages. He pretends not to
understand long words and makes fun of people who use them. He employs

a special form of punctuation, capitalizing words usually written with a small letter, as is done now only in theatrical and film publicity. But in the Pooh books the effect is reversed: Milne capitalizes to show that though the character takes something seriously, the reader need not do so. When Pooh remarks "I have been Foolish and Deluded" the words are weakened by the capital letter; to have said that Pooh was foolish and deluded would have been much stronger.

A side effect of this is to weaken words that are conventionally capitalized, and by extension things they stand for. Milne was aware of this; in an essay on his poem "The King's Breakfast" he makes a suggestion for reading aloud the lines:

> The King asked
> The Queen and
> The Queen asked
> The Dairymaid

Don't be afraid of saying "and" at the end of the second line; the second and third words have the same value, and you need not be alarmed because one is a royal noun and the other is only a common conjunction.

When he uses a word it means what he tells it to mean; his Bears and Expeditions are of a very special kind. He makes the rules; he determines what things and emotions will be allowed into his books and on what terms.

In the same way, when Milne came to write his *Autobiography* he tended to remember selectively. His own childhood appears through a kind of golden haze:

> The sun is shining, goodness and mercy are to follow me (it seems)
> for ever,... fifty years from now I shall still dream at times that
> I am walking up Priory Road.

As Milne himself once announced, "Art is not life, but an exaggeration of it." And an exaggerated, sentimental—and also sometimes rather condescending—tone sometimes appears in the *Autobiography*, especially when he speaks of his father. Describing his own departure for boarding school, he writes:

> Farewell, Papa, with your brave, shy heart and your funny little
> ways; with your humour and your wisdom and your never-failing
> goodness;... "Well," you will tell yourself, "it lasted until he was
> twelve; they grow up and resent our care for them, they form their
> own ideas, and think ours old-fashioned. It is natural. But oh, to
> have that little boy again, whom I used to throw up to the sky,
> his face laughing down into mine—"

This nostalgic theme recurs in the Pooh books, particularly in the final chapter of *The House at Pooh Corner*[6]:

> "Pooh, when I'm—*you* know ... will you come up here sometimes?"
> "Just Me?"
> "Yes, Pooh."
> "Will you be here too?"
> "Yes, Pooh, I will be, really. I *promise* I will be, Pooh."
> "That's good," said Pooh.

This is also sentimentality, but a sentimentality which rises into pathos, via the pathetic fallacy. In fact, the world of childhood and the past, our discarded toys and landscapes, will not mourn us when we leave; the regret will be felt by our own imprisoned earlier selves. Milne ascribes to his father and to Pooh the passionate regret he feels for his own lost paradise.

It is no wonder that this particular lost paradise, this small, safe, happy place where individuality and privacy are respected, should appeal to people growing up in a world of telegrams, anger, wire-tapping, war, death, and taxes—especially to those who would rather not grow up. Milne's loosely-organized society of unemployed artists and eccentrics, each quietly doing his own thing, might have a special attraction for counter-culture types. For them, Pooh Corner would be both the ideal past and the ideal future—at once the golden rural childhood they probably never knew, and the perfect commune they are always seeking.

Notes

1. Sung by Kenny Loggins on "Sittin' In" by Kenny Loggins with Jim Messina, Columbia Records. I am grateful to my student, Laurence Bassoff, for calling this album to my attention.
2. Frederick C. Crews, *The Pooh Perplex, a Freshman Casebook* (New York, 1963).
3. Roger Sale, with characteristic daring, was the first American to break this silence, in "Child Reading and Man Reading: Oz, Babar, and Pooh," *Children's Literature*, Volume 1, 1972.
4. A.A. Milne, *Winnie-the-Pooh* (New York, 1926).
5. A.A. Milne, *Autobiography* (New York, 1939).
6. A.A. Milne, *The House at Pooh Corner* (New York, 1928).

5

Prickles under the Frock

The Art of Beatrix Potter

SETH SICROFF

Beatrix Potter's prose style bears a resemblance to Mrs. Tiggywinkle's plain print frock; underneath the deceptively simple dress there are prickles. The apparently simple, guileless point of view of the narrator is betrayed by an understated humor which depends on the complications of word games and the interplay between details of text and illustration. The premise of anthropomorphism is not accepted and ignored, but continually recalled to mind by sly references and incongruities. To see the importance of the deliberately bland and aphoristic sentence structure, one need only compare the taut understatement of Potter's "your Father had an accident there; he was put in a pie by Mrs. McGregor" with the wordy French translation: "Un accident affreux arriva a votre pauvre père dans ce maudit jardin. Il fut attrapé et mis en pâté par Madame McGregor." In this case, less *is* more.

Beatrix Potter has a feel for unusual words, which glow "with a hard and gem-like flame" against the backdrop of deliberate simplicity. In most of the books, there are one or two of these elegant words: Tommy Brock snored "apoplectically" in *The Tale of Mr. Tod*, and in *The Tale of the Flopsy Bunnies*, the effect of the lettuce is very "soporific."[1] In these passages, the word draws attention to an important idea. The soporific effect of eating lettuce is responsible for the rabbits' capture; Tommy Brock's deceptively apoplectic appearance encouraged Mr. Tod to risk setting the booby trap. In most cases, these incongruously elegant words are used in such a way as to emphasize the incongruity of the characterization. Jemima's high aspirations move her to complain of the "superfluous hen." The technical language in *Ginger and Pickles* suggests the awesome complexity of the problems besetting the dog and the cat: "Send in all the bills again to everybody, 'with compts', replied Ginger."

Potter indulges in a number of little games which remind the reader of the ambiguous position of her inventions, between man and beast. An important trick is juxtaposition, as in *Mr. Tod*:

> Mr. Tod was coming up Bull Banks, and he was in the very worst of tempers. First he had been upset by breaking the plate. It was his own fault; but it was a china plate, the last of the dinner service that had belonged to his grandmother, old Vixen Tod. Then the midges had been very bad. And he had failed to catch a hen pheasant on her nest.

Sentimental human regrets are set cheek by jowl with the practical concerns of a predator.

The juxtaposition is of a more complicated sort when mother pigs give advice. In *The Tale of Pigling Bland*, Aunt Pettitoes gave these instructions to her children, before they set off to market:

> "Now Pigling Bland; son Pigling Bland, you must go to market. Take your brother Alexander by the hand. Mind your Sunday clothes, and remember to blow your nose"—(Aunt Pettitoes passed round the handkerchief again)—"beware of traps, hen roosts, bacon and eggs; always walk upon your hind legs."

Aunt Dorcas gave similarly garbled instructions to Robinson:

> "Now take care of yourself in Stymouth, Nephew Robinson. Beware of gunpowder, and ships' cooks, and pantechnicons, and sausages, and shoes, and ships, and sealing-wax."

The reminders on manners and the errands might have been addressed to a human child. "Bacon and eggs," "shoes," "sausages," and "sealing-wax" are objects which represent death to pigs. Some of the advice means nothing, except in retrospect, later on. "Hen roosts" prove a dangerous locale to Pigling Bland—though how Aunt Pettitoes could have foreseen this is beyond explanation. The reason for avoiding ships' cooks is clarified when one kidnaps Robinson, and the need for prudence with respect to sausages and wax is also elaborated later on in *Little Pig Robinson*:

> Old Mr. Mumby was a deaf old man in spectacles, who kept a general store. He sold almost anything you can imagine, except ham—a circumstance much approved by Aunt Dorcas. It was the only general store in Stymouth where you could not find displayed

upon the counter a large dish, containing strings of thin, pale-coloured, repulsively uncooked sausages, and rolled bacon hanging from the ceiling.

"What pleasure," said Aunt Dorcas feelingly—"What possible pleasure can there be in entering a shop where you knock against a ham? A ham that may have belonged to a dear second cousin?"

. . . Finally (the man) begged to have the honour of showing him over a ship engaged in the ginger trade, commanded by Captain Barnabas Butcher, named the "Pound of Candles."

Robinson did not very much like the name. It reminded him of tallow, of lard, of crackle and trimmings of bacon.

(One wonders at the menace posed by "pantechnicons"—moving vans; was it simply that the noise of passing carts prevented Robinson from hearing old Mr. Mumby's anxious warning?)

The little reminders about the nature of the characters do not emerge inevitably from the dialogue and the action. Potter's complicity is apparent not only in the improbability of some of the things said by characters, but also in the peculiar vocabulary of the narrator. When she tells us that "Timmy Willie had been reared on roots and salad" (*Johnny Town-mouse*), she is slyly mixing mouse and human realities. Mr. Brown, in *Squirrel Nutkin*, is clearly not dressed in human clothing, but Potter tells us that he puts the unfortunate squirrel in his waistcoat pocket. Again, some of the animals do live in houses, but others live in less human abodes. The mice who wink at Peter in the garden, we are told, are "sitting on their doorsteps," although the picture shows them sitting in an ordinary niche. Certain loaded phrases acquire a generalized meaning. Mrs. McGregor's example of making rabbit pie is followed, improbably enough, by Mr. Brock ("Tommy Brock did occasionally eat rabbit-pie . . . " *Mr. Tod*). The phrase, which makes some sense in the domestic context of Mrs. McGregor's home, has been exported to the woodlands. The reverse occurs with the phrase "rabbit-tobacco." This makes some sense as an item in Old Mrs. Rabbit's shop: "she also sold herbs, and rosemary tea, and rabbit-tobacco (which is what *we* call lavender)." But when Mr. and Mrs. McGregor start talking about buying rabbit-tobacco (*Flopsy Bunnies*), it is Potter who is winking at *us*.

The above examples are relatively logical, compared with some of the other tricks by which Potter recalls the basic absurdity of the stories. When Pigling Bland approaches Piperson's farm, the hens try to warn him away, in very peculiar language:

"Bacon and eggs, bacon and eggs!" clucked a hen on a perch. "Trap, trap, trap! cackle, cackle, cackle!" scolded the disturbed cockerel. "To market, to market! jiggetty jig!" clucked a broody white hen roosting next to him.

There is no intrinsic logic in what the hens say; rather, their words, like the Pie's "gammon and spinach," are logically non-sensical, like real-life chicken garble. Again, like the Pie's "gammon and spinach," which are foods and therefore somehow relevant to Duchess's strangulation, the words are sensible to the other party (and to the reader). "Bacon and eggs," "henhouse," and "trap" have come to mean the equivalent of "danger." "To market, to market! jiggetty jig" is a line from a nursery rhyme, which we may understand as either a reminder to Bland of his destination, or a prediction of Piperson's intention "to catch six fowls to take to market in the morning."

Potter's nonsense is often of the sort that draws attention to her art rather than to her "subject." The fact that Aunt Pettitoes gives her instructions in rhymed verse, and that Aunt Dorcas gives hers in alliterative doggerel, does not tell anything particular about the pigs. Instead, Potter develops a personal way of looking at things in terms of nursery rhymes, incongruities, and puns.

The puns are often of a peculiar sort: although many are spoken between characters, the joke is usually between author and reader. Ribby seems to be as little responsible for the humor of her puns as for the humor of cats' wearing clothes: "He's a bad kitten, Cousin Tabitha; he made a cat's cradle of my best bonnet last time I came to tea. Where have you looked for him?" (*The Roly-poly Pudding*). The same is true of Duchess's pun in *The Pie and the Patty Pan*: "Shall I run for the doctor? I will just look up the spoons!" "Oh, yes, yes! fetch Dr. Maggotty, my dear Ribby: he is a Pie himself, he will certainly understand."

The pictures play an indispensable role as a complement to the text. It is important to be able to see Peter Rabbit's world—the scenery, the little houses, and especially the dressed-up animals. But the illustrations do not simply show what is going on in the text.

Chronologically, the pictures are not limited to the scene described in the text. In *Johnny Town-mouse*, when the country mouse is explaining his tastes to the town mice, there is a flashback illustration of the way life used to be, when he was in the country. In *Two Bad Mice*, there are pictures drawn, as it were, in the conditional tense. "The little girl that the doll's house belonged to said, 'I will get a doll dressed like a policeman!'" The accompanying picture shows how the mice would react to this: Hunca-Munca is holding up her baby to meet the policeman, while two other mice crawl in at the window. On the next page, the nurse says she will set a trap; the picture shows how Hunca-Munca and Tom Thumb would teach their little children to deal with a mouse-trap.

In many cases, details are introduced in the pictures before they are mentioned in the text. In *The Tailor of Gloucester*, the text makes no mention of the mice until the bottom of page fourteen except "accidentally," when the tailor refers to the scraps as "tippets for mice and ribbons for mobs" (p. 13). Yet in the first illustration of the book, there are three mice inconspicuously stealing scraps of cloth behind the tailor's back, and in the next illustrations we are given pictorial evidence of the mice's craftsmanship, thirty pages before we are told as much in the text. In *Jemima Puddle-duck* the same thing happens. In the illustration of Jemima addressing the other animals in the barn, there is an egg hidden under the trough; later, we are told that although Jemima hid her eggs, they were always found and removed. The facing picture shows this happening, but there is also another egg under the rhubarb leaf which the boy does not seem to have noticed.

Often the pictures are necessary to explain the text. For example, when Potter tells us, in *Benjamin Bunny*, that "Peter let the pocket-handkerchief go again," we would be unsure of the significance of that remark, without the picture. Peter's clumsiness is due to apprehension: hand touching his chin, he is listening for sounds of the approach of Mr. McGregor. Sometimes the pictures tell the story more precisely than the text. The "pocket-handkerchief" worn by Peter is not rabbit-size, but man-sized; the discrepancies with regard to the mice's doorstep and Old Mr. Brown's waistcoat are similar.

In many instances, the illustrations allow the reader a more accurate perception of what is going on that than of a relatively naive narrator. For example, the narrator of *Jemima Puddle-duck* seems to share the duck's simple point of view. Nowhere in the text is the "sandy whiskered gentleman" explicitly identified as a fox. Where the text tells us simply that "the gentleman opened the door and showed Jemima in ... " and that "she was rather surprised to find such a vast quantity of feathers. But it was very comfortable; and she made a nest without any trouble at all," the pictures show the fox snickering behind her back, and a barrel-full of chicken parts in the corner. In another tale, when Ginger and Pickles are forced to close up shop, the narrator tells us that "Ginger is living in the warren, I do not know what occupation he pursues; he looks stout and comfortable. Pickles is at present a gameskeeper." The pictures make it clear that both have turned to poaching.

The fact that one can read the books over and over, forwards and even backwards, and still discover, at each reading, new and amusing details, is an important factor in the popularity of Beatrix Potter's stories. Potter's art is not polemic, elegiac, or philosophical, but it is amusing and intelligent. She does not take sides, or choose between animals and humans, or reality and fantasy. The distinctive quality of her work is a function of her ability to maintain a consistent literary world which exists between reality and fantasy, denying neither.

The various Tales are published by Frederick Warne & Co. Ltd., London and New York.

Some Meanings in Children's Literature

6

Notes on the Waist-High Culture

JOHN SEELYE

I want to state at the start my uneasiness about the classroom use of children's literature, for my position is on the side of the Luddites, even to Sans Culottism. I once wrote a book called *The True Adventures of Huck Finn*, which was originally titled *Huck Finn for the Critics*, in the hope that they would leave the original book alone; and if consistency is the hobgoblin of small minds, what I propose talking about is hobgoblins and small minds, anyway. If the author of "Goldilocks and the Three Bears" had meant for his work to be studied in the classroom, he would have written something along the lines of *Moby-Dick*, which as a children's poem became "The Hunting of the Snark." As a matter of fact he did, although few critics pay much attention to Southey's *The Doctor*; nor do many children, for all of that, though Southey has much to say on the subject.

What I find most fascinating about children's literature is that so much of it was not written for children but, like "Goldilocks," was created for an adult audience. Southey himself observes how a child may read *Pilgrim's Progress* for enjoyment, "without a suspicion of its allegorical import," for what "he did not understand was as little remembered as the sounds of the wind, or the motions of the passing clouds; but the imagery and the incidents took possession of his memory and his heart... Oh! what blockheads are those wise persons who think it necessary that a child should comprehend everything it reads!"[1] Or to put it in the vernacular of Huck Finn: "The statements was interesting, but tough." Children have likewise appropriated the interesting parts of *Robinson Crusoe*, *Gulliver's Travels*, and *The Leatherstocking Tales*, among others. They have not appropriated parts of *The Mill on the Floss* and *The Rise of Silas Lapham*, among others.

It is important to note somewhere that no children's literature was written by children, nor are children much interested in the stories other children tell. Most children aim their little fictions, as a matter of fact, at grown-ups, who likewise supply, intentionally or otherwise, the stories children prefer being told. Such were the golden oldies that Mother Goose laid, and such, I imagine, are skip-rope rhymes and the moron, elephant, and "baby" jokes that kids love to tell. "Higgledy, piggledy, pop!" wrote S. G. Goodrich, who as an author known as Peter Parley turned out—with the part-time help of Nathaniel Hawthorne—didactic literature for children: "The dog ate up the mop." Goodrich was mocking the simple-mindedness of nursery rhymes, which he detested, but his dactyls succeeded where his didacticism did not, and Peter Parley survives today because of "Higgledy, piggledy, pop!"

As a children's author, S. G. Goodrich was a latter-day product of the Enlightenment, which likewise produced Diderot's *Encyclopedia*, most definitely not a book for children, and J.J. Rousseau. He wrote *Émile*, which is about books for children and contains a recommended reading list of one volume, *Robinson Crusoe*. From *Émile*, which like *Sesame Street*, made learning fun, came the grand original for many subsequent books for children, *Sandford and Merton*, who begat *Swiss Family Robinson*, who begat *Masterman Ready* and *Coral Island*. Goodrich, that is to say, was representative of the Victorian age, a period greatly productive of children's literature and pornography, *Little Lord Fauntleroy* being a dandy case in point: from Burnett's pretty prig in velvet knickers it is not a far leap to Oscar Wilde, who gave us *The Happy Prince*, and to Swinburne, who gave us little boys blue and black, proving, I guess, that perversion is the other side of subversion.

Because subversion is what children's literature—that is, the literature preferred or even stolen by children—is all about. The rest, as Southey points out, is just wind. If Frances Hodgson Burnett's best book for children, *The Secret Garden*, was written in the Rousseauistic tradition, being intended as a treatise on how a child might be reformed by means of the Burpee seed catalogue, it also contains a thoroughly subversive dimension. For all of its pious horticulture, *The Secret Garden* also satisfies a child's deep psychic needs, because the important thing about the garden is not its flowers but its *secrecy*. Little girls need blooms of their own. The subversive element is the thing children seek in whatever literature they read, whether meant for adults or for themselves. Edgar Rice Burroughs did not write *Tarzan of the Apes* for children, but small boys read it with delight, not for the absurd Darwinian thesis but for the forbidden delights of climbing high trees. Among the Victorian writers for children, Lewis Carroll was perhaps the most sensitive to the subversive side of juvenile psyches, sending Alice down a rabbit hole into a world very much her own, in which authority figures speak nonsense and small is very large.

But before Carroll's tiny Alice, there was Alcott's *Little Women*. In Jo March we have a truly subversive figure, who manages to hold to her own while adopting protective coloration. To understand this best, however, you have to leave off at the end of the first part: the sequel, like all such, is a sell-out, though in marrying a much older man, while refusing the beautiful Childe Byron, Laurie, Jo most certainly continues her subversive operation, much as her early efforts at authorship are blood-and-thunder melodramas. Horatio Alger, who shares with Alcott her Protestant Ethical background, shared with her also a preference for dime novels as well as for Dickens, both providing the stuff from which he wove his rags-to-riches rugs.

Louisa May Alcott wrote *Little Women* on the basis of her experiences as a child growing up in what amounted to a fatherless family, since Bronson Alcott was generally away in some empyrean realm—say, over at Ralph Waldo Emerson's. But the Marches remain solidly middle-class people, maintaining the norm which, like plum pudding and one dying child, was Charles Dickens's gift to children's literature. The Marches may be suffering deprivation but it is not down-and-out poverty: at least Alcott's children have shoes. But Whittier's rural barefoot boy as Ragged Dick develops more cheek as he loses his tan: part Oliver Twist, part Artful Dodger, Ragged Dick lives the hand-to-mouth life of an urban Huck Finn, not from choice but from necessity. Alger, himself the son of an impoverished Unitarian minister, knew hardship but never the kind experienced by most of his young heroes. Still, he was familiar with the boys he wrote about—too familiar, by some accounts—and living among the poor newsboys of New York he was also intimate with his intended readers. Alger studied his audience, perhaps more intently than any other nineteenth-century American author for children, and he learned that if there is one thing small boys like more than a collection of dime novels, it is a collection of dimes jingling in their pockets.

The essential parable in *Little Women* harks back to the interesting part of *Pilgrim's Progress*, while the basic fable in *Ragged Dick* is lifted from Bunyan's American counterpart, the Enlightenment's gift to Philadelphia, the Republic's answer to Rousseau—Ben Franklin. It was Franklin who taught American writers that the best way to make money plentiful in your pocket is to write a book telling other people how it is done. Alger, it might be said, went Ben one better: by incorporating into his fiction the basic elements of a literature then forbidden to young boys, the dime novel, he eliminated the middle man—the parent—in speeding the dime into his own pocket. He died in poverty, but that was because he gave away all that he earned to needy children, thereby putting his own morality into action. For like all great writers for children, Alger remained something of a perpetual child, who believed in the literal truth of his fairy tales—the sign of true magicians and con men. It is enough to make one forgive Alger for reviving the Protestant Ethic in terms simple enough for comprehension by children and advertising men.

I suppose the most successful smuggler in America today is Maurice Sendak, who reminds me of Tom Lehrer's song about "The Old Dope Peddler," for Sendak's message is all massage. His stories seem a literary version of an acid trip, a kind of grooving with kids: ask not where the Night Creatures are, they are in your h-e-a-d. What Sendak gives kids is the Hobbit habit, for it was Tolkien who crossed Carroll's Alice with the Wizard of Oz and ended up with Bilbo Baggins. Or, in other terms, *The Lord of the Rings* is Tennysonian chivalrics in Beatrix Potter bunny feet, for Tolkien was as a children's writer the last of the great Victorians, on whose imperial imagination no sun ever set. This brings me to Peter Beagle, our most eminent candidate for the American Tolkien; indeed, Beagle has produced movie scripts for Tolkien's stories. *The Last Unicorn* is one more of those mysterious, charismatic works that operates in a twilight zone between childhood and a farther range, very much a product of the sixties and second cousin to *The Yellow Submarine*. Beagle in his works reminds me of Leonard Cohen, and like Cohen he is a singer as well as a writer, but where Cohen's fiction is x-rated fantasy, obviously inspired by *The Naked Lunch*, Beagle seems to have taken his fairy story not only from Tolkien but also from Tolkien's ultimate source, that deep psychic well of folklore. What Beagle knows is the oldest secret of all; to pursue and be pursued, to be captured and to escape, that is all ye know and all ye need to know in order to write for children. The rest is mere genius.

Still, I am curious to find out the extent to which Beagle's work is being appropriated by children for themselves. I wonder because my general impression is that children are not doing much appropriating these days, not in terms of literature, at any rate. I recently observed a gang of ten-year-old boys (accompanied by an oversized teenager obviously hired for the occasion) being turned away from a movie theater in which Blake Edwards's "10" was being shown, obviously an example of thwarted appropriation, recalling from my own childhood certain illustrated playing-cards and very small comic books. That kind of subterranean appropriation has been going on for a long, long time, as any student of the original versions of folktales can attest. Being a member of the waist-high culture puts your head at the visceral level, a metaphor which all aspiring writers for children should remember. For the child is closer to the ground than to the sky. Huck Finn, who as an eternal child beats Peter Pan all to hell, preferred that place to the other, having heard heaven described. Huck is subversiveness itself, a kind of Pied Piper eternally heading for his infernal hole in Holiday Hill, where Tom Sawyer's bandit gang waits for him, ready to act out another episode of their ongoing dime novel. A hole, contra Ruth Krauss, is not to dig. A hole is to crawl, creep, or fall into, down and down toward those subterranean realms where the real fun begins.

Note

1. [Robert Southey], *The Doctor&c.*, 2 vols. (New York: Harper & Brothers, 1836), 87.

7

On Writing for Children*

Emanuel Goldsmith, author of *Architects of Yiddishism at the Beginning of the Twentieth Century*, has described Isaac Bashevis Singer as "one of the most remarkable authors who has ever lived ... wiry, inescapable style, an intensely personal, inimitable vision, a Machiavellian wit, but above all else, it is the bracing, revivifying character of his insights that makes him important."

Mr. Singer is a born story teller beloved both by children and adults because of the warm humor and wisdom of heart embodied in his writing.

Question (Q). Most folktales and fairytales were originally intended for adults. Through the years they have been abandoned to the children. What kinds of behavior do these tales try to teach and what is the effect of these teachings on children?

I. B. Singer (A). I don't believe that most of the fairytales and stories were created to teach people anything, and this is a good thing, because once a story is made to teach, one can foresee what it is going to say. Fairytales I admire most. You read a story and then when the story is ended you ask yourself what does it teach? What is it saying? You are bewildered by their pointlessness, but they are beautiful anyhow and I think that children love these kinds of stories.

For example, my father used to tell me stories—religious kinds of stories—about a man who was a good man on this earth and then he died and went to Paradise. These kinds of stories used to bore me, because I knew already that the good people go to Paradise and the bad people are roasted in Hell. But sometimes my mother told me stories which were so

---

*Questions asked of Mr. Singer by students of Children's Literature at The University of Connecticut, April 3, 1977.

pointless that you really could learn nothing from them. Let's say that a bear swallows three children or something like this and then they cut open his belly and the children go free. A story like this had no meaning, but it had beauty. In children's literature the writers can tell a story with a moral, but they should be careful not to be too much on the didactic side. The stories should have beauty in themselves. The great works of literature actually teach us nothing. What does *Madame Bovary* teach us? That a woman that was unfaithful to her husband commits suicide? We know that not all women who betray their husbands commit suicide or are killed. Many of them live to an old age. When Tolstoy wrote *Anna Karenina*, the story was the same. Anna also betrayed her husband and she also committed suicide. We learn actually from *Anna Karenina* nothing, for whatever we had to learn we could already have learned from *Madame Bovary*. But the story is beautiful anyhow. I think it is a great tragedy that modern writers have become so interested in messages that they forget that there are stories which are wonderful without a message; that the message isn't everything. I once said that if all the messages would disappear and only the Ten Commandments would be left, you would have enough messages for the next 10,000 years. It is not the message which is so important but the story itself. A story has an independent life. It can exist without a message, although a message is sometimes good for it, but only sometimes.

Q. Were you a writer or storyteller as a child? Who told stories to you when you were a child?

A. Well, first of all my father and mother were both excellent storytellers. They told us stories. I heard stories all the time. In addition I used to read what they used to call storybooks in Yiddish. These were little books which cost a penny apiece. I used to buy them. I said once that if I would have a million rubles—I would buy all these storybooks. Actually there were not enough storybooks to buy them for a million rubles; there were only maybe a few score. I read the stories of the famous Rabbi Nakhman of Bratzlav, a famous rabbi who was not only a great saint and a great Jewish scholar, but also a great poet, one of the most puzzling personalities who has ever lived. And he told stories which his disciple wrote down and these stories influenced me immensely. I would say that although he was a rabbi and a saint there was no message in his stories. His disciple said that those who know the Cabala will find out what the message is. Since I was not a great Cabalist then and I am not yet today, I love the stories by themselves. I never found any message in them, but they are most fantastic and wonderful. I am astonished that these stories are not yet made as literature for children. I intend, if it's possible, to write a kind of digest of them. I still love stories and readers always call me up, since my telephone is listed in the telephone book, and if they tell me they have a story to tell me, I say immediately, "Come up! I want to hear it." I still think that the story is the very essence of literature. When writers forget the art of storytelling, they forget literature. It's a great tragedy that writers have forgotten their main aim, that they have to tell stories.

Q. Will you please explain the origin of Yiddish folktales and do you take all your children's stories from Yiddish folktales?

A. I don't take all my stories from Yiddish folktales because I invent stories myself. After all, these folktales were invented by someone; the people did not tell them all. There was always a man who talked out the story and then it became a part of folklore. I would say I use both methods. If I find some that are beautiful folktales, especially those which were told to me by my mother and father, I would use them. And if not, I say to myself, "I am a part of the folk myself. Why can't I invent stories?" And, of course, I have invented a number of stories. Sometimes I hear a little story, a spark of a story, and then I make from the spark a fire. At least this is what I try to do. My mind is full of stories and to me the human history is actually an aggregation of millions of little stories. If a day passes in my life without a story, I am disappointed. But thank God, one way or another, the Almighty is always sending stories to me. As far as the origin of the stories, their origin is the human imagination. What else?

Q. In your lecture here a year ago, you stated that "Symbolism is not good for children because although by nature a child is a mystic, he is also by nature a realist." In what ways is a child a mystic and a realist, and how conscious are you of simplifying the symbolism for children for the sake of clarity?

A. As a rule every good story is symbolic and if it doesn't have a symbol, you can try to find a symbol or invent a symbol. Children have a great feeling for mysticism. They believe in the supernatural; they believe in God; they believe in angels; they believe in devils. They don't question you if you tell them a story which is connected with the supernatural. But children don't like nonsense. There are some writers who think that if they write a story which doesn't make any sense, just because it makes no sense it is full of symbols. Symbolism is often a wall behind which unable writers hide in order to make themselves important. I have seen many writers who think that a child can take nonsense, and it isn't true. A child will believe in the supernatural, but even in a supernatural story, the child wants logic and consistency. I once read a story where a man said that three little stones fell into a kettle and out came three little monkeys. The child just does not believe in these things. Although I am very much against Russia, I think that they are right about one thing: that writing nonsense and telling children things that are completely unbelievable is not good for the child's mind. Because although the child has less experience than the adult, the child has already a sense of logic and knows what makes sense and what doesn't make sense. Distortion of reality is not symbolism; distortion of reality is bad writing. The great symbols don't come from nonsense but from sense. The stories from the Bible and the Book of Genesis are full of sense and at the same time highly symbolic. Many of these little books which make no sense at all are doing damage to children's literature; if you are not bound by any logic and by any consistency, everybody can be a writer. The child, good and independent reader that he is, is also a severe critic. The wonderful thing about children is that you cannot hypnotize a child to read a story because the author was a great man. You can tell him it was written by Shakespeare or by the Almighty himself, but the child does not care about authority. If the child doesn't like a story, the child will reject it immediately. The same thing is true about reviews. No child will read a story because it got good reviews. Children, thank God, don't read reviews. Of course, children don't care at all about advertising. If the story was advertised on the whole page of *The New York Times* it will not change the child's mind about the story. I wish that our adult readers would be as independent in this respect as the children are. And because they are great readers and independent readers and because they are not hypnotized by all this mishmash, one should be very careful with them.

Q. When asked why your stories for children always have happy endings you have been quoted as saying, "If I have to torture someone, I would rather torture an adult than a child." In what other specific ways do you alter your writing for children?

A. I try to give a happy ending to a story for a child because I know how sensitive a child is. If you tell a child that a murderer or a thief was never punished and never caught, the child feels that there is no justice in the world altogether. And I don't like children to come to this conclusion, at least not too soon.

Q. Many of your children's stories include traditional folk material from Jewish culture. Would you call yourself more of a storyteller or a story creator?

A. First of all the reason why they all come from Jewish tradition is that I believe literature must have an address. You cannot write a story just about people. When you tell a story to a child, "There was somewhere a king," the child would like to know where the king was. In Ireland, in Babylonia? The same thing is true about adult literature. Literature, more than any other art, must have an address. The more the story is connected with a group, the more specific it is, the better it is. Let's say we write a letter to Russia. First, you say it's to Russia. Then you have to say, what city? What part of Russia? What is the number of the house and so on and so on until you come to the specific person, and when you mail it, it will come right there to the intended person. The same thing in a way is true about literature. The more specific it is the more influence it has on a reader.

Q. Critic Marilyn Jurich argues that the nature of Yiddish folk humor is to urge acceptance. She says, "Change for the poor, oppressed, cannot be realized, not by the ordinary man. To urge change is to meet despair or destruction. Only deliverance is from God and the only joy is in experiencing God's presence in whatever peace is attainable." Do you feel this urging of acceptance is a characteristic of your writing for children?

A. I would say that all generalizations, especially about literature, are false. Of course, there may be such stories also, but to say that all Jewish stories are of this kind is false to me. By the way, I don't really understand exactly what she means by "accept." Of course, if we write a story we want it to be accepted. What is the meaning of the word "acceptance"? She wants the poor people to be accepted by the rich? You explain it to me. Do you know what this critic is saying?

Q. Well, I think that she is saying by acceptance to accept that which is given to you, if it is suffering, to accept suffering. If it be fortune, to accept fortune.

A. I don't really try to teach my readers that they should accept all the troubles in the world. In other words, if there was a Hitler, they should accept Hitler? Actually the Jew has not accepted the badness of the world. It is a Christian idea that we should accept everything. I would say that a Jew, although he believes that everything is sent by God, he is also a man of great protest. Of rebellion. Fighting evil. And because of this to say that the Jewish story is of acceptance is kind of a generalization, which does not really jibe with our reality. We have accepted neither Hitler nor Haman, none of the enemies of humanity. The opposite. We fought them. It is true that in the Hitler holocaust, the Jew who fought Hitler was like a fly fighting a lion. But just the same it is not in our nature to be passive when the evil powers come out.

Q. What do you think about the study and criticism of children's literature in the universities?

A. I know that the universities teach writers who want to write for children and it's a wonderful thing; and I am very happy to see so many people here interested in this. But I really don't know enough about the universities to come to any generalization. I would say that wherever I go, people are interested. Children's literature is not anymore a stepchild of literature. It's becoming a very legal kind of literature. Of course, children's literature is still very young. One hundred years ago it almost did not exist. It did not exist among the Jewish people in my time. We didn't have such a thing as literature for children. I think that children's literature has a great future because it is still telling a story. In this respect it has never become ultra-modern.

Q. Some children's book experts believe in a prescribed vocabulary for children at various age levels. Your stories, even for the very young, contain much vocabulary that some might call too advanced for young children. How conscious are you of your vocabulary when writing for children?

A. I would say that if you don't remember all the time that a child is a child and you treat him as an adult, there is a good chance that the child will act like an adult; if not one hundred percent at least fifty percent or sixty percent. Because of this I am not very careful about using words which people think that the child will not understand. Of course, since I write in Yiddish sometimes these words in Yiddish may be more simple than they come out in English but I will say a child will not throw away a book because there are a few words that he does not understand. The opposite—the child will be intrigued and will look into a dictionary or it will ask the mother or the teacher what the word means. A child will throw away a book only if there is no story, if it doesn't make sense and is boring. Amongst the adults there is lately a theory that a good book has to be boring; that the greater a bore, the better writer he is; some writers even boast about it—how boring they are. The great masters tried their best to be easy and to be understood. Any child can read *Anna Karenina* or even *Madame Bovary* if it has a feeling for love and sex. So I am not afraid of difficult words.

Let's not forget about one hundred years ago, eighty years ago or even fifty years ago, whole generations were brought up on poetry. They were brought up on Pushkin and Byron. A book of poetry was in every house. Many young women and young men learned poetry by heart. But what happened to poetry now-a-days? It has become so erudite, so confused and so obscure, that people just stopped enjoying it. So now the biggest publishing company publishes a book of poetry in 800 copies and 500 are given away to reviewers and other poets. The poet of today began to speak to other poets. He speaks to nobody else. There is a great danger that this may happen to adult literature altogether. It will become so profound and so erudite that it will be like a crossword puzzle, only for pedantic minds who like to do these puzzles. I am often afraid that this may happen to children's literature. I know that it cannot happen, because the child will say, "No," in a big voice.

Q. In a discussion of the conditions necessary for you to write, you spoke of three things. You must have a plot, you must have a passion to write, and you must feel that you are the only one that can write that particular story. What special thing do you think that you have that you share with children?

A. I would say that I see to it that the stories which I tell the children no other writer would have told them. This does not mean that they are better than other stories. When you read a story by Andersen, you will know that this is not a Grimm story. It is an Andersen story. When you read a story by Chekov, you say this is not a Maupassant story, but a Chekov story. The real writer manages to put his seal on his work. He tells you a story which others cannot tell. Only if I see that this story has my "seal," it is sort of, say, my story, I will tell it. And this is the reason I will not just write stories about abstract things which any other writer might be able to do. A Russian story must be Russian and a French story must be French. You may be an internationalist, you may be cosmopolitan, you may think that all the nations are clannish and we should unite. But when it comes to literature, you cannot really move away from the group and its culture.

When I write a story, whether it's adult or for children, I have to say, "This is my story."

8

On Not Writing for Children

P. L. Travers

"On Not Writing for Children"—what an odd title for a lecture, you will say, especially from one whose books are largely read by children! But I hope they are also read by grownups, as you will see by what I'm going to say. I think that grownups are a very important part of children's literature, so called. I'm not sure that I believe in children's literature, but as I go on, you'll see why. Well, you know, I'm not writing for children. This seems to suggest that there exists some particular reason for the fact that I don't write for children, and that I am proposing to explain it: a sort of secret recipe that, with luck, can be divulged.

But if there is a secret, I am not going to divulge it, not because I will not, but because I cannot. I cannot tell you how it's done. There is something in me that hesitates to inquire too closely into this business of writing; fear perhaps that if one discovered the "how" of it, the way it's done, one might be tempted to make use of it and let it become mechanical. There is something in me that could go on writing and writing, book after book about Mary Poppins; and maybe I will do that, but if I know how to do it, I shan't be able to do it at all. To me it is a mystery, and I think it should remain a mystery. Some of you will know, perhaps, that one of the most annoying aspects of a character in a book of mine is that she never explains. There is a Chinese ideogram called *pai* that has, I am told, two different meanings, depending on the context. One is "explain," but the other one is "in vain." How can I add anything to that? It is in vain to explain that the Chinese know better than we, even though they are doing all those terrible things to Confucius.

And yet I feel bound to clarify this feeling I have. No, it is stronger than a feeling—this conviction I have, that very few people v ite for children.

Not long ago, an American journalist, Clifton Fadiman, a well-known writer and collector of children's books, asked me for (and I quote) "your general ideas on literature for children, your aims and purposes and what led you to the field." Well, this flummoxed me. I hadn't any ideas, general or specific, on literature for children and I hadn't set out with aims or purposes. I couldn't say that anything I had done was intended or invented. It simply happened. I said it was a strong belief of mine that I didn't write for children at all, that the idea simply didn't enter my head. I am bound to assume, and I told him this, that there is such a field. I hear about it so often, but I wonder if it is a valid one or whether it has not been created less by writers than by publishers and booksellers—and perhaps indeed by people who teach Children's Literature. I am always astonished when I see books labeled "For from 5 to 7" or "From 9 to 12" because who is to know what child will be moved by what book at what age? Who is to be the judge? I'm not one; I can't tell.

Nothing I had written before Mary Poppins had anything to do with children and I have always assumed, when I thought about it at all, that she had come out of the same well of nothingness (and by nothingness, I mean no-thing-ness) as the poetry, myth, and legend that had absorbed me all my writing life. If I had been told while I was working on the book that I was doing it for children, I think I would have been terrified. How would I have had the effrontery to attempt such a thing? For, if for children, the question immediately arises, "for what children?" That word "children" is a large blanket; it covers, as with grownups, every kind of being that exists. Was I writing for the children in Japan, where Mary Poppins is required reading in the English language schools and universities, telling a race of people who have no staircases in their homes about somebody who slid up the bannisters? For the children in Africa, who read it in Swahili, and who have never even seen an umbrella, much less used one? Or to come to those nearer my own world, was I writing for the boy who wrote to me with such noble anger when he came to the end of the third book where Mary Poppins goes away forever, "Madum (he spelt it M-A-D-U-M), you have sent Mary Poppins away. Madum, I will never forgive you. You have made the children cry." Well, what a reproach! What a picture! The children weeping in the world and I alone responsible! The labels "From 5 to 7" or "9 to 12" can have no relation to such a letter. It came straight out of the human heart, a heart that, no matter what its age, was capable of pain. That boy had already begun to know what sorrow was and he reproached me for his knowledge.

Or was I writing for the children in Trinidad, a group of whom asked me to talk to them when I was in the library at Port of Spain? It was they, however, who did the talking, telling me more about the books than I could ever have known. But I noticed that the smallest child, a little dark plum-colored boy, was silent. Had he read the book? I asked. Yes. Then what was it he liked about Mary Poppins? He shook his head sombrely. "I don't like her," he said. Well, this immediately charmed me. Praise is something you feel shy of trusting, but blame—ah, blame is where you learn your lessons. "No?" I asked with interest, hoping to hear the reason why. But then the solemn face suddenly broke, like a cracked melon, into a smile. His eyes shone with his secret joke. "I don't like her, I love her." Well, what an answer, what a declaration! Was I writing, could I even dream of writing, for creatures who understood so much and in particular for this one child, hardly more than six years old, who already knew and could strictly evaluate the shades of feeling between liking and loving? This was an extraordinary thing to happen.

Or for that other child who was asked to write an essay on his favorite subject or his favorite book? It was short, just five or six lines, but his teacher thought so well of it that she kindly sent it to me. It said, "The Lord is the Father of all things and Mary Poppins is the Mother of all things and they are married, or has been married, and they are both a miracle." Well, I find that moment of uncertainty in the "has been married" very touching and I think I see the reasoning behind it. The Lord doesn't figure in any of the books—He's never mentioned. Clearly, therefore, at some stage, he and Mary Poppins must have agreed to part. I like to think that this was not due to any fundamental incompatibility but rather that the pair came to an amicable agreement to function in different spheres. Now, could I dare, could I presume to write for such a child? Perhaps, indeed, it was he who was writing for me, teaching me what to look for in my own work. For a writer is, after all, only half his book. The other half is the reader and from the reader the writer learns.

Then there was the boy of sixteen who called to me from an upper room in my house and earnestly asked me to make him a promise. With some hesitation, I agreed, uncertain where it would lead me. And what do you think the promise was? "You must never, never be clever," he said. "I have just been reading *Mary Poppins* again and I have come to the conclusion that it could only have been written by a lunatic." Well! I have never had thoughts of being clever, so I accepted the epithet lunatic as I believe he meant it, as a sort of praise. And here, again, a reader had given me a clue. Moonstruck! A writer needs to be moonstruck, which is to say absorbed in, lost in, and in love with his own material. Perhaps that's part of the secret—to be in love with one's own material, to be moonstruck by it.

If I go back to my own childhood—no, not back but if I, as it were, turn sideways and consulted—wasn't it James Joyce who said, "My childhood bends beside me"? If I go back or if I turn sideways, I am once again confronted with the question of who writes for children. We had very few books in our family nursery. There were all the Beatrix Potters, the Nesbits, and the two Alices which I loved then and still love, for there is nothing in them that I have left behind or rejected as belonging specifically to childhood. What was worth reading then is worth reading now. And of course, there were the fairy tales and row upon row of Dickens and Scott, which I inched through simply because they were something to read and I was a reading child. There was also, now I come to think of it, Strewel Peter, which is nowadays thought to be cruel. Probably none of you has heard of Strewel Peter, but it's a very old book, far older than I am—from back into my mother's childhood. But nothing in him frightened me. My parents, I knew, would never let me be drowned in ink or have my thumb cut off by the Great Long Red-Legged Scissors Man. And it is worth asking here, I think, why we grown-ups have become so squeamish that we bowdlerize, blot out, gut, and retell the old stories for fear that truth with its terror and beauty should burst upon the children. Perhaps it is because we have lived through a period of such horror and violence that we tremble at the thought of inflicting facts upon the young. But children have strong stomachs. They can be trusted with what is true.

I once bowdlerized a book for a child, a child very dear to me. It was *Black Beauty*. Do you know that *Black Beauty* is the best seller in the world other than the Bible? It's an extraordinary thing to think of. Well, there's a part where Ginger, Black Beauty's friend, is to be killed. I quickly foresaw this and made up the story that Ginger was sent to a buttercup field to end his days in happiness, and it went down very well. Then I went away and my sister was left to read *Black Beauty* again to this child who adored it. And when I came back, I found a stony face to greet me, and I said, "Aren't you pleased to see me?"

"No," he said, "I'm not."

"Why, what have I done?"

"You've lied to me. Ginger is dead!"

"Oh," I said, "I've always tried not to lie to you, but I thought you wouldn't be able to bear it, so I put him into a buttercup field."

He said to me with tears in his voice, "Of course I could have beared it, you should have trusted me."

You should trust the children; they can stand more than we can.

As a child, I had a strong stomach myself. For, as well as the then unbowdlerized fairy tales, I had a great affection for a book that I found on my father's shelf called *Twelve Deathbed Scenes*. I read it so often that I knew it by heart, each death being more lugubrious and more edifying than the one before it. I used to long to die—on condition, of course, that

I came alive the next minute to see if I, too, could pass away with equal misery and grandeur. Now, I wonder about the author of that book. Nobody in his lifetime could have accused him of being a writer for children. He would not have made such a claim himself. And yet, in a sense, he was writing for children since one loving reader of ten years old was keeping his memory green.

It was the same with my mother's novels. Every afternoon, when she fell asleep, I would slip into her room, avidly read for half an hour, and sneak away just as she was waking. Those books fascinated me, not because they were so interesting but because they were so dull. They dealt exclusively with one subject, which seemed to be a kind of loving. But love, to me, was what the sea is to a fish, something you swim in while you are going about the important affairs of life. To the characters in these books, love was something strange and special. They pursued it avidly while leading what to my mind was a completely stationary existence. They never played games, never read a book, no teeth were ever brushed, no one was reminded to wash his hands, and if they ever went to bed it was never explicitly stated. I looked forward to those stolen half-hours as, I suppose, a drunkard does to a drinking bout. It was not so much pleasure as a kind of enthrallment. I was ensnared, as by a snake-charmer, by such a distorted view of life. But what of the authors? Did they, in their pursuit of love, see themselves as writers for children? Surely not, surely not. Yet for one child indeed they were.

Who, then, writes for children? Who, I wonder? One can, of course, point to the dedication pages as proof positive that somebody does. One thinks of Beatrix Potter's Noel and Lofting's children. But I wonder if such names are not really a sort of smoke screen. A dedication, after all, is not a starting point, but rather a last grand flourish. You do not write a book for this or that person. You offer it to him when it is finished. Nothing will persuade me, in spite of all his poetic protestations, that Lewis Carroll wrote his books for Alice, or indeed for any child. Alice was the occasion but not the cause of his long, involved, many-leveled confabulations with the curious inner world of Charles Lutwidge Dodgson. Of course, when it was all over, when he had safely committed it to paper, he could afford a benignant smile and the assurance that it had been done for children. But do you really believe that? I don't.

It is also possible that these dedicatory names may be a form of unconscious appeasement, perhaps even of self-protection. A writer can excuse himself to society for having invented the pushme-pullyou animal with a head at both ends, which you will remember in Dr. Dolittle, by saying with an off-hand laugh, "After all, it's for children." And if a man happens to find himself in the company of a white rabbit, elegantly waistcoated and wearing a watch, scurrying down a rabbit hole and afraid of being late for the party, he does well to clap a child's name on the book. He may then well hope to get off lightly.

But in the long run, truth will out, as it did when Beatrix Potter declared, "I write to please myself!"—a statement as grand and absolute in its own way as Galileo's legendary "Nevertheless, it moves." There is, if you notice, a special flavor, a smack of inner self-delight, about the things people write to please themselves. Think of Milne, think of Tolkien, think of Laura Ingalls Wilder—those books not written for children, but that children nevertheless read.

For a long time I thought that this assertion, "I write to please myself," backed up by C. S. Lewis' statement that a book that is written solely for children is by definition a bad book, were the last words on the subject of writing or *not* writing for children. But the more I brooded, the more I saw that, as far as I was concerned, neither of these comments was the complete answer. And then, by chance, I turned on the television one evening and found Maurice Sendak being interviewed about his book, *Where the Wild Things Are*. All the usual irrelevant questions were being flung at him—Do you like children, have you children of your own? Ridiculous questions for anybody who has written a book. And to my astonishment I heard my own voice calling to him in the empty room. "You have *been* a child. Tell them that!" And his screen image, after a short pause, said simply and with dignity. "I have been a child." Well, it was magical. He couldn't possibly have heard me and yet, distant in space but at the same moment of time, we had both come to the same point. "I have been a child."

Now, I don't at all mean by this that the people who write the books that children read, are doing it for the child they were. Nothing so nostalgic, nothing so self-indulgent, nothing so sentimental. But isn't there, here, a kind of clue? To be aware of having been a child! Many people forget this; but who are we but the child we were? We have been wounded, scarred, and dirtied over, but are still essentially that child. Essence cannot change; to be aware of and in touch with this fact is to have the whole long body of one's life at one's disposal, complete and unfragmented. You do not chop off a section of your imaginative substance and make a book specifically for children; for if you are honest you have, in fact, no idea where childhood ends and maturity begins. It is all endless and all one. And from time to time, without intention or invention, this whole body of stuff, each part constantly cross-fertilizing every other, sends up—what is the right word?—intimations. And the best you can do, if you are lucky, is to be there to jot them down. This being there, this being present to catch them, is important; otherwise they are lost. Your role is that of the necessary lunatic who remains attentive and in readiness, unselfconscious, unconcerned, all disbelief suspended, even when frogs turn into princes, and nursemaids, against all gravity, slide up the bannisters. You have, indeed, to be aware that on a certain level, not immediately accessible, perhaps, but one that one derides at one's peril—on a certain level the frog is lawfully a prince and the transcending of the laws of gravity—up the bannisters or up the glass mountain, it really makes no difference—is the proper task of the hero. And heroes and their concomitant villains are the very stuff of this kind of literature.

Now these matters, I submit, have nothing to do with the labels "From 5 to 7" or "From 9 to 12"; they have nothing to do with age at all. Nor have they anything to do with that other label, "Literature for Children," which suggests that this is something different from literature in general, something that pens off both child and author from the main stream of writing. This seems to me hard both on children and on literature. For if it is literature indeed, it can't help being all one river and you put into it, according to age, a small foot or a large one. When mine was a small foot, I seem to remember that I was grateful for books that did not speak to my childishness, books that treated me with respect, that spread out the story just as it was, Grimm's Fairy Tales, for instance, and left me to deal with it as I could. If they moralized, I was not offended. I let them do it because of the story. If they tried to explain, I humored them, again for the sake of the story. Book and reader communed together, each accepting the other. So, remembering my own experience as a reader, could I, as a writer, speak to a child by way of his childishness?

Childlikeness—ah, that's a different matter. It is a quality that can be found in child and grown-up alike. It has nothing to do with age. Not very long ago, a woman journalist came to see me and told me how she had read *Mary Poppins* to her child very quietly so as not to disturb the father, who was working in the same room. And night after night, with increasing irascibility, he protested against this quietness. He was not being disturbed, he said, and begged her not to mumble. If there was one thing he detested, he said, it was the sound of somebody mumbling. And at the end of a week of such protestations, when he was going away for a night, he took the child aside and whispered, "Listen carefully to the story and when I come back you can tell me all that has happened." He, himself, had been listening all the time.

Well, I have a feeling of affection for that father for I think there was something in him that would agree with me, if I put it to him, that what is real, is real for everyone, not *only* but *also* for children. And he would not, I think, think me frivolous if I suggested that the country where the fox and the hare say goodnight to each other, this country is the place we are all seeking, child and grown-up alike. We are looking for miracles, looking for meaning. We want the fox not to eat the hare, we want the opposites reconciled. Child and grown-up alike, we want it. And I hope *you* will not think me frivolous when I say that it is not only children but many grown-ups, lunatic grown-ups if you will, who in their own inner world are concerned at the Sleeping Beauty's sleep and long for her to be wakened.

And here it is worth while remembering, since we are discussing Not Writing for Children, that neither the Sleeping Beauty nor Rumpelstiltzkin was really written for children. In fact, none of the fundamental fairy stories was ever written at all. They all arose spontaneously from the folk and were transmitted orally from generation to generation to unlettered listeners of all ages. It was not until the nineteenth century, when the collectors set them down in print, that the children purloined them and made them their own. They were the perquisites of the grown-ups and the children simply took them. I remember a poem of Walter de la Mare's which begins, "I'll sing you a song of the world's little children magic has stolen away." Well, I could sing you a song of the world's magic the children have stolen away. For in the long run it is children themselves who decide what they want. They put out their hands and abstract a treasure from all sorts of likely and unlikely places, as I have tried to show. So, confronted with this hoard of stolen riches, the question of who writes or who does not write for children becomes small and, in fact, irrelevant. For every book is a message, and if children happen to receive and like it, they will appropriate it to themselves no matter what the author may say nor what label he gives himself. And those who, against all odds, and I'm one of them, protest that they do not write for children cannot help being aware of this fact and are, I assure you, grateful.

That's all I have to say.

9

Webs of Concern

The Little Prince and *Charlotte's Web*

LAURENCE GAGNON

Any literary work is susceptible to an indefinite variety of interpretations. In this respect works of literature are like formal systems. Our understanding of the sequences of words in a novel or poem, or the sequences of symbols in a logico-mathematical system is not completely determined by those sequences of words or symbols, still less by any intentions of the author(s). We achieve an understanding of a literary work or a formal system when we associate with it some model of the way things are or, at least, of a way they could be. Sometimes in order to do this we may have to suspend (temporarily) some of our beliefs about what is the case. But such are the demands of imaginative interpretation.

One type of model which can be used with great success in interpreting works of children's literature and adult fantasy is a Heideggerian model. By associating parts of Martin Heidegger's philosophy with certain parts of these literary works, we can achieve a novel, if not profound, understanding of them. Two cases in point are *The Little Prince* by A. de Saint Exupéry and *Charlotte's Web* by E. B. White.[1] It has even been reported that Heidegger himself once considered *The Little Prince* to be "one of the great existentialist books of this century."[2]

Stated as simply and untechnically as possible, the particular Heideggerian model appealed to here is one concerned with persons and their capabilities.[3] Now persons are capable of many things, of flying planes and watering flowers, of eating leftovers and killing insects. Yet these are rather superficial capabilities, not being characteristic of persons as such but rather only of persons as pilots or gardeners, omnivores or killers. Among the more fundamental capabilities are those of being aware of oneself, of being concerned about things in the world, of dreading one's death, and of living authentically. Since each person as such is unique and irreplaceable, this ultimate capability is also the ultimate personal obligation: to live authentically. Under the present interpretation, *The Little Prince* and *Charlotte's Web* are about various personal struggles to live authentically. In each of these works there are characters who find themselves thrown into existence, as it were, amidst other beings with whom they end up being concerned, all the while being confronted with the difficult and inescapable task of truly becoming what they alone can be— even unto death. This is precisely the task of living authentically. The ever-present danger here is that of losing one's sense of personal identity by becoming part of the crowd or by becoming overly concerned with other beings.[4]

In *The Little Prince*, neither the stranded pilot nor the prince himself have succumbed to the temptation of becoming a people-self; i.e., a faceless, anonymous part of a crowd. Since he was six years old, the time at which he produced his famous drawings of a boa constrictor digesting an elephant, the stranded pilot has been of the opinion that grown-ups are not only concerned with inconsequential "matters of consequence," such as bridge and golf, politics and neckties, but also terribly dense when it comes to discussing such important matters as boa constrictors, primeval forests and stars. "So," he says, "I have lived my life alone, without anyone that I could really talk to . . . " (p. 5).

The little prince has not been so lonely, having his flower to talk to. However, his opinion of grown-ups is much the same as that of the stranded pilot. They are not merely strange, nor even "very, very odd," but rather "altogether extraordinary" in their denseness and their concerns (pp. 47, 50, 52, 57). The king who has no subjects except a rat, the conceited man who has no admirers except himself, the tippler who drinks to forget that he is ashamed of drinking, the businessman who values his accounts but not what they are of, the geographer who knows nothing in particular about geography—none of these receives nor deserves the admiration of the little prince, for none are living authentically. Worse yet there is little hope that they will change, since they neither take care of things nor care for persons. What interest they take in the little visitor is selfish. Living on their respective planets, the little prince would at best be treated as an extension of themselves, not as a distinct individual worthy of their concern. It is not just physically that they lead isolated lives.

Only on asteroid 329 does the little prince find a man whom he could possible befriend—the lamplighter—who at least takes care of his lamp. "But his planet is indeed too small. There is no room on it for two people . . . " (p. 61). On earth there is at least room. Here, of course, the little prince finds friendship. He tames the willing fox. He establishes ties with the not-so-willing, stranded pilot. He becomes forever responsible for them, and they in turn for him.

But there is always a danger here; one can lose oneself to the things one takes care of and the persons one cares for. One can become so concerned with other beings that one identifies with them rather than striving for the unique identity proper to oneself. As long as one does this, one cannot live authentically. Before he began his wanderings, the little prince was too concerned with his rose; in his conscientiousness he had become a slave to her and she in her vanity and pride encouraged his servitude. This was not good for either of them. At that time it was important to both that she be the only flower of her kind in the whole universe. Because of all this, his agony in the garden is inevitable, when he discovers that there are thousands upon thousands of roses like his own. Yet none are his rose. This the tamed fox enables him to see. What makes his rose precious is not its physical appearance but the time he has "wasted" on it. "It is only with the heart that one can see rightly; what is essential is invisible to the eye" (p. 87). This truth, which men have forgotten, sets the little prince free; while he still has ties with his rose, he is no longer tied down to her.

In this regard the stranded pilot has much to learn. Although his initial concerns are taking care of his damaged plane and caring for himself, he eventually manages to become deeply concerned for his little visitor. But in this new concern, he becomes overly attached to his new friend. He understands that the little prince must leave but he cannot accept it as the fox has done. He asks for comfort and implores his readers to send him word of the little man's return. Yet this is understandable, for the stranded pilot is neither as wise and patient as the fox nor as young and innocent as the little prince. He requires more time.

The wisdom of the fox is not the only wisdom which the little prince discovers on earth. He also learns that while taking care of one's possessions and caring for others are necessary for one to live authentically, they alone are not sufficient, even when done without attachment. One must also recognize that life, especially one's own life, necessarily involves death, not as a termination of these concerns but rather as a culmination of them. This is the wisdom of the snake who always speaks in riddles. With a certain resoluteness, the little prince advances toward his own death, even though he is somewhat afraid and anxious. As the stranded pilot discovers, it was not by chance that little man was "strolling along like that, all alone, a thousand miles from any inhabited region" (p. 98). Death is always a solitary experience.

But since the little prince is a star-child, innocent and true, there is a resurrection. His "was not such a heavy body" after all (p. 109). Yet even with the element of resurrection, the question of what comes after death ought not to arise. For dying is the ultimate individual act of which a person is capable. The stranded pilot cannot quite accept this. He still ponders the mystery of what happens afterwards: "What is happening on his planet?"; "Has the sheep eaten the flower?" (pp. 109, 111).

These questions are not important in themselves, but only in so far as they symbolize the ties which have been established between the little prince and the stranded pilot. What is important is stated by the star-child:

> In one of the stars I shall be living. In one of them I shall be laughing. And so it will be as if all the stars were laughing, when you look at the sky at night ... You—only you—will have stars that can laugh! ... And when your sorrow is comforted (time soothes all sorrows) you will be content that you have known me. You will always be my friend.
>
> (p. 104)

And this would be true, even if there were no resurrection.

In *Charlotte's Web*, a rat, a pig, and a spider find themselves thrown into existence together, inescapably confronted with the task of truly becoming what they can be—even unto death. The rat, Templeton, commits himself to an inauthentic existence. In a miserly fashion he acquires things without thereafter tending to them. Merely storing rotten eggs like banking stars does not involve taking care of one's possessions. Not having developed even this capacity, he cannot develop his capacity of caring for others. He must be enticed to go to the fair and bribed to pick up the egg sac. He could care less whether Wilbur, the pig, died of a broken heart or whether Charlotte, the spider, died of exhaustion and old age (pp. 168–169). Nor does he really confront the possibility of his own death. He lives for the present, especially when it is "full of life" in the form of feasting and carousing (pp. 147, 175). Of course, his death will come sometime. But he sees it as coming in the distant future, as the end of his life, rather than as a distinctive part of his life. "Who wants to live forever?" he sneers (p. 175).

Wilbur, on the other hand, is not committed to inauthentic existence but he is tempted in a variety or ways to live inauthentically. As a young pig, he does not have an especially strong personality. His attitudes and opinions can easily be swayed by outside influences: a few words from the goose, a pail of slops, a rainy day, the bad news from the old sheep, the reassuring promise of Charlotte. As a result he is always in danger of becoming a people-self rather than a distinctive person. If Charlotte's web says that he is "some pig" and people believe it, Wilbur believes it. If it says that he is "terrific" and people believe it, he not only believes it but also really feels terrific. If it's "radiant," then radiant Wilbur is. (Only with the last, prophetic message is there a genuineness in Wilbur's attitude—he has finally become more of himself, a humble pig.)

Wilbur refuses to face the fact that he might be killed next Christmas time and turned into smoked bacon and ham. " 'I don't *want* to die' ..." he moans, "... 'I want to stay alive, right here in my comfortable manure pile with all my friends' " (p. 51). He does not see his dying as an integral part of his life. He sees it as the end of it all.

Left to his own devices, the selfish and insecure Wilbur would remain a people-self. But "out of the darkness, came a small voice he had never heard before ... 'Do you want a friend, Wilbur?' it said. 'I'll be a friend to you' " (p. 31). Charlotte tames him. From the ties thus established, Wilbur gradually grows to care for the large grey spider who lives in the upper part of the barn doorway. Since he naturally tends toward being a people-self, his initial reaction is to identify himself with his new found friend by imitating her. So he tries in vain to spin a web, ignoring Charlotte's profound observation, "... 'you and I lead different lives' " (p. 56). When Charlotte says she's glad she's a sedentary spider, Wilbur replies, " 'Well, I'm sort of sendentary myself, I guess' " (p. 61).

Gradually Wilbur realizes that he and Charlotte are different, even though friends. They are different not merely generically, as pig and spider, but also individually, as distinctive persons. But persons are beings-unto-death. So Wilbur and Charlotte must also differ in their dying.

It is only after the Fair has ended, the crowd dispersed, and Wilbur's hour of triumph over that he turns his attention away from himself toward his dying friend. " 'Why did you do all this for me? ... I don't deserve it. I've never done anything for you' " (p. 169). With her characteristic wisdom, Charlotte replies, " 'You have been my friend ... That in itself is a tremendous thing' " (p. 164).

Now more than ever, Wilbur wants to preserve the ties that have been established between him and the lovely grey spider. He throws "himself down in an agony of pain and sorrow," sobbing "... 'I can't *stand* it ... I won't leave you here alone to die'" (p. 165). But Wilbur is being ridiculous. He can't stay with Charlotte. For if he stayed, he would not be true either to Charlotte or himself. His call of conscience is to return to the farm with Charlotte's egg sac. With amazing agility (for a pig) Wilbur accepts this call to authenticity. "All winter Wilbur watched over

Charlotte's egg sac as though he were guarding his own children" (pp. 175–176).

In the spring the young spiders came. But there is sorrow in this resurrection. Being unique themselves, none can live the life Charlotte did. So Charlotte's children sail away. "This is our moment for setting forth" (p. 180). However, Wilbur is not left totally alone. Three of them stay. To them Wilbur pledges his friendship, "forever and ever" (p. 183). Yet "Wilbur never forgot Charlotte. Although he loved her children and grandchildren dearly, none of the new spiders ever quite took her place in his heart. She was in a class by herself" (p. 184). From the beginning Charlotte had resolutely advanced toward her own solitary death, all the while taking care of her magnificent web and caring for her humble friend. She saves Wilbur from an undistinctive death and gives him both the situation and the time to heed his own call of concern.

> Nobody, of the hundreds of people that had visited the Fair, knew that a grey spider had played the most important part of all. No one was with her when she died. (p. 171)

Thus a stranded pilot and a little prince, a young pig, and a grey spider struggled to live authentically, each necessarily in his own way and time. Because of them, laughing stars illuminate webs of concern in the dead of night.

Notes

1. All references cited in the text will be to the following editions of these works: A. de Saint Exupéry, *The Little Prince*, trans. by K. Woods (New York: Harcourt, Brace & Jovanovich, 1971). E. B. White, *Charlotte's Web* (New York: Harper & Row, 1952).

2. C. Cate, *Antoine de Saint-Exupéry* (New York: G. P. Putnam's Sons, 1970), p. 465.

3. Some of the passages in M. Heidegger's, *Sein und Zeit*, which are relevant to the present model are: pp. 12, 42–43, 53–57, 121–30, 142–45, 175–76, 191–96, 231–36, 245–80, 296–310, 325–26, 386, 424–26. These are indicated in the margins of J. Macquarrie and E. Robinson's translation of the work (New York: Harper & Row, 1962). Of course, if other passages are emphasized or other works used, different Heideggerian models will result.

4. The details of the model are worked out in the subsequent interpretations of the two works. For a lucid exposition of the model, see: J. Demske, *Being, Man, and Death* (Lexington: University of Kentucky, 1970).

10
Death in Children's Literature

FRANCELIA BUTLER

C. S. Lewis, whose "Narnia" fantasies for children are one expression of his religious philosophy, observed that "a children's story is the best art form for something you have to say."[1] Like a parable—or sometimes, an epitaph—the limpid simplicity of the form makes it easier to see into the depths, even of death.

Once upon a time, children and adults shared the same literature and together understood what there was to be understood about death. That time was from the beginning of literature up until the end of the seventeenth century, when a separation began to take place between the literature of adults and that of children. From then on, the treatment of death became part of a larger problem—the commercial and psychological exploitation of children through a special literature aimed at them alone.

Indications are that the separation might have begun with the "Warnings to Apprentices," published by commercial interests in the seventeenth century. These bear a striking resemblance to the warnings to little children, the "deathbed confessions" of children who disobeyed moral "laws" and reformed too late. Numerous books of these confessions were published in England and America by the Puritan merchant class in the late seventeenth and eighteenth centuries. These deathbed confessions and other dire warnings to children were continued in the hundreds of Sunday School tracts which grew out of the Sunday School movement begun by Robert Raikes. Raikes, a wealthy shipowner, acknowledged that he began the Sunday Schools to keep working children from depredations on Sundays.[2] These tracts distorted goodness itself by getting children to do the right things for the wrong reasons. Raikes' family ties with John Newbery, who is considered to be the "father" of children's literature, could be one indication that the establishment of children's literature as a separate field had an economic basis.

Before the seventeenth century, children learned about death in literature shared with adults. They heard Bible stories, fables, legends, ballads, folk tales, or folk plays or read them themselves. Death could be seen in proper perspective because in this literature all the convictions, fears, and hopes of people about many things were gathered up and transmitted.

For the most part, this literature encouraged hopes for life after death in some form. Stith Thompson's *Motif-Index of Folk Literature* abounds with references to restoration to life, either by magical reassemblage of the body's dispersed members, or by administration of the water of life, or by medicines, or in various other ways. Men may come back as women or women as men. People may become children, dwarves, monsters, princes or princesses, stars or angels or gods. They can return to earth as fish, horses' heads, donkeys, cows, bulls, oxen, calves, buffalo, swine, wild boar, goats, cats, dogs, lions, wolves, rabbits, foxes, deer, seals, bears, hyenas, jackals, elephants, monkeys, rats, otters, ducks, owls, hawks, eagles, swallows, cuckoos, doves, pigeons, ravens, quails, partridges, herons, cranes, geese, peacocks, parrots, snakes, lizards, crocodiles, tortoises, or frogs. Or they may come back as bees, butterflies, fleas, weevils, bedbugs, salmon, goldfish, sharks, whales, leeches, scorpions, crabs. Again, they may turn into trees, roses, lilies, lotus, grass, straw, herbs, bramblebushes, tobacco plants, peanut plants, eggplants, musical instruments, dishes, fountains, balls, wind, stones, salt, smoke, rainbows, minerals, meteors, hills, flour vats, hoes, hoe-handles, mussels, or currants. Or, after a variety of transformations, they may return to their original human form.[3] In any case, the possibility of coming back as an eggplant or a fish, for instance, should sharpen one's interest in ecology. The hopeful note in folk literature is that people *do* tend to come back.

In North American Indian tales, as Jaime de Angulo's beautiful crystallization suggests, life and death are closely related, are at times interchangeable states.[4] However, in some American Indian tales, people stay dead:

> Nearly all North American Indian tribes offer some explanation of the origin of death. The most widespread tale is that of an early controversy between two characters, either animal or human. One character wants people to die and be revived, the other wants death to be permanent. The second character wins the controversy. Often, a little later, a close relative of his, such as the

son, dies and the parent wishes the decision reversed. His opponent reminds him, however, that he himself has already decided the matter.[5]

A similar matter-of-fact acceptance of death is occasionally found in European folktales, as in Grimm's story, "The Death of Partlet," a story left out of most Grimm collections. As the story ends in Grimm,

> Chanticleer was left alone with his dead Partlet. He dug her a grave and laid her in it, and raised a mound over it, and there he sat and mourned her till he died too. So they were all dead.[6]

Children themselves seem to begin with this same simple acceptance of death. In the still very active oral tradition, in the skip-rope rhymes jumped by children from the age of six on, and chanted much earlier, children treat death quite matter-of-factly:

> Little Miss Pink
> Dressed in blue
> Died last night
> At quarter past two
> Before she died
> She told me this:
> When I jump rope
> I always—miss.[7]

By writing the American Field Service, which solicited the rhymes from foreign lycées, and also through writing foreign embassies in Washington, I have made a collection of these rhymes. One contributed by the New Zealand Embassy goes:

> There was an old woman and her name was Pat,
> And when she died, she died like *that*,
> They put her in a coffin,
> And she fell through the bottom,
> Just like *that*.[8]

Restoration to life is the general rule in children's play, however. "Bang bang, you're dead!" is only a figure of speech.

One of the many stories of restoration to life in the Grimm collection is the famous "Juniper Tree" story. In this story, a little boy who has been murdered by his jealous stepmother and made into a tasty stew for his father, comes back as a bird to reward his loving father and little sister and to drop a millstone on his stepmother's head. As a bird, he sings about what has happened to him:

My mother made a stew of me,
My father ate it all.
My little sister wept to see
Marlene, my sister small,
Then gathered my bones in her silken shawl,
And laid them under the Juniper tree.
    Sing, hey! What a beautiful bird am I.[9]

After the stepmother's death, the bird becomes a little boy again and rejoins his family. When the stepmother dies, however, she dies for good; for the wicked, death often provides irreversible retribution. It brings death or rigidity, turns one to a statue or a stone.

Andrew Lang's Fairy Books of various colors date back to the nineteenth century, but they have always been loved by children and furnish an excellent cross section of the folk tales from all parts of the world. In these volumes, there are at least a dozen stories of special interest which relate to death. In *The Orange Fairy Book*, there is a story from India entitled, "The King Who Would See Paradise."[10] The theme here seems to be that though Paradise may be one's lot eventually, one should not hasten the process, but prepare for the end by performing as perfectly as possible one's duties while on earth. *The Pink Fairy Book* contains a Spanish story, "The Water of Life," in which a sister, wiser and more courageous than her brothers, fetches the magic water and restores not only her brothers, but "a great company of youths and girls" who have been put under an evil spell and turned to stones.[11] *The Red Fairy Book* contains a Rumanian story which attempts to explain death. People feel impelled to follow a mysterious Voice and are never seen again. When the source of the Voice is finally located, it turns out to be nothing but a vast plain. After that, people don't bother to follow the voice anymore, but simply die at home.[12] *The Crimson Fairy Book* has a more cheerful story— one of a prince who seeks immortality and gets it. In this Hungarian tale, the Queen of the Immortals and Death himself fight over a youth. The Queen wins.[13] *The Yellow Fairy Book* has a North American Indian story which combines elements similar to those in the story of Pygmalion, and the Orpheus and Eurydice legend. When an Indian's wife dies, he makes a wooden doll just like her and dresses it in her clothes. The doll comes to life, but the husband is under a prohibition not to touch her until they have returned to their own village. He can't wait and she becomes a doll again.[14] In *The Violet Fairy Book* are two Swahili stories in which animals, in one a gazelle and in the other, a snake, sacrifice their lives so that human beings may live.[15] *The Lilac Fairy Book* contains another Swahili tale— this one about a clever monkey who professes to keep his heart in a safe place at home, when he travels. This idea of an external heart or soul is not infrequent in folk tales. It is a means of safeguarding one's immortality by keeping it stashed away—not putting all one's organs in one's body, so to speak. The other tale has to do with a fish who achieves immortality. A tree arises from his buried bones. This tale is unusual because, even in Christ's use of them in the New Testament, fish are expendable . . . one of the innocuous animals that ends up as food for people and the act of killing fish is blotted out, some way.[16]

Though there are a variety of approaches to the subject of death in these stories, all in all the approach is not morbid. Generally in folk tales, the magic potion which conquers death is love. One sees this in the German folk tale, "Briar Rose," or essentially the same, the French story, "The Sleeping Beauty." As G. K. Chesterton observes in his essay, "The Ethics of Elfland,"

> There is the terrible allegory of "The Sleeping Beauty," which tells how the human creature was blessed with all birthday gifts, yet cursed with death; and how death also may perhaps be softened to a sleep.[17]

Nor does this death-conquering love have to be sexual. Stravinsky's ballet, "The Firebird," has acquainted many westerners with the Russian folk tale of "Prince Ivan, the Firebird, and the Gray Wolf." Murdered by his evil brothers, "Prince Ivan lay dead on that spot exactly thirty days; then the gray wolf came upon him and knew him by his odor:

> Then the gray wolf sprinkled Prince Ivan with the water of death, and his body grew together; he sprinkled him with the water of life, and Prince Ivan stood up and said: "Ah, I have slept very long!"[18]

In the legends enjoyed by children, the hero has power, even over death. In the Norse legend of "Thor's Unlucky Journey," Thor is challenged to a wrestling match with Utgard-Loki's old nurse, Eli, who, unbeknownst to him, is Old Age or Death: "It was a marvel," said Utgard-Loki, "That you withstood so long and bent only one knee."[19]

In Caxton's version of *Le Morte d'Arthur*, from which many children's versions, including Lanier's *Boy's King Arthur*, stem, Arthur commands Sir Bedivere to throw Arthur's sword, Excalibur, into the water. Bedivere throws the sword far out, and sees an arm and hand reach above the water, take the sword, brandish it three times and vanish. Then Sir Bedivere takes the dying King on his back and carries him to the waterside. Here a barge is drawn up, with many fair ladies in it, all of them wearing black hoods. At the King's command, Bedivere puts him on the barge, and the barge moves away:

> Than sir Bedwere cryed and seyde,
> "A, my lorde Arthur, what shall becom of me, now ye go frome
>   me and leve my here alone amonge myne enemyes?"
> "Comforte thyselff," seyde the kynge, "and do as well as thou
>   mayste, for in me ys no truste for to truste in. For I muste
>   into the vale of Avylyon to hele me of my grevous wounde.
>   And if thou here nevermore of me, pray for my soule!"[20]

Roland, in all versions of the Charlemagne cycle, blows a note of defiance in the face of death. Here is a version for children:

> Count Roland's mouth was filled with blood. His brain had
> burst from his temples. He blew his horn in pain and anguish.
> Charles heard it, and so did his Frenchmen. Said the King:
> "That bugle carries far!"
> Duke Naimes replied:
> " 'Tis that a hero blows the blast!"[21]

When The Cid dies, in a current children's version of this Spanish legend, the embalmed body of The Cid leads a victorious charge against the enemy:

> It was The Cid himself who led the charge, mounted upon
> Babieca, his sword Tizone gleaming by his side! This was too much
> for Yusuf and too much for his army. The legends were all true!
> This Cid was really a demon from hell! Here he was, raised from
> the dead, charging relentlessly down on them![22]

Best known of the many retellings of the Robin Hood story for children is probably that of Howard Pyle. Here, too, Robin Hood seems to be in control, even of his death:

> His old strength seemed to come back to him, and, drawing the
> bowstring to his ear, he sped the arrow out of the open casement.
> As the shaft flew, his hand sank slowly with the bow till it lay
> across his knees, and his body likewise sank back again into Little
> John's loving arms; but something had sped from that body, even
> as the winged arrow sped from the bow.[23]

Universally, in folk plays, which are shared both by children and adults, there is an element of wonder, of fantasy, in the ritual death so often portrayed and inevitably followed by restoration to an even more vigorous life.[24] Fertility symbol or whatever it may be, this death and resurrection is accepted both by audience and the players—and these plays continue in some sections of the world.[25] In the mummers' play of St. George, for instance, St. George may kill the Turkish Knight (there are many versions of the play), but then the Doctor invariably enters with a special medicine:

> It will bring the dead to life again.
> A drop on his head, a drop on his heart.
> Rise up, bold fellow, and take thy part.[26]

Also, in the Punch and Judy shows, which in their present form probably date to the eighteenth century but which may date back to the fertility rituals in Greek and Roman mimes, Punch literally triumphs over Death, or the Devil.[27]

One finds in folk drama the concept of life as a journey towards death, a journey in which children and adults move on together, the morality, "Everyman," being the notable example of this theme. In such plays, the traveler is guided by the various tenets of his faith, his deeds being the mileposts of his progress.

The strong dramatic element in life as a journey is found in many folk tales, including those among Indians in the Middle American area, where "The underlying theme is that the soul on its way to the afterworld is confronted by dangers and difficulties which must be overcome."[28] Some of these, such as going between clashing rocks or over a body of water, are reminiscent of the Greek or Roman epics. The idea of life as a journey toward death peeps through most notably, perhaps, in children's literature in the nineteenth century in Louisa May Alcott's *Little Women*, where Meg, Jo, Amy, and Beth (who is about to die) go on a pilgrimage from cellar to attic—a more realistic journey than that in Bunyan—and later receive small copies of *Pilgrim's Progress*, in colored bindings, under their pillows as Christmas gifts.[29] Andersen's "Little Mermaid" also must make a journey from sea to land and undergo much suffering—must die that others may love—before she wins an immortal soul. Nor is it enough purgation for Tom, the chimney sweep in Charles Kingsley's *The Water-Babies*, to be brutally beaten by his Master and maltreated by everyone in contact with him. Even after he drowns and becomes a water-baby, he still must undergo a long Jungian journey and spiritual purification—must help someone he doesn't like (his old Master, Grimes).[30]

Besides folk tales and folk drama, another form of literature for children which has ancient roots is the fable. Though there is currently no satisfying popular edition, there are several bowdlerized editions of *Aesop* published by various companies every year. We know that Caxton's translation of *Aesop* was read both by children and adults, and John Locke repeatedly recommends *Aesop* for children.[31] Here the relation of all as-

pects of human experience is quite complete—including sexual experience—complete enough to make spicy reading for *Playboy*. (But this
shouldn't bother us if we have seen the rhymes chanted today by children
themselves and recorded in the seventy-fifth volume of the *Journal of
American Folklore*.) Here is one of the "death" fables from Caxton's *Aesop*:

> Many one ben whiche haue grete worship and glorye/ But noo
> prudence/ ne noo wysedom they haue in them whereof Esope
> reherceth suche a fable/ Of a wulf which found a dede mans hede/
> the whiche he torned vp so doune with his foote/ And sayd/ Ha a
> how fayr hast thow be and playsaunt/ And now thow hast in the
> neyther wytte/ ne beaute/ yet thow arte withoute voys and without
> ony thought/ And therefore men ought not only to behold the
> beaute and fayrenesse of the body/ but only the goodnes of the
> courage/ For somtyme men gyuen glorye and worship to some/
> whiche haue not deseruyd to haue hit/.[32]

Alas, poor Shakespeare and Milton, who were limited to reading like this,
instead of having the benefit of such contemporary emptiness as *Michael
Is Brave* (a frightened little boy learns courage by showing a little girl how
to go down a slide), or any of the other hundreds of commercial books
(we shan't call them literature) by one-message tacticians in the Puritan
tradition, who—no matter how they may try to sugar coat the message—
talk down to children. Sir Roger L'Estrange's *Aesop*, which came out two
years after Locke had recommended *Aesop* for children's reading, states
specifically in the preface that it is designed for children and has nothing
unsuitable for childish ears.[33] Yet it is just as explicit about all areas of
human experience as is Caxton's.

A more recent book for little children, *Life and Death*, by Herbert
Zim and Sonia Bleeker, also is explicit, but the focus is on factual and
scientific information:

> Long ago people had the idea that death was like a long sleep.
> Children think so too. This belief is far from the truth. A sleeping
> animal or a sleeping person is alive. He breathes, his heart beats,
> he moves, dreams, and will react to a touch or a poke. Someone
> who is dead does none of these things.[34]

Later on, the book candidly tells the child:

> After burial a body, which is composed of nearly three-quar-
> ters water, soon changes. The soft tissues break down and dis-
> appear first. Within a year only bones are left.[35]

Such man-in-the-white-coat treatment lacks warmth and beauty and is certainly not sufficient for initiating children to the subject of death. In many commercial books for children now, there is a paucity of imagination, a lack of philosophical reflection, something missing. Their spiritual nihilism is in itself a moral message in the Puritan tradition. Truth, these books imply, can only be determined by scientific testing. Zim and Bleeker stand for no philosophical truth. Instead, they indifferently display various beliefs on a kind of religious lazy Susan: "There is no way," they say, "to know if these beliefs are true or not. They are beyond our power to test or experiment."[36]

The inadequacy of such books as literature for children on the subject of death is commented on by Sheila R. Cole in an article which appeared in *The New York Times Book Review*. Miss Cole summarizes her observations as follows:

> All of these stories were written with a didactic purpose: to give a child a way of looking at death and living with the knowledge of it. All of them try to diffuse the finality and fearfulness by presenting death as just another natural process. But to most adults in our culture, death is more than just another natural process. It is an occasion surrounded with mystery and deep emotions. Presenting it to a child as just another change we go through is less than candid. Adults often present a prettier reality to children than actually exists. But to give easy answers to a child's questions about death is to deny reality and to diminish both life and death and, ultimately, to turn our children from our counsel.
> —"For Young Readers: Introducing Death" (September 26, 1971), p. 12.

In the nineteenth century, the neurotic writers of the classics for children expressed at least some honest emotion. Freud wasn't around yet, and they felt safe in exploding their problems—homosexuality or other—into childish rhymes and fantasies. Filled with guilt, these writers were constantly aware of death. In Lear's limericks, supposedly light rhymes designed both for children and adults, death is a leading topic, as Alison White has pointed out.[37] There was, for example, "The Old Man of Cape Horn, / Who wished he had never been born/ So he sat on a chair till he died of dispair." Professor White surmises (as Elizabeth Sewell suggested earlier in *The Field of Nonsense*) that "in his limericks Lear, like all of us, is trying to get used to death, to dull its sting."[38]

Perhaps Professor White's explanation will also serve for the grim death jokes which critics have noticed in *Alice in Wonderland*:

"Well!" thought Alice to herself, "after such a fall as this, I shall think nothing of tumbling down stairs! How brave they'll all think me at home! Why, I wouldn't say anything about it, even if I fell off the top of the house!" (which was very likely true.)[39]

Children themselves have many grimly comic—"mini-dramas"—about death:

> Look, look, mama!
> What is that mess
> That looks like strawberry jam?
> Hush, hush, my child!
> It is papa
> Run over by a tram.
>
> Ushy gushy was a worm
> A little worm was he
> He crawled upon the railroad track
> The train he didn't see.
> Ushy gushy![40]

Besides Lear and Carroll, two other writers of the nineteenth century who seem to have given vent to their emotional problems in their writings for children were J. M. Barrie and Oscar Wilde. *In Fifty Works of English and American Literature We Could Do Without*, J. M. Barrie is accused of making *Peter Pan* the vehicle for his triple theme of incest, castration, and homosexuality.[41] Barrie is also criticized for his treatment of death in the play. Say the authors:

> It's not enough, however, for Barrie to betray children. He betrays art. He does it brilliantly. That superb piece of engineering (the engineering, however, of an instrument of torture), the scene where Peter Pan appeals to the children in the audience to keep Tinker Bell alive by clapping to signal their belief in fairies is a metaphor of artistic creation itself.... Peter Pan blackmails the children, cancels the willingness of the suspension of disbelief, and disrupts the convention on which all art depends when he threatens to hold the children morally responsible for Tinker Bell's death unless by a real act—an act done in the auditorium, not on the stage—they assert their literal belief in what they know to be an artistic fiction.[42]

In Barrie's defense, one can say that he is asking the children to do what many fairy tales do—that is keeping the protagonists alive through an act of love.

All five of Oscar Wilde's famous fairy tales for children have death as their theme. In the best known of the tales both "The Selfish Giant" and the little boy he loves die. The little boy is identified as Jesus. "The Happy Prince" (a statue) persuades a swallow to pluck the ruby from the Prince's sword, the sapphires from the Prince's eyes, and the gold leaf from his body and give it to the poor in the city. By the time these acts of charity have been accomplished, it is too late for the swallow to fly South for the winter.

> "I am glad that you are going to Egypt at last, little Swallow," said the Prince, "you have stayed too long here but you must kiss me on the lips, for I love you."
>
> "It is not to Egypt that I am going," said the Swallow. "I am going to the House of Death. Death is the brother of Sleep, is he not?"
>
> And he kissed the happy Prince on the lips, and fell down dead at his feet.
>
> At that moment a curious crack sounded inside the statue, as if something had broken. The fact is that the leaden heart had snapped right in two.[43]

The saddest of Wilde's stories is "The Nightingale and the Rose." A little nightingale sees a student weeping for a red rose. The student's girl has said she would dance with him if he brought her such a rose. The nightingale seeks a rose for the youth, and is told by a tree that the only way such a rose can be obtained is for the nightingale to build it out of music and stain it with her own heart's blood. The nightingale must sing to the tree all night, with her breast against a thorn (an old English belief, by the way, as to how nightingales sing). The thorn must pierce her heart, and her life-blood must flow into the tree. "Death is a great price to pay for a red rose," cried the Nightingale:

> So the Nightingale pressed closer against the thorn, and the thorn touched her heart, and a fierce pang of pain shot through her. Bitter, bitter was the pain, and wilder and wilder grew her song, for she sang of the Love that is perfected by Death, of the Love that dies not in the tomb. . . .
>
> "Look, look!" cried the Tree, "the rose is finished now;" but the Nightingale made no answer, for she was lying dead in the long grass with the thorn in her heart.[44]

The Student finds the rose outside his window and presents it to the girl, but she spurns it as the Chamberlain's nephew, meanwhile, has sent her some jewels. Disgusted, the Student throws the rose down in the street, and a cartwheel runs over it.

> "What a silly thing Love is," said the Student as he walked away. "It is not half as useful as Logic, for it does not prove anything, and it is always telling one of things that are not going to happen, and making one believe things that are not true. In fact, it is quite unpractical, and, as in this age to be practical is everything, I shall go back to Philosophy and study Metaphysics."
>
> So he returned to his room and pulled out a great dusty book, and began to read.[45]

Cynically, the Student throws away the emotional and picks up the scientific.

Even though these stories sound like dreams recounted on a psychoanalyst's couch, they do have the ring of honesty, which can be tested by comparison with the Puritan educational propaganda for children, in which death is a punishment for sin. Closely related in theme to the "Warnings to Apprentices" of the late seventeenth century, numerous deathbed confessions of young children stemmed from James Janeway's *A Token for Children: Being an Exact Account of the Conversions, Holy and Exemplary Lives, and Joyful Deaths of Several Young Children* (1671). These continued to be printed in small American towns during the eighteenth and nineteenth centuries. The Connecticut Historical Society in Hartford has a number of these little books[46] and several are listed in the A.S.W. Rosenbach catalog of *Early American Children's Books*.[47] Their reflection is seen in *The New England Primer*, many editions of which contained these verses:

> Tho' I am young yet I may die,
> And hasten to eternity:
> There is a dreadful fiery hell,
> Where wicked ones must always dwell.[52]

As if the poor American Indian children had not suffered enough, even they were subjected to these deathbed confessions, and in 1835, *Triumphant Deaths of Pious Children* was translated into Choctaw by Missionaries of the American Board of Commissions for Foreign Missions.[49] What is more, these deathbed confessions of children merged imperceptibly with the nineteenth century Sunday School literature, so that we have, for instance, *An Authentic Account of the Conversion, Experience, and Happy Deaths of Ten Boys*, designed for Sunday Schools, and published in New Haven (1820).[50]

Here is a quotation from one of the early nineteenth century Sunday School booklets published for children by the American Tract Society in New York. Since I have not located it elsewhere, I am quoting from a copy in my own collection:

> Why should you say, 'tis yet too soon
>   To seek for heaven, and think of death?
> The flower will fade before 'tis noon,
>   And you this day may lose your breath.
>
> Then 'twill for ever be in vain
>   To cry for pardon and for grace;
> To wish you had your time again,
>   Or hope to see the Savior's face.[51]

This gloomy literature allied itself easily with the sentimental attitude toward death in the mid-nineteenth century, famous examples being Hans Christian Andersen's stories of "The Little Fir Tree," "The Steadfast Tin Soldier," and "The Little Match Girl." Then there is the death of Little Eva in Harriet Beecher Stowe's *Uncle Tom's Cabin.* Often, in the sentimental literature, the child does not die for his own sins but for the adultery of adults—his parents—and the trend here is found in adult literature as well, as in Mrs. Wood's *East Lynne.*[52] Always quick to penetrate hypocrisy, Mark Twain in *Tom Sawyer* has the boys, supposedly dead, return to witness their own funeral and to hear themselves eulogized as saints by those who hated their humanity while they were alive in the town:

> First one and then another pair of eyes followed the minister's, and then almost with one impulse the congregation rose and stared while the three dead boys came marching up the aisle, Tom in the lead, Joe next, and Huck, a ruin of drooping rags, sneaking sheepishly in the rear! They had been hid in the unused gallery listening to their own funeral sermon! (*Tom Sawyer*, Chapter 17)

Thus, the boys have the double satisfaction of getting back at their parents or parent-figures and, at the same time, of witnessing their own "death" and resurrection.

In our own time, one of the best known instances of death as a punishment for a mistake (or at least, death as closely associated with the mistake or sin) is that of the death of the good Thorin in Tolkien's *Hobbit.* Thorin's greed for the great jewel, the Arkenstone, to which he feels rightly entitled, leads to a fight. Though the quarrel is resolved, Thorin dies and the Arkenstone is buried with him. Thus Thorin (and possibly the readers) learns the worthlessness of material things.

One of the most notable treatments of death in children's literature is by E. B. White in *Charlotte's Web*. White makes an interesting blend of fantasy and realism: when the little spider dies, she lives on through her 500 offspring, through the memory of the extraordinary web-writing she did above the stable door, and through the love of her friend, the pig Wilbur. White is to be commended for facing a subject which most writers for children now avoid—though not all children are content, I find, with the prospect of a selective immortality for those with children or extraordinary ideas or (short-lived) friends. Still, such lines as these have beauty, pathos, and, above all, sincerity:

> Nobody, of the hundreds of people that had visited the Fair, knew that a grey spider had played the most important part of all. No one was with her when she died.
>
> (*Charlotte's Web*, Chapter 21)

For the fullest treatment of death in children's literature, we must return to the nineteenth century, to the fantasies of George MacDonald, most notably to *At the Back of the North Wind* and *The Golden Key*. George MacDonald (1824-1905) was a Scottish preacher influenced by Paracelsus, Boehme, Swedenborg, Blake, Wordsworth, Novalis, and negatively, by Calvinism. He in turn exerted an influence on Lewis Carroll, Ruskin, C. S. Lewis, Charles Williams, and J.R.R. Tolkien. Since most of his family died of tuberculosis, including four of his own children, MacDonald (who also suffered from the disease) was understandably preoccupied with the subject of death.[53]

To some extent, his writings combine the various attitudes toward death, for they embody a simple acceptance of death and fear of death and the conviction finally that death is "more life."[54] He believed that child-like qualities are eternal; he believed that all life goes through a mystic evolution, each step of which on the way up is attended with sacrifice; and one is tempted to conclude from his fantasies that he believed that through love, faith, and the imagination one can create one's own Paradise and make it real.

But one must be careful not to be too explicit about meanings in MacDonald's fantasies about death. What they say is all the more effective because it is not pinned down. One must simply make the leap of faith into his stories. As W. H. Auden says in his Afterword to MacDonald's *Golden Key*,

> But to hunt for symbols in a fairy tale is absolutely fatal. In the Golden Key, for example, any attempt to "interpret" the Grandmother or the air-fish or the Old Man of the Sea is futile:

they mean what they are. The way, the only way, to read a fairy tale is the same as that prescribed for Tangle at one stage of her journey.[55]

And Auden quotes the following passage from the story:

> Then the Old Man of the Earth stooped over the floor of the cave, raised a huge stone from it, and left it leaning. It disclosed a great hole that went plumb-down.
> "That is the way," he said.
> "But there are no stairs."
> "You must throw yourself in. There is no other way."[56]

My own feeling is that the vagueness of MacDonald's fantasies is not a deliberate artistic accomplishment but an accident induced by an imperfect fusing of his own thought with his reading in Paracelsus, Boehme, and Novalis.

I think he wrote the fantasies because he needed deeply to believe them, but that ultimately he did not altogether trust them. The despondent silence of his last five years might serve as evidence. But I also believe that he wrought better than he knew, and that the blurred picture he produced was intuitively good, for it frees the imagination of the reader.

In St. Exupéry's *The Little Prince*, which Martin Heidegger is said to have regarded as "one of the great existentialist books of the century,"[57] the Little Prince deliberately goes out to meet the snake which he knows will return him to the earth, cause his death:

> There was nothing there but a flash of yellow close to his ankle. He remained motionless for an instant. He did not cry out. He fell as gently as a tree falls. There was not even any sound, because of the sand.[58]

The supreme act of giving is his death. It washes over him like a great wave and returns him to the cycle of nature. His courageous act of faith is not unlike the leap demanded of Tangle in *The Golden Key*. And it bears a striking symbolic resemblance to the leap demanded of all human beings in a strange Vietnamese folktale, "The Well of Immortality." In this folktale, the God Nuoc comes to earth and stations himself at the bottom of a deep well. He calls up that those who have the faith to leap down to him will become immortal. But people hesitate. Instead of leaping, they dip their fingers and toes and the tops of their heads in the water. And this is all the immortality they get—their nails and hair continue to grow after death.[59]

After the disturbing reaches of the fantasies of MacDonald or of St.

Exupéry, it is rather a relief to turn to the old-fashioned Christian Platonism of C. S. Lewis' Narnia series, concluded in the seventh book *The Last Battle*:

> "The Eagle is right," said the Lord Digory. "Listen, Peter. When Aslan said you could never go back to Narnia, he meant the Narnia you were thinking of. But that was not the real Narnia. That had a beginning and an end. It was only a shadow or copy of the real Narnia, which has always been here and always will be here: just as our world, England and all, is only a shadow or copy of something in Aslan's real world. You need not mourn over Narnia, Lucy. All of the old Narnia that mattered, all of the dear creatures, have been drawn into the real Narnia through the Door. And of course it is different; as different as a real thing is from a shadow or as waking life is from a dream." His voice stirred everyone like a trumpet as he spoke these words: but when he added under his breath "It's all in Plato, all in Plato: bless me, what *do* they teach them at these schools!" the older ones laughed. It was so exactly like the sort of thing they had heard him say long ago in that other world where his beard was grey instead of golden.[60]

How is it best to introduce a child through literature to the idea of death? Folk literature, the amalgam of human experience, and some of the great fantasies seem to indicate that the honest and warm human approach is best—not talking down to the child because of his age, for death knows all ages, but simply telling him what we know, what we don't know, what we fear, and what we hope. We find this approach in folk literature, which, as Tolkien might put it, is the very bones of the stock of human experience[61] in which there is frequently a close and friendly relationship between life and death. The predominant attitude toward death is simple acceptance, combined very often with a belief that death is not final, that it is to be accepted, even actively embraced with the sure knowledge that through love, a resurrection will occur.

Notes

1. See the editorial Afterword, "About the Author of This Book," to any of the Penguin Books in the Narnia Series (Middlesex, England, 1965).

2. Edna Johnson, Evelyn R. Sickels, and Frances Clarke Sayers, *Anthology of Children's Literature* (Boston, 1970), p. 1155. And see all of J. Henry Harris, *Robert Raikes, The Man and His Work* (Bristol, 1899?).

3. Stith Thompson, *Motif-Index of Folk Literature*, Vol. II (Bloomington, Indiana, 1956), pp. 402-517.

4. Jaime de Angulo, *Indian Tales* (New York, 1969). First edition, 1953.

5. *The Standard Dictionary of Folklore, Mythology, and Legend*, Vol. I (New York, 1949), p. 300.

6. *Grimm's Folk Tales*, tr., Eleanor Quarrie. The Folio Society. (London, 1965), p. 189. For the matter-of-fact acceptance of death by primitive man, see Paul Radin, *Primitive Man as Philosopher* (New York, 1957), pp. 97-113. First published, 1927.

7. For "Little Miss Pink," see Francelia Butler, *The Skip Rope Book* (New York, 1963).

8. The New Zealand rhyme may also be found in Brian Sutton-Smith, *The Games of New Zealand Children*, University of California Folklore Studies, No. 12 (1959), pp. 73-88.

9. *Grimm's Folk Tales*, p. 25.

10. Andrew Lang, ed., *The Orange Fairy Book* (New York, 1968), pp. 24-28. First published, 1906.

11. ———, ed., *The Pink Fairy Book* (New York, 1967), pp. 184-90. First published, 1897.

12. ———, ed., *The Red Fairy Book* (New York, 1966), pp. 182-85. First published, 1890.

13. ———, ed., *The Crimson Fairy Book* (New York, 1967), pp. 178-91. First published, 1903.

14. ———, ed., *The Yellow Fairy Book* (New York, 1966), pp. 149-51. First published, 1894.

15. ———, ed., *The Violet Fairy Book* (New York, 1966), pp. 127-47; 263-269. First published, 1901.

16. ———, ed., *The Lilac Fairy Book* (New York, 1968), pp. 42-53; 209-15. First published, 1910.

17. Gilbert Keith Chesterton, *Orthodoxy* (New York, 1908), p. 89.

18. Aleksandr Nikolaevich Afanasiev, "Prince Ivan, the Firebird, and the Gray Wolf," in *The Twelve Dancing Princesses and Other Fairy Tales* (New York, 1964), pp. 122-23.

19. Johnson, Sickels, and Sayers, p. 447.

20. *The Works of Sir Thomas Malory*, ed., Eugene Vinaver (London, 1954), p. 871.

21. Johnson, Sickels, and Sayers, p. 534.

22. Robert C. Goldston, *The Legend of the Cid* (Indianapolis, 1963), p. 154.

23. Howard Pyle, *The Merry Adventures of Robin Hood* (New York, 1968), p. 295. First published, 1883.

24. Sir Edmund Chambers, *The English Folk-Play* (London, 1969), pp. 50-59; 200-10. First published, 1933.

25. One has only to consult the English Folk Dance & Song Society for a current calendar of performances in English villages.

26. Chambers, p. 8.

27. George Speaight, *Punch & Judy A History* (London, 1970), pp. 8-10. First published as *The History of the English Puppet Theatre* (London, 1955).

28. *The Standard Dictionary of Folklore, Mythology, and Legend*, p. 300.

29. Louisa May Alcott, *Little Women* (Boston, 1919), Chapters I and II.

30. Charles Kingsley, *The Water-Babies*. University Microfilms (Ann Arbor, 1966), p. 222. First published, London, 1863.

31. *The Educational Writings of John Locke*, ed., James L. Axtell (Cambridge, Eng., 1968), pp. 259, 271, 298, 349, 364.

32. *Caxton's Aesop*, ed., R. T. Lenaghan (Cambridge, Mass., 1967), p. 98.

33. See, for instance, Sir Roger L'Estrange, *Fables and Storyes Moralized, Being a Second Part of the Fables of Aesop . . .* (London, 1699). In his introduction, L'Estrange writes, "Now *This Medly*, (such as it is) of *Salutary Hints*, and *Councels*, being Dedicated to the *Use*, and *Benefit* of *Children*, the *Innocence* of it must be preserved *Sacred* too, without the least Mixture of any Thing that's *Prophane*, *Loose*, or *Scurrilous*, or but so much as *Bordering* That way." He then includes stories that would be considered too gross for *Playboy*. (The writer of this paper examined this copy at Guildhall Library, London.)

Unfortunately, a current edition of L'Estrange (New York, 1967) is so badly bowdlerized that it constitutes merely a poor sample. The publishers nevertheless avoid acknowledging that L'Estrange intended the book for children.

34. Herbert S. Zim and Sonia Bleeker, *Life and Death* (New York, 1970), p. 20. See also Sara Bonnett Stein, *About Dying* (New York: p. 74) and Jill Krementz, *How It Feels When a Parent Dies* (New York, 1981).

35. Ibid., p. 46.

36. Ibid., p. 55.

37. Alison White, "With Birds in His Beard," *Saturday Review* (January 15, 1966), p. 27.

38. Ibid.

39. *The Annotated Alice*. By Lewis Carroll, with an introduction and notes by Martin Gardner (New York, 1960), p. 27. Here also Gardner refers to William Empson's comments in *Some Versions of Pastoral* on the numerous death jokes in *Alice*.

40. Rhymes familiar to Gertrude and Bruce McWilliams of Southend-on-Sea, England, now of Pound Ridge, New York.

41. Brigid Brophy, Michael Levey, and Charles Osborne, *Fifty Works of English and American Literature We Could Do Without* (New York, 1968), p. 109.

42. Ibid., p. 112.

43. *The Best Known Works of Oscar Wilde* (New York, 1927), p. 519.

44. Ibid., pp. 523-24.

45. Ibid., p. 524.

46. In the Albert C. Bates and Maria E. Hewins Collections, Library of The Connecticut Historical Society, Hartford.

47. A.S.W. Rosenbach, *Early American Children's Books* (New York, 1971), pp. 18, 31, 82, 133, 196. First published, 1933.

48. For instance, in *The New England Primer*, published by Ira Webster (Hartford, Conn., 1843).

49. Rosenbach, p. 285.

50. Rosenbach, p. 126.

51. *A New Picture Book*. Series 1 No. IV. American Tract Society (New York, 19--). Arnold Arnold, in *Pictures and Stories from Forgotten Children's Books* (New York, 1969), shrewdly observes that "the manipulative school of child literature has its counterpart in our own day" in "psychologically manipulative" stories which "tend to be written according to formula and confining, anti-literate, age-grouped vocabularies." p. 2.

52. Peter Coveney, *Poor Monkey: The Child in Literature* (London, 1957), pp. 136-49.

53. Robert Lee Wolff, *The Golden Key: A Study of The Fiction of George MacDonald* (New Haven, 1961), pp. 4, 9, 48, 138, 146, 373-75, 388.

54. George MacDonald, *The Golden Key* (New York, 1967), p. 71.

55. George MacDonald, *The Golden Key.* "Afterword'' by W. H. Auden, p. 85.

56. Ibid., p. 57.

57. Curtis Cate, *Antoine de Saint-Exupéry* (New York, 1970), p. 465.

58. Antoine de St. Exupéry, *The Little Prince* (New York, 1943), p. 89.

59. Ruth Q. Sun, *Land of Seagull and Fox: Folk Tales of Vietnam* (Rutland, Vermont, 1967), pp. 19-20.

60. C. S. Lewis, *The Last Battle* (Penguin: Middlesex, Eng., 1969), pp. 153-54. First published by The Bodley Head, 1956.

61. J.R.R. Tolkien, "On Fairy Stories," *The Tolkien Reader* (New York, 1966), pp. 19, 30, 31.

Poetry Can Say It Best

11

The Evolution of the Pied Piper

In the English-speaking world, the Pied Piper of Hamelin has achieved status as a standard figure of reference. According to context, he can be cited as typifying the cheated journeyman who exacts a terrible revenge, the piper who must be paid by anyone who has called for a tune, the seducer of the young, or the mysterious and sinister sorcerer who lures the susceptible to disaster by the irresistible sweetness and charm of his spell.

His physical appearance, attributes, dress and background are likewise well established. Tall, swarthy, lean, blue-eyed, clean-shaven, clad in an old-fashioned costume of red and yellow, he is a poor wandering musician who earns the respect and patronage of the wealthy and powerful—Caliphs, Nizams, Chams and their like—for his extraordinary skills in the extermination of animal pests.

In the children's literature of other languages and cultures, the character and outward showing of the piper are more prosaic and less clearly marked. A flutist, ratcatcher, or run-of-the-mill magician, he simply appears from nowhere and departs again in the half-light of legend, without offering any information on his origins or background. He comes. He clears Hamelin of its rats. The townspeople fail to deliver the promised reward. The magus collects the children of the place and leads them to a nearby mountain. With the children, he passes into the mountain, never to be seen again.

The more vivid and circumstantial version of the story, and its widespread circulation in English, is undoubtedly due to its treatment by Robert Browning in the long poem that has become a classic of children's literature. Browning originally composed the work in 1842 for the amusement of a little boy who was confined to his room by illness. The child was William C. Macready, Junior, eldest son of William Macready, the highly popular and successful tragedian with whom Browning had long been friendly and for whom he had written several theatrical pieces. The poet intended Willie to use his verses as the subject of drawings or paintings in the production of which he had already shown some talent.

For source material, Browning apparently turned to a version of the legend printed in Nathaniel Wanley's "Wonders of the Little World" (1678). He may further have consulted Richard Verstegen's "Restitution of Decayed Intelligence in Antiquities," published in 1605. It is possible also that he added details picked up from verbal accounts narrated inside his own family circle, or taken down from story-tellers encountered during his journeys through Germany in 1834 and 1838. The accounts found in the publications of Wanley and Verstegen both repeat uncritically the substance of earlier printed works in German. The tradition of the Piper had attracted the attention of chroniclers and historians at the period when the printing press was giving circulation in fixed and permanent form to narratives which had up to that point mainly been current only in oral form.

The first known version of the story in print is in the "Wunder-zeichen" of the theologian Hiob Fincelius, which appeared in 1556. Fincelius reports that about 180 years before, the Devil had appeared in Hamelin and attracted many children, through his piping, to follow him to a hill where they were lost. He adds that the whole story is written in the Town Chronicle of Hamelin where many people of the better sort have read and heard it.

This reference to official town records suggests an obvious line of research for investigation of the origins and growth of the legend. Several studies have been written, and an admirably thorough and scholarly summary of their findings has been made by Dr. Heinrich Spanuth.[1] Dr. Spanuth opens his survey with a brief overview of the condition of Hamelin in the latter years of the thirteenth century. With an abbey dating from the eighth century, and a regular market from the tenth, it had become a Hansa town with full charter privileges granted in 1200. In 1259, it was purchased by Bishop Wedekind of Minden from the Abbot of Fulda for 500 marks of silver. The chronicles record that on July 28, 1260, the menfolk of the town sallied out on a military expedition against the town of Sedemünder and were, to a man, either killed or taken into captivity. The ecclesiastical registers indicate that a requiem mass was said yearly for the repose of their souls.

Of the appearance of a piper in Hamelin on June 26, 1284, there is no contemporary report. On the other hand, a record has survived concerning the transfer, on July 23, 1284, the Eve of the Feast of St. John the Baptist, of a hide of land to the neighbouring hamlet of Honrode, and the names are recorded of the Burgomeister and his fellow signatories to the transaction. Only after the lapse of nearly a century does any record appear of an occurrence which might be construed as relating to the mysterious piper.

The reference is found as a note in the end-papers of a manuscript copy of the *Catena Aurea* of Heinrich von Herford which can be dated about 1370. Although the existence of this Luneburger Manuscript was noted in other textual references, the text itself was lost for centuries until located by Dr. Spanuth himself in 1936. Written in Latin, a loose un-polished rendering into English would suggest the following narrative . . .

"To be noted is a marvellous and truly extraordinary event that occurred in the town of Hamelin in the diocese of Minden in the year of the Lord 1284, on the very feast-day of Saints John and Paul. A young man of 30 years, handsome and in all respects so finely dressed that all who saw him were awestruck by his person and clothing came in by way of the bridge and the Weser Gate. On a silver pipe which he had, of wonderful form, he began to play through the whole town, and all the children hearing him, to the number of 130, followed him beyond the eastern wall almost to the place of the Calvary or Gallows field, and vanished and disappeared so that nobody could find out where any one of them had gone. Indeed, the mothers of the children wandered from city to city and discovered nothing. A voice was heard in Rama and every mother bewailed her son.[2] And as people count by the years of the Lord or by the first, second and third after a jubillee, so they have counted in Hamelin by the first, second and third year after the exodus and departure of the children. This I have found in an old book. And the mother of Herr Johann de Lude, the deacon, saw the children going out."

Dr. Spanuth refers to the local church records of the period which contain references to a Deacon Johann von Lude who died on March 12, 1378. The allusion to his mother, as a little girl of perhaps ten years of age, seeing the children leave Hamelin in 1284, therefore seems acceptable as a statement of truth, rather than an improbable invention.

Other references to the passage of a piper are found among the sur-viving archives of the town. A Council Record Book known as 'De Brade', dating from the last years of the fourteenth century, contains an account of 130 children being lost, after following a piper dressed in multi-coloured clothing through the Eastern Gate of Hamelin on June 26, 1284. The same date, with some kind of allusion to the exodus of the children, was also reproduced in various inscriptions on buildings in the town. Some of these, on chimney-breasts or lintels, have been preserved. Others, such as a carved stone on an old Town Gate, have disappeared and are now known only from descriptions and sketches in literary texts left by observers.

With the passage of time, however, succeeding versions of the story tend to vary as to the day and year of the event, and to gain in embellishments of commentary and interpretation what they lack in historical precision.

Whether the story-tellers claim to have collected their accounts from conversations with the townspeople of Hamelin, or to have based their writings on older texts which they have consulted, they concur in colouring the events with overtones of magic, witchcraft and diabolic intervention. By the mid-sixteenth century, the accretion of narratives from folk-rhymes, quotations from chronicles and pious explanations, had solidified. It now becomes an account of wickedness attracting its merited punishment.

The seventeenth century saw a corresponding reaction, when the burghers of the prosperous and developing township attempted to redeem their reputation by denying the truthfulness and historical accuracy of the legend. Pamphleteers and historians were forthcoming who sought to discount the story of the piper and the children as a mere folk-fable without any greater factual substance than the unlikely invention of an ignorant, unlettered and superstitious populace seeking wonders and portents. Controversies and literary polemics developed, with exchanges of charges and counter-charges, assertions and challenges, accusations and denials. The ebb and flow of the debate makes for interesting and amusing reading, but the detail is of little value for the present survey. What is important is that the writers concerned were more intent on promoting their particular interpretations rather than on any systematic review of what objective evidence might still be accessible to scrutiny.

When the cooler intellectual climate of the Enlightenment arrived, writers of eighteenth century Western Europe were therefore content to repeat in different languages, and with varying details, the stories that they inherited as coherent narratives. Usually, the presentation was of a quaint old story—an unexplained curiosity of folk-tradition from the remote past.

The Romantic movement, with new attitudes to the heritage of the past and to the cultural treasury of popular traditions revived interest in the legend of the piper. In Germany, the brothers Grimm collected and published one account, and Johann Wolfgang Goethe made it the subject of a poem. Robert Browning was only one among many writers of the time to note the tale or to include a treatment in his literary output. The story also became the starting-point or inspiration for nineteenth century musical plays, songs and operas. Researchers who have sought some real event in history as the origin of the legend, have therefore had to contend with these many overlays of fictional exaggeration or outright falsification.

Some have seen the exodus of the young people of Hamelin as a distorted memory of an episode in the Children's Crusade of 1212, when the youth of Western Europe in their thousands followed Nicolas of Cologne to disaster along the shores of the Mediterranean. Others have argued that the children must have been carried off in some epidemic typical of the period. Exponents of this theory place the rats in the foreground of the story as carriers of the vermin that propagated diseases such as bubonic plague. When rats were plentiful, sickness and death would be widespread. The survivors from any outbreak of pestilence would develop some kind of immunity, from exposure to non-fatal attacks of the infection. At some later date, when rats returned and the plague with them, it would be chiefly the new generation of children who would have no developed resistance to the disease and who would therefore be borne away. The theorists who argue for some rational explanation along these lines suggest that the legend, in the form that Browning found and perpetuated, combines strands from different sources in the folk memory.

There are references, for example, in German popular tales to acts of revenge by sorcerers who are cheated out of what they consider to be their just dues. A story is found about the town of Lorch, which was beset by a plague of ants. A hermit arrived and was promised a fee for eliminating this nuisance. He led the ants away, but was not paid, so he took away all the pigs of the place, with a magic charm. The next year, a plague of crickets invaded Lorch. A charcoal burner was found who was promised money to rid the town of them. When he did, and was refused the agreed reward, he led away all the sheep. In the third year, came a plague of rats. An old man of the mountains arrived and promised to clear them for a price. When the rats disappeared and his payment was not forthcoming, he led all the children after him, playing on a pipe, to the Tannenberg.

The argument runs that if a migrant version of such a story were to be transferred to Hamelin, instead of Lorch, it would require little local colouring or associations for the story of the piper to become irrevocably linked to the name of the town. The fate of a Hamelin contingent vanishing in the Children's Crusade, or in the disastrous expedition to Sedemünder, or in the onset of some pestilence, would provide the necessary connection.

The children, or young people, might even have succumbed to an outbreak of the Dancing Madness, another frightening phenomenon of mediaeval Europe, in which dozens of the inhabitants of a locality would inexplicably be seized by a collective impulse to rise and roam together in a jerking, twisting frenzy, until they literally danced themselves into collapse and even death. Modern medical researchers suggest that the Dancing Madness originated in the toxic effects of a fungus which infected growing grain crops, and which would survive and ferment to produce hallucinogenic substances such as ergot throughout the processes of being harvested, stored under unsatisfactory conditions, milled into flour and baked into bread. Instances have been investigated in recent years of similar outbreaks in country districts of Europe.

Against such ingenious and intriguing theories, however, stands the more prosaic and factual evidence of the note appended to the Luneburger Manuscript. There is no mention in this oldest reference either of any event requiring a supernatural explanation, nor any act of revenge for non-payment of an agreed price for banishing rats from Hamelin. Dr. Heinrich Spanuth points out that the scribe's account could refer in all respects to a visit to Hamelin by a herald or crier, acting as Lokator, or recruiting agent. It was a common practice at the period for the overlords of territories requiring immigrant populations to send a Lokator through their domains to preach the merits of far-off locations and invite those discontented with their present lot to venture out into the unknown in search of a brighter future. In 1284, Rudolph von Hapsburg, as Holy Roman Emperor, had recently acquired by conquest extensive new possessions in Moravia. The Pied Piper of Hamelin may therefore in fact have been one of Rudolph's emissaries, clad in a colourful tabard carrying the heraldic blazon of a coat-of-arms, and blowing flourishes on his trumpet to attract onlookers. On that Monday, June 26, 1284, on the Feast of Saints John and Paul, the little market-town held perhaps some two thousand souls. The sudden and unexplained departure *en masse* of one hundred and thirty young people must certainly have been a grievous loss to the townspeople who remained.

It may well have been, however, that those who followed the piper simply joined a convoy of emigrants waiting out of sight on the road beyond the Koppelberg.

The suggestion contained in the Browning poem, that the children of Hamelin became in time the ancestors of the inhabitants of Saxon towns in Transylvania, or elsewhere in Eastern Europe, may therefore reflect a historical fact.

Notes

1. *Der Rattenfänger von Hamelin: Vom Werden und Sinn einer alten Sage* (Hamelin: Verlag C. W. Niemeyer, 1951).
2. Jeremiah 31:15. Matthew 2:18.

12

The Sane, the Mad, the Good, the Bad

T. S. Eliot's *Old Possum's Book of Practical Cats*

MARION C. HODGE

In general, T. S. Eliot's poetry is intellectual, subtle, static, lyrical. Nothing much happens in it. There are few characters, and they do little except think. Prufrock takes a walk, climbs stairs. Gerontion is "an old man in a dry month / Being read to by a boy, waiting for rain."[1] In *The Waste Land*, Madame Sosostris tells fortunes, Phlebas the Phoenician drowns, and, at the conclusion, the narrator sits "upon the shore / Fishing ..." In *Ash-Wednesday* and *Four Quartets*, there are no characters at all, no activity; there is only meditation. The most vigorous narratives in Eliot's "serious" work are those concerning the sexual grubbiness of the typist and "the young man carbuncular" in *The Waste Land*, and that of Sweeney in several short poems. For the most part, then, Eliot's poetry is thought and symbol, state of mind, state of consciousness. His themes are commonly the emotional and moral sterility of modern civilization and the hope for the renewal of an abiding, satisfying faith, a mythology that will order the present chaos and evil. Implicit in these themes is a vision of humanity as vulgar, powerless, and depraved.

But when Eliot writes for children, some things are different. In *Old Possum's Book of Practical Cats* there is much more action, more narrative, little abstraction, no stream of consciousness. There are many characters in these poems, several of whom are criminals, and there is a great deal of violence, although Eliot here is less serious than in his other work: sometimes he is downright playful.

But even when writing for children, the moralist in Eliot cannot be suppressed. Just as he is drawn to the symbol in his "serious" poems, he is drawn to the fable in these poems for children. In *Prufrock*, in *The Waste Land*, in *Four Quartets*, he preaches to adults. In *Old Possum's Book of Practical Cats*, he preaches to children (and adults). He dispels any doubts about his intentions, any doubts that the cats he describes are not symbols for human beings, in the concluding poem of the series, "The Ad-dressing of Cats":

> You now have learned enough to see
> That Cats are much like you and me
> And other people whom we find
> Possessed of various types of mind.
> For some are sane and some are mad
> And some are good and some are bad...
> ws (11.5-10)

Nor is Eliot's vision of mankind's depravity and violence changed. The most obvious theme of these beast fables is the imperfectibility of catkind/ mankind. This theme is explored through the many criminals who are main characters, and, except for a few instances, through those cats who are not outlaws but are nevertheless subjects of satire rather than praise. The second important theme of *Practical Cats* is that of order in a violent, chaotic world.

The imperfectibility of mankind is a stated theme in three poems, "The Old Gumbie Cat," "The Rum Tum Tugger," and "Mungojerrie and Rumpelteazer."

"The Old Gumbie Cat" describes the attitudes and actions of Jennyanydots, a reformer of the "let's be up and doing," "learn a trade and become a productive member of society" school of thought. Part of the Gumbie Cat's nature is to be idle: "All day ... / She sits and sits and sits and sits /" (11.3-4), and so she seems to be an idle rich type. During the night she becomes active, and sneaks into the basement, being "deeply concerned with the ways of the mice" (1.9), cockroaches, and beetles who live there.

From what are these unsavory characters to be saved by their social and cultural superior? Well, Jennyanydots does not like the mice because "Their behaviour's not good and their manners not nice" (1.10) and because they "will not ever be kept quiet" (1.19). She is disgusted by the cockroaches' "idle and wanton destroyment" (1.32). Jennyanydots, like many of her ilk, is prone to think in stereotypes.

Because the indictment of the mice, cockroaches, and beetles is no more serious or specific than this, and because the Gumbie Cat's solutions are quite specific, Eliot is satirizing the Gumbie Cat herself. He obviously does not agree with her that teaching the mice "music, crocheting, and tatting" (1.12) will do any lasting good—neither will giving the cockroaches "employment" (1.31), forming "from that lot of disorderly louts, / A troop of well-disciplined helpful boy-scouts ..." (11.33-34), or organizing the beetles into a tattoo (1.36). If these activities work, why is it necessary for Jennyanydots to make visit after visit to the basement? Eliot knows that when the Gumbie Cat turns her back the mice and cockroaches and beetles will resume their boisterous destruction. He has chosen these creatures for symbols of the lower class specifically because of such hopeless activity. It is their nature. They cannot be improved. Eliot puts distance between himself and the Gumbie Cat when he says that "*she thinks that the cockroaches just need employment*" (1.31, my italics). Moreover, he qualifies his statement on the effectiveness of her reforming activities: "So for Old Gumbie Cats let us now give three cheers—/ On whom well-ordered households depend, it appears" (11.37-38). "It appears" shows the precariousness of Eliot's situation. Regarding this problem he, like many of us, is in somewhat of a moral and intellectual bind, for he admires the Gumbie Cat's efforts to rehabilitate the basement dwellers even while he smiles at her naiveté.

So while the Gumbie Cat receives faint praise, she is also damned. She is damned, above all, because she does not realize the depth of man's depravity; and secondly, because she thinks a few lessons in arts and crafts will be sufficient to alter the situation in the basement; and thirdly, because her efforts are superficial—she is not vitally interested in the mice and cockroaches, for if she were, she would not sit all day in the "warm and sunny spots" (1.14) winding the curtain-cord and tying it into sailor-knots (1.21), that is, doing nothing.

The imperfectibility of catkind/mankind is also a theme in "The Rum Tum Tugger." The Rum Tum Tugger is a "curious beast" (1.23) and a terrible bore" (1.12). He is a "bore" because he is not satisfied with anything:

> The Rum Tum Tugger is a Curious Cat:
> If you offer him pheasant he would rather have grouse.
> If you put him in a house he would much prefer a flat,
> If you put him in a flat then he'd rather have a house,
> If you set him on a mouse then he only wants a rat,
> If you set him on a rat then he'd rather chase a mouse. (11.1-6)

He is a "beast" for several reasons: he is "disobliging" (1.24) and "artful and knowing" (1.31), he is generally an unloving creature who "doesn't care for a cuddle" (1.32)—a cuddle being something which satisfies both owner and cat—but who will sometimes selfishly "leap on your lap in the middle of your sewing" (1.33). Also, he is a thoroughly modern and thoroughly democratic cat who "only likes what he finds for himself" (1.28). We may infer that he doesn't appreciate the civilizing influences of such surrogate experience as is found in history and literature. Finally, the Rum Tum Tugger is a "beast" because he likes chaos: "there's nothing he enjoys like a horrible muddle" (1.34). What can be done about such a cat? Can he be made to see his errors and to correct them? No, "For he will do / As he do do / And there's no doing anything about it!" (11.9-11). In this poem, Eliot is more emphatic than elsewhere in the series about mankind's moral and spiritual sterility; he makes these words a refrain with which each stanza (and so the poem itself) concludes.

Similarly, the final line of "Mungojerrie and Rumpelteazer" shows Eliot's insistence that the crimes of these two "highly efficient cat-burglars" (1.18) cannot be curtailed: "there's nothing at all to be done about that!" "Mungojerrie and Rumpelteazer" seems at first to be a playful poem, less serious than either "The Old Gumbie Cat," or "The Rum Tum Tugger," but it is a very serious poem indeed. For example, a cook, "in a voice that was *broken with sorrow*" (1.25, my italics), announces to a family that they "must wait and have dinner *tomorrow!*" (1.26) because the two thieves have stolen the "Argentine joint" (1.27). If such cruelty is not bad enough, Eliot underscores the family's powerlessness. They are reduced to mere frustrated exclamation: "It's that horrible cat! / It was Mungojerrie—or Rumpelteazer!" (11.28-29). Apparently having no recourse, or at least feeling they have none, "most of the time they left it at that" (11.16, 29). This kind of detail makes the narrator's final statement even more poignant—a desperate cry of mixed rage, frustration and resignation in the face of man's depravity: "And there's nothing at all to be done about that!"

In *In Defense of Reason*, Yvor Winters has written that "Eliot's position is one of unmitigated determinism... [Eliot believes] that the individual lacks the private and personal power to achieve goodness in a corrupt society...."[2] These three poems in particular, and the series of poems in general, corroborate Winters' contention. Eliot's often raucous versification and his vigorous rhymes tend to muffle the pessimism of the moral, but it is there nevertheless; and it is present as well in the several poems which depict the activities of criminals.

"Growltiger's Last Stand" is a swiftly moving little narrative which describes the violent death of Growltiger, "the roughest cat that ever roamed at large" (1.2). Growltiger is hated and feared so much that his death at the hands of the Siamese is celebrated in England as well as in Bangkok. At the beginning of the poem, the narrator describes Growltiger's appearance, reputation, and belligerent personality. Growltiger is a rough-looking character, wearing a "torn and seedy" coat and "baggy" trousers (1.6). One ear has been torn off in a fight and he is missing an eye (11.7, 8). He has such a terrible reputation that "people shuddered at his name" (1.10), and

They would fortify the hen-house, lock up the silly goose,
When the rumour ran along the shore: GROWLTIGER'S
ON THE LOOSE!

(11.11-12)

Growltiger revels in his infamy, "Rejoicing in his title of "The 'Terror of the Thames' " (1.4). His title is accurate, for besides being a thief, Growltiger is a brawler and murderer, preying on the "weak canary" (1.13), "pampered Pekinese" (1.14), or "any Cat" with whom he "came to grips!" (1.16). Growltiger reserves his greatest hatred for those "of foreign name and race" (1.18), and particularly the "Persian and the Siamese ... / Because it was a Siamese had mauled his missing ear" (11.19-20).

Growltiger makes his last stand when one Gilbert leads "his fierce Mongolian horde" in a surprise attack. Growltiger's defenses have been relaxed on "a peaceful summer night" (1.21) so that he might enjoy the company of "the lady GRIDDLEBONE" (1.30). Growltiger's closest aides, Grumbuskin and Tumblebrutus, have left the ship, and his crew is sleeping below deck.

As Growltiger and Griddlebone sing to each other, Gilbert and his men slip aboard the ship and imprison Growltiger's sleeping crew. Griddlebone slinks away when the attackers are discovered and escapes, but Growltiger is forced to walk the plank. This is an ironic punishment, Eliot points out, but one that is justified:

He who a hundred victims had driven to that drop,
At the end of all his crimes was forced to go ker-flip, kerflop.

(11.51-52)

The final stanza describes the international celebration which follows the death of Growltiger. In England Growltiger's death is cause for such acts as "dancing on the strand!" (1.54) and roasting whole rats (1.55), while in Bangkok "a day of celebration was commanded" (1.56).

What Eliot had in mind by writing "Growltiger's Last Stand" is difficult to say unless it was to present catkind in one of its most deplorable states. The very brevity of the poem argues against psychological or dramatic sophistication, and its superficiality of detail makes it unsatisfactory as a story. The characters possess little virtue and resort to violence to attain their goals. Growltiger is a thief, a murderer, and a bigot. His lover, Griddlebone, is another of Eliot's jaded females, being "Disposed to relaxation, and awaiting no surprise" (1.35). She is also, as we have noted, a coward, obviously feeling no loyalty to Growltiger. Growltiger's best friends have abandoned him to drink and seek out more victims (11.25-28). Thus, Eliot seems primarily concerned to present another pessimistic picture of catkind.

But as with his other "simple" children's poems, Eliot infuses into "Growltiger's Last Stand" a measure of complexity. Growltiger is not entirely devoid of admirable qualities. He is sometimes "disposed to show his sentimental side" (1.24). He apparently cares deeply for Griddlebone, and she is attracted to him by his singing ability:

> Growltiger had no eye or ear for aught but Griddlebone,
> And the Lady seemed enraptured by his manly baritone...
>
> (11.34-35)

But Eliot's tone is inconsistent, and his narrator lacks seriousness. Griddlebone is said to be "skeered" (1.45) when Gilbert attacks; and instead of a more forceful metaphor for walking the plank, Growltiger is said "to go ker-flip, ker-flop" (1.52).

Mungojerrie and Rumpelteazer are criminals too, but they are not as vicious, not as hated as Growltiger. They are "very notorious (1.1) as "highly efficient cat-burglars" (1.18) with remarkable skills as "knockabout clowns, quick-change comedians, tight-rope walkers and acrobats" (1.2). They are the kind of criminal that society often tolerates and even admires to some degree, "plausible fellows" (1.20) who have "a very unusual gift of the gab" (1.17) and therefore will even "engage a friendly policeman in conversation" (1.20).

Unlike Growltiger, Mungojerrie and Rumpelteazer are not brutal cats; they concentrate on the taking of property rather than the taking of lives. And although their crimes, as we have already seen, often cause their victims a great deal of grief, they cause no terror or bodily harm. These two cats, however, are destructive, knocking tiles "loose on the roof / Which presently ceased to be waterproof..." (11.9-10), smashing and crashing things in dining-room, pantry, and library (11.34-37). Moreover, they often steal from the very people who can afford it least, the "family" to whom the loss of a cut of meat means the loss of a meal, the family who buys fake, cheap "Woolworth pearls" (1.14).

In "Macavity: The Mystery Cat" we find a character much more like Growltiger than either Mungojerrie or Rumpelteazer. T. S. Matthews may be right when he says that "It is possible to see the origin" of this poem "in a rarely fortunate day at the dentist's—*Macavity's not there!*"[3] But the cat that Eliot presents here is responsible for emotions quite different from the pride and relief one experiences after a favorable dental report. While his "powers of levitation" (1.7) and his ability to disappear may cause awed admiration, Macavity is "a fiend in feline shape, a monster of depravity" (1.18). As a matter of fact, the narrator reports the opinion of many that Macavity is the worst criminal of them all; that, in fact, the others are his subordinates:

> And they say that all the Cats whose wicked deeds are widely known
> (I might mention Mungojerrie, I might mention Griddlebone)
> Are nothing more than agents for the Cat who all the time
> Just controls their operations: the Napoleon of Crime!
>
> (11.39-42)

Like Growltiger and Mungojerrie, Macavity is a thief and destroyer, and like Growltiger again, he is a murderer:

> And when the larder's looted, or the jewel-case is rifled,
> Or when the milk is missing, or another Peke's been stifled,
> Or the greenhouse glass is broken, and the trellis past repair—
> Ay, there's the wonder of the thing! *Macavity's not there!*
>
> (11.23-26)

The activity that separates Macavity from his criminal colleagues is his taking of state and military secrets:

> And when the Foreign Office find a Treaty's gone astray,
> Or the Admiralty lose some plans and drawings by the way,
> There may be a scrap of paper in the hall or on the stair—
> But it's useless to investigate—*Macavity's not there!*
>
> *(11.27-30)*

Macavity is different from the ferocious, physically battered Growltiger in that he is "outwardly respectable" (1.21). Whereas Growltiger "scowled upon a hostile world," returning the hatred society feels for him, Macavity is debonair, preferring to dupe society rather than to confront it:

> He sways his head from side to side, with movements like a snake;
> And when you think he's half asleep, he's always wide awake...
> Macavity, Macavity, there's no one like Macavity,
> There never was a Cat of such deceitfulness and suavity.
> He always has an alibi, and one or two to spare:
> At whatever time the deed took place—MACAVITY WASN'T THERE!
>
> (11.15-16, 35-38)

Macavity possesses all the attributes of the urbane cat who can operate outside and against the social order successfully:

> Macavity's a Mystery Cat: he's called the Hidden Paw—
> For he's the master criminal who can defy the Law.
> He's the bafflement of Scotland Yard, the Flying Squad's despair:
> For when they search the scene of crime—*Macavity's not there!*
>
> (11.1-4)

Up to this point, we have been looking at two important facets of *Old Possum's Book of Practical Cats*: Eliot's conviction that catkind/mankind is prone to crudity, cruelty, and violence, and is beyond reformation. The several examples reflect that conviction by the fact that criminals figure prominently in the poems. Now we will turn to a second important element, the quest for order.

For Eliot, order is an essential goal. In a famous little essay, "*Ulysses*, Order and Myth," Eliot discusses order and his belief that literature can be can effective means of creating it. Joyce's "mythical method," his use of *The Odyssey* as a pattern for the structure of *Ulysses*, Eliot says, "is simply a way of controlling, of ordering, of giving a shape and a significance to the immense panorama of futility and anarchy which is contemporary history."[4] We must not expect Eliot to be dogmatic in his desire for order. As we shall see, to Eliot "order" is not a synonym for repression, but rather the condition of love, justice, mercy, and harmony toward which catkind must always strive, but in which it will never find itself.

The majority of poems in *Practical Cats* show various types of disorder. From burglary to mob violence, disorder abounds among Eliot's cats. Only a few manage to overcome it. The disorder in the basement is one of the things that motivates the Old Gumbie Cat. The Rum Tum Tugger is an anarchist of sorts, loving nothing so much as a muddle. And the outlaws, Growltiger, Mungojerrie, Rumpelteazer, and Macavity, live disorderly, desperate lives and are responsible for disrupting the lives of their victims.

The theme of order is important even in the least serious poem in the series, "Mr. Mistoffelees." Mistoffelees is a superior magician, "The Original Conjuring Cat" (1.2):

> At prestidigitation
> And at legerdemain
> He'll defy examination
> And deceive you again.
>
> (11.10-13)

The result of such deceit is some apparently harmless mystery and disorder:

He holds all the patent monopolies
For performing surprising illusions
And creating eccentric confusions.

(11.7-9)

Order is also a theme of the poems which describe the three most "practical" cats in the series: Gus, Bustopher Jones, and Skimbleshanks. For these three, order is respectively: a method of attaining superiority, a way of living a long life, and a way of achieving security.

The title character in "Gus: The Theatre Cat" is a retired actor, now forced to make his living by manning the theater door. When he gets together with his friends, Bus "loves to regale them, if someone else pays, / With anecdotes drawn from his palmiest days" (11.13-14). These anecdotes consist of his own exploits on the stage and the characters he portrayed:

He once played a Tiger—could do it again—
Which an Indian Colonel pursued down a drain.
And he thinks that he still can, much better than most,
Produce blood-curdling noises to bring on the Ghost.
And he once crossed the stage on a telegraph wire,
To rescue a child when a house was on fire.

(11.39-44)

And when he gets a little smashed, Gus will remark on the relative merits of modern actors and the actors of his own time. Notice the emphasis he puts on order and discipline:

And he says: "Now, these kittens, they do not get trained
As we did in the days when Victoria reigned.
They never get drilled in a regular troupe,
And they think they are smart, just to jump through a hoop."
And he'll say, as he scratches himself with his claws,
"Well, the Theatre's certainly not what it was.
These modern productions are all very well,
But there's nothing to equal, from what I hear tell,
   That moment of mystery
   When I made history
As Firefrorefiddle, the Fiend of the Fell."

(11.45-55)

When compared to the past, the present is usually chaotic. The perspective that age gives us is narrow. For Gus, being "trained," being "drilled in a regular troupe" is the proper way to be educated, and the difference, he thinks, between the present and the past is that the past was a time of order while the present, by implication, is a time of disorder and disarray. Order and discipline, Gus feels, made him and his colleagues superior to the actors of the present generation. Opposed to his own versatility and creativity is the modern cat's cheap trick, merely a physical act of no importance.

In "Bustopher Jones: The Cat About Town," the orderly life accounts for physical well-being. Bustopher Jones does little all day except walk from one club to another enjoying the cuisine of each, and that is the reason that he is "remarkably fat" (1.2). Bustopher dresses fashionably; this shows him to be superior to his fellows, and he enjoys their admiration:

> He's the Cat we all greet as he walks down the street
> In his coat of fastidious black:
> No commonplace mousers have such well-cut trousers
> Or such an impeccable back.
> In the whole of St. James's the smartest of names is
> The name of this Brummell of Cats:
> And we're all of us proud to be nodded to bowed to
> By Bustopher Jones in white spats!
>
> (11.5-12)

His friends are aware of his increasing obesity, but Bustopher is unwilling to admit it. He is in good shape, he thinks, because he leads a well-ordered life:

> It can be no surprise that under our eyes
> He has grown unmistakably round.
> He's a twenty-five pounder, or I am a bounder,
> And he's putting on weight every day:
> But he's so well preserved because he's observed
> All his life a routine, so he'll say.
>
> (11.31-36)

The narrator agrees. Bustopher leads a good life, founded solidly on routine, on order.

The theme of "Skimbleshanks: The Railway Cat" is that peace, satisfaction, and security derive from order. " 'The Night Mail just can't go' " (1.8) unless Skimbleshanks is in control of the operation of the train, organizing services, protecting and pampering the passengers. When it seems that Skimbleshanks will not make the train on time, "The guards and all the porters and the stationmaster's daughters" (1.5) panic.

After he has given the signal and the train has departed, Skimbleshanks sets to work to insure that things go smoothly. Like Bustopher Jones, Skimbleshanks is a cat who lives by routine:

From the driver and the guards to the bagmen playing cards
He will supervise them all, more or less,
Down the corridor he paces and examines all the faces
Of the travellers in the First and in the Third:
He establishes control by a regular patrol
And he'd know at once if anything occurred.

(11.19-24)

He is also prescient, dictatorial, and powerful. He does not allow any disorderly behavior:

He will watch you without winking and he sees what you are
    thinking
And it's certain that he doesn't approve
Of hilarity and riot, so the folk are very quiet
When Skimble is about and on the move.
    You can play no pranks with Skimbleshanks!
    He's a Cat that cannot be ignored;
    So nothing goes wrong on the Northern Mail
    When Skimbleshanks is aboard.

(11.25-32)

Skimbleshanks' control produces creature comforts and security. The passenger's berth is found to be "very pleasant" (1.33) and "very neat with a newly folded sheet / And there's not a speck of dust on the floor" (11.35-36). He even follows the attendants around to make sure they perform courteously and conscientiously:

Then the guard looks in politely and will ask you very brightly
"Do you like your morning tea weak or strong?"
But Skimble's just behind him and was ready to remind him,
For Skimble won't let anything go wrong.

(11.41-44)

Skimbleshanks appears to be the kind of cat who could maintain order in any situation, but the environment in which he works would seem to be well-regulated without him. Eliot creates a character called the "Great Rumpuscat" to take charge in an unusual circumstance, a riot, a scene of general violent disorder.

"Of the Awefull Battle of the Pekes and the Pollicles: Together With Some Account of the Participation of the Pugs and the Poms, and the Intervention of the Great Rumpuscat" describes a confrontation between two breeds of dogs who "everyone knows, / Are proud and implacable passionate foes ..." (11.1-2). The Peke and the Pollicle, the narrator explains—and here we encounter racial and nationalistic biogtry—are, on the one hand, "Heathen Chinese" (11.26,31) and, on the other, "a dour Yorkshire tyke" (1.33) who are constantly fighting. Pugs and Poms are usually passive, but sometimes lend their voices to the terrible din of barking that precedes a battle.

It is a moment of great tension, and the observers are terrified:

> Now when these bold heroes together assembled,
> The traffic all stopped, and the Underground trembled,
> And some of the neighbours were so much afraid
> That they started to ring up the Fire Brigade.
> (11.46-49)

But now the Great Rumpuscat appears, "suddenly, up from a small basement flat" (1.50).

He displays a curious combination of vehemence and boredom:

> His eyes were like fireballs fearfully blazing,
> He gave a great yawn, and his jaws were amazing;
> And when he looked out through the bars of the area,
> You never saw anything fiercer or hairier.
> And what with the glare of his eyes and his yawning,
> The Pekes and Pollicles quickly took warning.
> (11.52-57)

It is as if the Great Rumpuscat has been involved in such situations so many times that the only emotion associated with them is boredom and contempt for the parties so childishly embroiled.

He does not ignore the situation, as one without moral scruples might very well do. However, we are given no indication that he is particularly concerned with morality, or even with order. He seems contemptuously detached from it all even when he moves to disperse the opposing mobs:

> He looked at the sky and he gave a great leap—
> And they every last one of them scattered like sheep.
> (11.58-59)

That's all. The Great Rumpuscat is not challenged. His authority, based only on his physical superiority and his fierceness, is absolute.

"The Song of the Jellicles," is the only poem in the series which celebrates harmony and joy:

> Until the Jellicle Moon appears
> They make their toilette and take their repose. . . .
> They're quiet enough in the morning hours,

> They're quiet enough in the afternoon,
> Reserving their terpsichorean powers
> To dance by the light of the Jellicle Moon....
> They are resting and saving themselves to be right
> For the Jellicle Moon and the Jellicle Ball.
>   (11.17-18, 25-28, 35-36)

The Jellicles, fully confident that the time for the ball will eventually arrive, possess none of the vulgar impatience, none of the nervousness that characterizes those who have little faith in the future.

Size is an important element in the Jellicle cats' personality. They are described somewhat inconsistently as being "rather small" (1. 2), "not too big" (1. 14), "of moderate size" (1. 22), and "small" (1. 30). Their smallness might be concomitant with a lack of sophistication, for certainly they cannot be said to be world weary, as are most of the cats in these poems. They "develop slowly" (1. 13) we are told, and in this case at least, such immaturity is a positive trait. As a matter of fact, except for their patience, the Jellicles are rather like children. They are embodiments of potential. They are physically active. They lack sophistry. They are "merry and bright" (1. 7), "pleasant to hear when they caterwaul" (1.8), and they have "cheerful faces" (1. 9) with eyes that are "bright black" (1. 10) and "moonlit" (1. 24).

"The Song of the Jellicles" might be a depiction of heaven, but it is as much of a heaven as catkind/mankind can create for itself on earth. It is a heaven of "repose" (1. 18) and of dancing "a gavotte and a jig" (1.16), of innocence and harmony, of happiness and satisfaction. It is a heaven of the best kind of order—inherent and welling up from the spirit and expressed in the movement of the body. In *Ash-Wednesday*, Eliot prays that God will "teach us to sit still"; but here the goal is not stasis but movement, a dance in the half light of the future:

> Jellicle Cats come out tonight,
> Jellicle Cats come one and all,
> The Jellicle Moon is shining bright—
> Jellicles come to the Jellicle Ball.
>   (11.1-4)

Wherever Eliot looks in the world he sees aspects of "the immense panorama of futility and anarchy"; he sees violence, licentiousness, and disorder. It follows from such a vision that the criminal's act may be seen as a type of the moral and ethical crimes and failings that beset us but for which we are not considered dangerous, and that order is a positive ideal. It is a vision that does not exclude the possibility of finding joy and harmony, or of creating it, as the dancer and the poet do. Eliot says much the same things to children in *Old Possum's Book of Practical Cats* as he says to adults in his other work.

Notes

1. *The Complete Poems and Plays: 1909-1950* (New York: Harcourt, Brace, and World, 1952), p. 152. All quotations of the poems are from this edition.

2. 3rd ed. (Chicago: Swallow Press, 1947), p. 487.

3. *Great Tom: Notes Toward the Definition of T. S. Eliot* (New York: Harper and Row, 1974), p. 191, note.

4. M. H. Abrams and others, eds., *The Norton Anthology of English Literature*, v. 2 rev. (New York: Norton, 1968), p. 1824.

5. "Lewis Carroll and T. S. Eliot as Nonsense Poets," *T. S. Eliot: A Symposium for His Seventieth Birthday*, Neville Braybrooke, ed. (London: Hart-Davis, 1959), rpt. in Hugh Kenner, ed., *T. S. Eliot: A Collection of Critical Essays*, Twentieth-Century Views (Englewood Cliffs, N.J.: Prentice-Hall, 1962), p. 71.

13

"Over the Garden Wall / I Let the Baby Fall"
The Poetry of Rope-Skipping

FRANCELIA BUTLER

Through the act of skipping, of overcoming the demonic power of the rope, the child achieves a bodily and psychic loosening of emotional strictures. The rhymes, ancient in origin, durable and widely distributed, are a way for unconscious elements in the personality to surface. Skipping rope is practiced in widely diverse countries and cultures.

In Belfast, for example, children in large families are often forced to tend younger brothers and sisters, and their frustration may come out in rope-skipping rhymes. One child commented that her mother didn't like her to skip too much, since it wore out her shoes. Then she began:

> My wee brother is no good.
> Chop him up for firewood.
> When he's dead
> Cut off his head,
> Make it into gingerbread.

Another skipper in Belfast added this one:

> Eni eni mino mo
> Set the baby on the po [pot]
> When it's done
> Clean its bum
> And give it a lump
> Of sugar plum.

However, babies can be a nuisance to skippers everywhere. In England and New Zealand children chant:

> Over the garden wall
> I let the baby fall.

My mother came out
And gave me a clout
Over the garden wall.

And in the United States, baby care is a problem, too:

I had a little brother,
His name was Tiny Tim.
I put him in the washtub
To teach him how to swim.
He drank up all the water,
He ate up all the soap.
He died last night
With a bubble in his throat.

Most rope-skipping rhymes about family relations have to do with a skipper's relationship to his or her mother. Often the mother appears as disciplinarian, as in this rhyme I heard in Belfast in two versions, the first from a girl's, the second from a boy's point of view:

My mother said
I never should
Play with gypsies
In the wood.
If I should
She would say,
"Naughty girl to disobey
"Disobey disobey,
"Naughty girl to disobey."
I wish my mother would
Hold her tongue.
She had a boy
When she was young.
I wish my father would
Do the same.
He had a girl
with an awful name.

The boy's variant of this rhyme:

My mother said
I never should
Play with gypsies
In the wood.
The wood was dark,

> The grass was green,
> In came Sally
> With a tambourine.
> I went to the sea—
> No ship to get across.
> I paid 10 shillings
> For a blind white horse,
> I was up on his back
> And was off in a crack,
> Sally told my mother
> I would never come back.

The girl with the "awful name" that father had in the first version sounds like Sally "with a tambourine" in the second—the kind of girl who causes sons to repudiate motherly advice about sex outside marriage. Once that taboo is broken, the youth may be "at sea" for a while until he sets up his own code of conduct. The Platonic rider, reason, must ride the horse, the emotions. He may not see his way at first, but some Sally will get the message back to his mother that he will never return to the old emotional dependency.

As disciplinarians, mothers can be monsters. This Scottish rhyme was given to me by Reginald Oakes:

> Kilty kilty Calder
> Couldn't play his drum;
> His mother took the bellows
> And blew him up the lum.

"Lum" is Scottish for chimney. A mother, presumably, scolds her daughters in this rhyme, which I heard in the Slovenian section of Yugoslavia:

> Katarina, Barbara,
> Look how you've cared for the house!
> A chicken's been stolen
> The feathers all plucked—
> Eaten no doubt in Ljubljana.

Everywhere, mothers and food are closely associated. In this French rope-skipping rhyme a mother is calling to her children:

> Soup's on, on, on!
> Come and get it, get it, get it!
> Never leave the rope empty,
> The one who does gets punished.

And a succession of children keep the rope warm and turning—just as their mothers have kept the pot of soup warm for generations at the back of an old French stove.

Another French rhyme tracked to the 16th century and associated with the image of Rabelais's Gargantua goes:

> Pan, pan, pan.
> Mama is at Caen.
> I've eaten 10 eggs,
> The heads of two cows,
> A hundred pounds of bread,
> And still I am hungry!

The mother figure, food and religion are combined in this rhyme jumped in Italy:

> Jump, Pilate!
> The Holy Mother takes you in her arms—
> Gives you a spoon of rice—
> Leap into Paradise!

By this leap of faith, any naughty child who identifies with Pilate is forgiven, and in passing through the ordeal of the rope, symbolically reaches a better world on the other side of it.

In a Greek school rhyme, a child expresses guilt for ingratitude over a mother's goodness:

> How can I hurt my mother
> To make her upset?
> Sings all day and night
> For my own good she tries.

I heard this skipped recently in Athens by Victoria Antoniou, a visitor to Athens from Volos, Greece. She was jumping in one of the numerous parks in Athens called "Joy of Children," this particular one having been planned about 15 years ago by Demetrios Pikionis, a famous architect. Small in size, it gave the impression of being much larger because of the varied levels of woods and water. It was a hot day, but children were comfortable either in the wooded parts or in two play areas covered with thatched roofs. In another "Joy of Children" park, boys, too, were doing a kind of rope-skipping—vigorous jumping over a ring of elastic held taut around the legs of two other children facing each other. Not so common in America, this game is very popular in Greece, India, Afghanistan, Turkey and Argentina.

Mother is not always regarded respectfully. Here's an American look at her:

> My mama and your mama live across the way.
> Every night they have a fight and this is what they say:
> Acka backa soda cracker
> Acka backa boo
> Acka backa soda cracker
> Out goes you!

In a Belgian rhyme, there are suggestions that the mother may not be all she might be:

> My mother bought a herring,
> A herring without a head.
> She put it in front of the window.
> Two policemen came and took my mother along.
> My mother began to yell,
> And did my mother yell!
> Did my mother yell!
> Still another one, that makes two.

As for father, he sometimes appears as disciplinarian, as in this French rhyme:

> "Papa, give me some tea!"
> "No my daughter, after dinner."
> Daughter in a tantrum
> Breaks the teapot
> Father, furious,
> Pulls her hair.

The father as disciplinarian also appears in this extinct Frisian rhyme, used for swinging and possibly skipping in Germany in the area of Norden in 1875. It was given to me by Heinz Kurth, an author of children's books.

> Jan Plojet's son fell through the floor,
> Fell on his nose
> In the peppernuts vat.
> Come out, you thief! Come out, you scamp!
> He has been too long in the swing [or rope].
> One last push
> Another shove
> And let the swing [rope] come to rest.

Like many rope-skipping rhymes that have a rhythmic quality, displaying their ballad origin, this rhyme was originally sung.

Grandmothers come in for attention in the rhymes, as in this one from Belfast:

> Granny in the kitchen doing a bit of stitchin'
> In comes a bogeyman and chases Granny out.
> "Oh!" says Granny. "That's not fair!"
> "Oh!" says the bogeyman. "I don't care."

A French rhyme considers grandmothers and death:

> A.B.C.D.
> My grandmother is buried
> In a field of chicory.
> When the chicory begins to sprout,
> My grandmother will come out.

There are variants of this rhyme, all reflecting the idea that life does go on in a cycle from death to rebirth, that is part of nature's plan—an idea accepted matter-of-factly by many children.

The position of sisters and aunts is sometimes ambiguous, as in these two Belfast rhymes:

> My Aunt Nellie had a bile [boil] on her belly.
> She rubbed it up and down.
> She sold pigs' feet at the bottom of the street,
> And a policeman knocked her down.

> My sister Fanny walks very canny.
> For she isn't very steady on her feet,
> She spends all her money
> Drinking with her honey
> In the pub at the corner of the street.

Unlike Aunt Nellie, Aunt Jane is well thought of by Belfast skippers. The following rhyme is included in a prize-winning rope-skipping program produced by David Hammond for the B.B.C. in 1971. It is old, but I have heard it several times in Belfast:

> My Aunt Jane she called me in.
> She gave me tea out of her wee tin.
> Half a bap and sugar on the top,
> Three black lumps out of her wee shop.
> My Aunt Jane she's awful smart.

She bakes wee rings in an apple tart.
And when Halloween comes round,
Fornenst that tart I'm always found.
My Aunt Jane, she's a bell on the door,
A white stone step and a clean swept floor.
Candy apples, hard green pears,
Conversation lozengers.

A "bap" is a large round bun, like a hamburger bun. "Fornenst" means "beside," and "conversation lozengers" are little round candies in a tube with love messages on each candy wrapper, such as "I love you," "Be mine," "Take me home."

In the rhymes that refer to siblings, jealousy of a new brother is a common theme, as is illustrated by this well-known American rhyme:

Fudge, fudge,
Call the judge.
Mama's got a baby.
Ain't no girl
Ain't no boy,
Just a plain old baby.
Wrap it up in tissue paper.
Put it on the elevator.
First floor, miss!
Second floor, miss!
Third floor, miss!
Fourth floor—
Kick it out the door.

The same theme appears in this one, also frequently skipped in America:

Johnny over the ocean.
Johnny over the sea.
Johnny broke a milk bottle
And blamed it on me.
I told Ma.
Ma told Pa.
Johnny got a lickin'—
Ha! Ha! Ha!

Occasionally, the rhymes suggest incest, as in this one from Belfast:

Two little girls in blue, lad,
Two little girls in blue.
They were sisters; we were brothers,

And learned to love the two.
One little girl in blue, lad,
Who won your father's heart,
Became our mother.
I married the other,
But now we have drifted apart.

Skipping is done at a period when sex roles are not yet clearly differentiated. Children prefer the company of their own sex and in general girls do more rope-skipping than boys. There is rivalry between the sexes, as in this rhyme from Belfast:

Georgie and Jack are dressed in black,
Silver buckles behind their backs.
Foot for foot
Knee for knee
"Turn back Georgie and come with me."
"I have a leg for a stocking,
"I have a foot for a shoe,
"I have a kiss for a bonnie wee lass,
"But I have none for you."

Jack has his answer. Georgie is growing up. Such buried meanings in the rhymes are often sexual, and represent a catharsis for the child who acts out his or her fantasies through the chants.

The act of skipping itself is a discharge of tension. For this act, the prop, the rope, is a cheap and readily available toy. I have seen children use clothesline, a leather strap (Spain), a rope made on a string loom (France), plaited straw (Hungary), elastic (Greece) or a stiff wicker (Sweden). I have seen Cherokee Indian children using honeysuckle vines, and I am told that in India ropes of roses are sometimes used.

Often, rhymes are concerned with the process of growing up, of self-mastery. One interesting rhyme I have heard in England, Ireland and America consists of a series of questions:

What are you doing here, Sir?
Drinking up the beer, Sir.
Where'd you get the beer, Sir?
It wasn't far nor near, Sir.
Why do you speak so bold, Sir?
Because I've got a cold, Sir.
Where'd you get the cold, Sir?
Up at the North Pole, Sir.
Pray, what is your name, Sir?

My name is—[and the child jumps to the letters of his name.]

One wonders if these questions reinforce the magic of the rope, the demon, and the primitive association, as Neal Raisman, U. of Massachusetts, reminds me, of the moving rope with the magical protection of the circle. If the right answers are given and stumbling on the rope is avoided, the child can loosen himself from family relationships and begin to enter the adult world. The final line is concerned with name magic, with personal identity.

A French rhyme is about lettuce, whose fate is to be eaten in a salad once it reaches maturity. This rhyme is popular not only in France but also in Vietnam, where it no doubt arrived during the French occupation.

> O, the salad!
> When it grows up,
> People will eat it
> With oil—
> And with vinegar!

At the word, "vinegar," the rope is turned very fast—a custom common in several countries, where "pepper" and "vinegar" denote speed.

The "Teddy Bear" rhyme seems to be universal. In his quest for self-mastery, the little hero, the rope-skipper, goes through certain motions:

> Teddy Bear, Teddy Bear,
> Turn around.
> Teddy Bear, Teddy Bear,
> Touch the ground.
> Teddy Bear, Teddy Bear,
> Show your shoe.
> Teddy Bear, Teddy Bear,
> That will do.

Many Americans consider this rhyme a purely American product of the Teddy Roosevelt period, but I have found it in South Africa, Luxembourg, Ecuador and the Niigata prefecture in central Japan, where the rhyme is regarded as old. Teddy Bear is generally referred to as "Mr. Bear."

The hazy, ambiguous quality of many rope-skipping rhymes relates them to dreams as a way of expressing the inexpressible. Scraps of material from the unconscious seem to emerge in the following rhyme given to me by Litizia Maroni Lumbroso of Rome:

> There were three children on the seashore.
> Turnips, onions, five cents a bunch!
> The prettiest and tiniest began to sail.

While she sailed, her ring fell in the sea.
She raised her eyes to the wave,
Turnips, onions, five cents a bunch!
She saw a fisherman.
"O, fisherman of the wave,
"Come and fish over here."
"When I have caught turnips, onions, five cents a bunch,
"What will you give me?"
"Ten pieces of gold, an embroidered purse,
"Onions, turnips, five cents a bunch."

A child has lost a ring, a symbol, perhaps, of psychic wholeness. She seeks help from the fisherman, who draws on the source of all life, the sea.

There is an element of fear, perhaps a warning against strangers, which is frequently suggested in rhymes, in this rhyme from the Dominican Republic:

A little coach driver
Asked me last night
If I would like
To have a ride.

And I told him,
With lots of thanks,
That I get seasick
Riding in coaches.

Erotic rhymes are found almost everywhere. In this one, which I heard in Belfast, the child tries to foresee his own emotional future, possibly with premonitions arising from his family life:

The wind, the wind, the wind blows high,
The rain comes tumbling from the sky.
[Child's name] says she'll die
If she doesn't get a man with a rosy eye.
She is handsome, she is pretty
She is a lass from Belfast City.
A knock at the door and a ring at the bell—
Ah, my true love, are you well?

Though speech seldom accompanies the rope-skipping ritual in Greece, see-sawing is a different matter there. No test of skill is involved—only the erotic back-and-forth movement of a father's leg—or, for older children, the seesaw board. For this game there are rhymes, some of which have sexual overtones. A psychic castration is suggested by some rhymes, perhaps a displaced hurt to compensate for entering the taboo area of incest:

> See-saw, I see-saw myself.
> I fall and I hurt myself badly.
> And I hurt my knee,
> And my Pagona weeps for me.
> And I hurt my nail,
> And my sister-in-law weeps for me.

Another expresses romantic interest:

> Come up, apple,
> Come down, pomegranate, for me to ask you:
>
> "What's the girl doing?"
> "She's knitting a string to give to Ramandam
> "And he will give her a glass and a comb and a little stool for her
> to sit and talk to the earth."

One is reminded of the Delphic Oracle on her little tripod as she breathes in knowledge of the future through a crevice in a rock on Parnassus.

In her book "Picasso's World of Children," Helen Kay describes a painting and a statue by Picasso that portray his daughter Paloma skipping rope:

"In the canvas, Paloma's eyes are concentrating on her feet; the rear foot is held high in the air as she soars, while the front foot just toes over the rope—the hands clutch the skip rope as tightly as a lifeline. Her torso is made up of angles and cubes, showing the body's movement. The whole is held together and framed by the loop of the rope itself. Paloma seems to hang in the air. Yet she is grounded by the rope that whirls underfoot.

"The sculpture is humorous, a parody of Paloma at play. It is made up of two old wicker wine baskets and a hemp of rope. Her hair is corrugated paper, cast in plaster, topped by a bow that resembles a small airplane, ready to take off. On the child's feet is an actual pair of oversized, discarded shoes. Here, too, the leaping child is anchored in the air by a rope underfoot—and suspended by it. . . . These are twin documents of a child's uninhibited play."

So Picasso captured for Spain and the universe the freedom expressed by the child in the ritual of skipping rope, a freedom expressed most directly in a final rhyme, chanted by a lonely child in Luxembourg:

> Little rope, little rope, oh my little rope,
> Unwind yourself from the round ball:
> Twirl round and round and high.

Take me outdoors to the air and the sun.
Out of the room, out of the house, the narrow house;
Nobody can catch us!
Little rope, little rope, oh my little rope,
Unwind yourself from the ball.

14

Breaking Chains
Brother Blue, Storyteller

JOHN CECH

I think we're all like frost on the window; we blow away so quickly, you know. So every time I go anyplace, I always hope that whatever I've done is for real, so in case I never appear again, you've got something you can use for life.

Brother Blue

Coming out of the subway in Harvard Square one cold February afternoon, I noticed a crowd gathered on the sidewalk. That fact alone was nothing unusual in and around the Square. Groups of passersby often stop to listen to musicians or political harangues, to appraise the jugglers, or to pick through the wares—spread out on an old army blanket—of a young, half-frozen peddler, squatting indifferently nearby. Harvard Square has the feeling of a medieval place, of somewhere cut out of present time, even during rush hour on an ordinary winter's day.

Yet today, at the center of this crowd, a man was dancing. He wore a thin blue turtle-neck, decorated with ribbons, bells, balloons, and butterflies that drifted down over his blue trousers and slippers and hovered over his black face and blue knit cap. He held aloft a multicolored umbrella with one hand and shook a fool's bells in the chilly air with the other. His lithe body moved with energy and grace despite the numbing cold. Every gesture seemed both spontaneous and deliberate. Behind him, and a part of him, was the force of black dance, from the shaman and the tribal celebrant to the scatman, the tapper, the prancer. He touched the air with broad and subtle strokes of mime genius—Chaplin, Keaton, Marceau. This dancing man was telling a story—groaning it, mugging it, tickling and slapping it into being.

He was sweating in the freezing afternoon, like a Tibetan initiate in the middle of a frozen lake in the dead of winter, who thaws and dries a pile of icy garments with his own body's heat and then draws on layer after layer of the now-supple clothing, in an act that calls for absolute concentration and, in the same moment, forgetfulness. There was, unmistakably, something of that same spirit and warmth that could challenge the cold in what the man was doing that day, as his body whirled and stomped and his snapping fingers burst with sound, a living punctuation mark. Those onlookers near the center of the semi-circle hung on each word, rooted in the charmed and magic place until the last syllable had been spoken to release them. The hecklers and the spellbound were equally held by that ever more rare phenomenon: the sheer presence of one man and his story.

That was my first glimpse of Brother Blue. Soon he seemed to me to be everywhere around Cambridge and Boston: telling stories on the late-night jazz radio stations or on a children's program; on television doing three-and four-minute stories for pre-school children; and as the subject of frequent "local color" articles in the Boston papers. It wasn't until a year or so later that I encountered a different Brother Blue and began to know the other man behind the persona of the storyteller who had thawed the ice in Harvard Square.

I remember a long conversation we had in an elementary-school cafeteria. It happened that we were neighbors, living only a block apart. He often dropped into my daughter's school to say hello, tell a story, or talk with the children and any parents who could reconcile themselves to the idea of a black man, "gotten up" in a bizarre costume, spending his days working at, of all things, storytelling. That day he was at rest. In fact, he seemed to be exhausted. He pulled his body slowly over the tiled floor and slumped into a tan folding chair. But his mind was awake, as he spoke in low, ardent tones about the oral tradition and the Yugoslavian bards, Huizinga and ludic man, Harvey Cox, the Jataka Tales, Mozart, old age, Mister Rogers, slavery, Sesame Street, and Shakespeare. The ideas—informed, articulate, sophisticated—took the place of his body's dance and wove around the table between the coffee cups and doughnuts, as he warmed up to a stranger he was meeting outside the special circumstances of a performance. It wasn't long before he was "on" again, lost in a ten-minute demonstration of his own version of *King Lear* for the streets. Carefully, gently, his wife, Ruth, who is always nearby, began to shepherd him toward the door. They had appointments to keep, and she knew the mile walk to Harvard Square could take twenty minutes or two hours, depending on whom he met and talked with or told a story for along the way. After another fifteen minutes of parting words he was gone. But, faintly, one could still hear the sound of his bells in the room.

He stayed long enough for me to see that behind the mask of the performer lived a soft-spoken, deeply—even painfully—sensitive individual. Keats might have said he lived on his pulse. On other days, I sensed, he might have lived closer to the vital nerve endings that were so near the skin of his experience. He had spoken that day of the spirit-touching, soul-enlivening qualities of storytelling, of his own "calling," his own "madness" to tell stories. In our secularized age, the words *spirit* and *soul* can sound thin and affected in our daily working vocabulary, but not in Blue's. He said them with awe and with passion, as I would later find he would say and do so many things in his life. Sitting across the table from him, I could not help wondering where it—or more accurately, where he—had begun.

The details of Brother Blue's identity must be gathered from newspaper and magazine articles; his six-page, single-spaced list of degrees, awards, performances; and, finally, from the stories he tells about himself. Blue sweeps aside any definitive, autobiographical statement. He believes the bare facts trivialize the experience and blur the focus on what he seeks to do. "People should get past details. What matters is what you are in the middle, in the soul. There are things to be done that can be carried out by late bloomers."[1] One feels, from his circumspect answers to any questions about his age, that he considers himself one of these. As with the Tantric yogis, the details of his past are important only to the extent that they can be transformed into the expressions of the book he himself lives. On the other hand, as I later discovered, nothing seemed to be lost or lacking in significance for someone who had grown up, as he did, in an oral, storytelling culture. Indeed, his life reveals itself as a series of magically charged events that have the effect of being more real than any raw biographical data could ever hope to be. The stories are the man, his person and his myth.

We do know that his given name was Hugh Morgan Hill and that he was born the son of a bricklayer whose hands were dyed red by his work, in Cleveland, in the 1920s, in poverty. Blue himself may become metaphysical if asked when he was born and say, "I was either born yesterday or a thousand years ago." He took the name "Blue," depending on the circumstances of his explaining his naming, either from his father's cousin's nickname or from the way his brother, Tommy, first pronounced "Hugh." On other occasions he may create another origin:

Before I came into the world I was doing command performances for the King, alright? And he said, "Wow, this kid's good! I think I'll send him down to do some stuff. I was under a blue tree and there were blue apples in the trees, see how it bees? And the King said, "Rap for me, Blue." And I said, "To-cope-o, to-cope-o-did-ee." And He said, "I'm going to send that cat into the world; I'm going to call him Blue." And that was you know who. Me. Blue.[2]

His wife will remind everyone present that he is a storyteller. She will lovingly admonish him, and he will then come as close as he can to a "straight" answer for her sake:

When I was a kid, Hugh was not a name you called black kids. A lot of people called me "Blue" as a nickname. It rhymed with Hugh and it was easier to say. So I took the name Brother Blue. I call it my soul name, my right-on-name, my night name, my tight name, my game name, my name name.[3]

For a group of elementary school children, he will turn it in yet another direction:

My blue is the blue of the morning sky,
the butterfly,
the sea,
the blue of beauty.
See the color of my skin?
It's black, but it's wrapped in blue sky.
That's my story, and it's blue.
That's your story, too,
And it's beautiful.[4]

Though his parents could barely read and write, the world of his childhood in Cleveland was alive with stories, of his mother picking cotton in Mississippi, of his father's youth in Alabama. Blue speaks with emotion about the effects of those early years on him; the events are yesterday fresh. Particularly he remembers the figure of his father, the first and most powerful storyteller in his life, standing over his bed at night, casting a huge shadow on the wall, or reading aloud from the Bible, "pacing the floor and reading, and it was like he was singing."[5] He recalls the preachers in his church, "where we had that *rocking*, black thing; we used to walk down town to go there, walk three or four miles to get there and to hear that man rock, in that ultimate, fantastic kind of theater, what they call today 'total theater.' The man got up there and he *showed* you God scooping out the valleys and putting up the mountains."[6]

One of those catalytic events in Blue's childhood that led him to become a storyteller, pinning objects to his clothes and dancing out whatever came, involved his entertaining and trying to communicate with his brother, Tommy, who was "retarded." Blue does not like the word, and he actually shudders noticeably at the sound of it. "I don't like calling them mentally retarded because in the soul is something perfect."[7] Tommy had grown up in the Hill household but was later transferred to a "Home for the Retarded." Within a few days of the transfer, Tommy died. Blue believes it happened because of the separation from his family. Blue has shaped this experience into one of his most moving stories. "Once I Had a Brother." He calls it his "soul story," the one he would tell if he were dying and had only one story left.

"Once I Had a Brother" begins in the livingroom of a man "so rich the carpets hit you around the knees." He is called Mr. Best, "since he was exponentially rich and had the best of everything." Blue has been brought by a friend to a party at Mr. Best's house. When he is introduced to him as Brother Blue, Mr. Best replies, "Why should I call you brother?" As the evening wears on, Mr. Best disdainfully questions him about the value of storytelling. "Are you making any money?" he asks. "Nary a penny," Blue responds. When they are alone in the livingroom, Mr. Best looks at Blue with cold blue eyes and demands, "Alright, now, what is your story?" Blue answers him with the story he has never told to anyone, not even his wife:

I had a brother once. He died on me.
He could have been you,
peekin' through your eyes of blue.
He couldn't read or write.
But he could read and write music in the air.
He lived for love.
I taught him how to say my name,
and that became our game.
One night he said, "Brother Blue."
I jumped over the moon with the cow and the spoon.
That's when I began to wear rainbow colors on my clothes.
I tried to teach him how to write his name.
He tried. He couldn't. Didn't want to hurt the pencil.
I tried to teach him how to read.
He tried. He couldn't. Afraid of the dragons in the book.
For those who can't read beauty in a book,
I try to wear it. I cook
it in my clothes.
One night when I was far away,
They put Tommy some place.
They locked him in one door,
then two, three and four.

He upped and cried and died so fast.
If I had been there, would he have flew?
It's a true story, true inside true.
And now, if I see someone on the street
—or if you do—
who's confused and unhappy, that's my brother.
And I'm gonna love him.
And you should, too.

Blue concludes, "Now whenever I see someone with an ugly cocoon, I always think of my brother. There may be a beautiful soul—a butterfly—within. That's why I wear butterflies."[8]

This condensed version of the story gives one only a fleeting taste of the full tale, which can take nearly a half hour to perform. One of the problems in transcribing any of Blue's stories is that words alone do not do justice to the telling, in this case with the story's satirical opening, its lengthy portrayal of Blue's relationship with Tommy, its frequent, lyric choruses, and its acoustical and visual rhythms. Each time I have heard it performed someone in the audience weeps. Blue varies its length and the impact he hopes to achieve with it, depending on the age, size, and place of his audience. But it is essentially, an intimate story, what he calls his *cante hondo*, the song that the flamenco singers save till the end of an evening when "all the chaff has been blown out."

Blue recalls that once when he told the story to a group of children in a mental health care center, one child who, like his brother, could not speak ran up to him afterwards:

The boy had the look of the sun and the rainbow. He was crying and smiling after I performed. He put his head to the middle of my chest, then backed off and spread his arms as if he were flying. As long as I live—if I never get another response—I've got that. He was responding from his soul to something in my soul. I call that the butterfly.[9]

The struggle of the caterpillar to change itself into a butterfly is Blue's archetype because "it's symbolic of the spirit. Even the body itself is the chrysalis, the cocoon. All of reality is the chrysalis, the cocoon of something contained within the measurable, tangible, audible, visual reality. You can call it the 'Life Spirit,' you can call it 'God,' you can call it 'butterfly.' "[10]

Ugly ducklings are consequently the most frequent visitors to the field of Blue's stories. His own version of the Andersen classic is called "Ugly Duckling, Soul Brother Number One, to Brother Blue, Ugly Duckling Number Two." In this story, a copy of which is in Andersen archives in Odense, Blue portrays the duckling as a gravelly-voiced child Satchmo, old before his time, an unappreciated musician and singer who moans spirituals and wails fragments of a blues song to the cynical creatures of the barnyard. In another story his nasty Rumplestiltskin is utterly changed and delighted by the queen's new baby and becomes the child's godfather. In Blue's version of "Jack and the Beanstalk," his underdog Giant—named "Boo'Hoo"—belongs to "a minority called tall, and tall ain't bad at all, y'all." The giant doesn't perish in his fall from the beanstalk. Instead, he survives and marries a midget, and they live happily ever after, bringing "perfect babies" into the world while Jack is sent off to reform school to ponder his thieving nature. Fairy tale purists may object, but Blue sees what appears to many to be the justice of the tales as a shocking injustice to the villains, whom he would prefer to have mercifully redeemed rather than punished.

A second experience from Blue's childhood reaches out, as he might say, from "the middle of the middle" of the mythic center of stories through which he defines himself. Again it is an ugly duckling story—this time about himself. Although his father—the mason—tried to square him off, make him fit like a brick, in elementary school (when he was eight, "always late") he was the sole black child in an all-white school, "the only black button in a field of snow." Quite literally, he wanted to die. He was a failing student and considered himself unattractive and stupid until a teacher, Miss Wunderlich, with her "blue eyes, true eyes," perceived his emotional predicament, recognized his potential and encouraged him in his studies. In the story he becomes a whiz at arithmetic, and every other subject after that, and he pops his fingers and beats rapid time with his feet, evoking the energy of his new-found abilities as "a numbers runner," wildly and correctly ticking off problems in his head for her. "Miss Wunderlich" would later win him a Corporation for Public Broadcasting prize for an "outstanding solo performance" when the story was aired on WGBM-FM radio in Boston in 1975.

After serving overseas in the army in World War II, he attended Harvard on scholarship, receiving an A.B. cum laude with a major in Social Relations. The cultural shock of coming to Harvard in the late 1940s was at first overwhelming; few blacks were attending the school and he was the only black at Lowell House. "I got to thinking about the world here. I said, 'These are the best minds.' At home I'd always been the smartest, but here there were guys whose minds could take them all over the world."[11] Eventually the ugly duckling realized that he "could cut it" and do quite well. But cultural differences surfaced, poignant ones that could not be breached then. His father, with his Alabama accent, had difficulty pronouncing "Harvard"; so, to ease matters, Blue told him to say he was attending "Howard" instead. His father knew that name. When Blue was an undergraduate, his father received a serious beating on the street when he refused to hand over Blue's scholarship money, which he was about to mail off to Cambridge, to some thugs who stopped him. "I don't mind how many beatings I have to take," he told the hoodlum, "as long as he gets through school." Blue recalls having no one with whom he could possibly share the sorrow of this moment or who might understand the circumstances of his origins.

As an undergraduate he promised himself that, if he ever made it through the intimidating atmosphere of Harvard, he would somehow try to carry his education, in some form, back to the world he had grown up in and the people he knew best: "I thought about people like my daddy, who could barely read or write, and was so noble, and I wondered, 'How can I bring him the beauty of what I was finding?' "[12] Later this commitment would grow into Blue's rationale for developing his own style and approach to storytelling. Since 1968, Blue has been taking his storytelling to the streets, prisons, hospitals, schools, and churches of the community. His repertoire includes not only his own stories about his life, but also his distillations and revisions of the classics of children's and world literature—the Panchatantra and Jataka tales; Aesop, Grimm, and Andersen; *Oedipus, Othello* ("Big O"), *Macbeth* ("Mac's Blues"), and *King Lear* ("Blues for Old"), to name just a few of the sources he draws on.

> What I want to do is take whatever I know and break it down for those who don't have the literary teeth, so they can gum it. You have to work at that. You have to *know* Shakespeare, you have to *know* Aristotle's *Poetics*. You have to do all the reading and bring it down to the people. And then you must bring the stuff from the people to the academy.[13]

After graduating from Harvard, he studied briefly in both Harvard's and Yale's divinity schools. His interest in the theater and writing led him to the Yale Drama School where, in the 1950s, he eventually took his M.F.A. in playwriting, winning the Blevins-Davis Award for Playwriting for the best original play of the year, "Song for a Broken Horn." By the 1960s he was back at Harvard again, writing and acting in the Boston area and studying in the Divinity School. He believed the ministry might provide the vehicle for touching people. But he later told Harvey Cox, the noted Harvard theologian who advocates making organized religion respond to secular needs, that most of what he was preparing himself to do as a clergyman was "a mystery" to him. Still, he planned on an academic career. He recalls being "very interested in that fusion of the spirit and esthetics. I wondered, 'Is there a place wherein our poetic, our musical,

our histrionic—all our gifts—are combined in the highest way?' And I
thought it was probably in worship." He was hoping "to do a dissertation
on the Byzantine Church, the Eastern Church, wherein I think there is
probably the greatest fusion of dance, sound, and theatrical elements on
this earth."[14]

In the 1960s he steeped himself in folklore and mythology. He studied
under A.B. Lord and became intensely interested in Lord's work on the
oral tradition. He differed fundamentally with Lord, though they have
remained friends, over the appropriateness of incorporating the energy of
black art forms and language, along with modern dance, music, and theater, into the mainstream of the storytelling tradition. He left Lord's class
when he decided that rather than do scholarly research on the oral tradition
he wished to become an active agent of it.

His "coming out" with his spontaneous, theatrical form of storytelling, blended with the spirtually affective powers of worship, took place
in 1968, when he gave a number of performances of his happening/play/
requiem "O Martin, O King," in homage to the spirit of the recently slain
black leader. Dr. King had been one of his lights—" fusion of the singer,
the chanter, the poet, who had the intellectual prowess as well. He bridged
two worlds."[15] After these moving performances, friends suggested that
he continue to develop and exercise the format and style he had launched
in "O Martin, O King." In 1972 the ideas and the acts crystallized in
what he called his SOUL THEATRE, for which he wrote an impassioned,
Blakean manifesto:

> I want to put a light on the dark places in our existence. I
> want to catch the shy bird. I want to show the invisible. I want
> to sound the inaudible. I want to reveal the landscape of the SOUL!
>
> What I hope to do in performance, what I try to do, is to
> communicate the deepest experience honestly. Trying, with my
> life—trying to be absolutely honest, no lies, no hiding. Trying to
> integrate singing, dancing, mime, tableaux, finger-popping,
> stomping, story-telling, acting out sequences, exploding them out,
> screaming cries, all sounds and motions of the body to tell the
> truth in the middle of me. I used to blow a blues harp and beat a
> tambourine, but now my body is my only instrument. I try to use
> it to the utmost, to fuse everything I've got, to move as freely as
> I can in all the means of expression open to my body.
>
> My style is highly improvisational. I never do a work the same
> way twice. It must be open. It must be free to catch that bird,
> that wild bird, that beautiful bird that comes so suddenly on the
> wind. I try to work like a jazz musician, blowing an old song from

my SOUL, but blowing it ever new. I'm not trying to do a slick thing. That's not my way. I'm just trying to do something for real, moving from the middle of me, moving in the spirit, trusting it completely—with my life! I come out of a trusting tradition—out of the wide open black church, out of rhythm and blues, out of shouts and hollers. That's all walking on water. That's all riding the wind.[16]

The only props Blue used in these performances were the slave chains that had been loaned to him several years before by his professor of American Church History at Harvard. Blue had said to him after class one day, "You've gotten to 1890 and you haven't discussed slavery at all." His professor replied, "We'll get to it." And the next meeting he came into class and dropped a paper bag on the table in front of Blue.

That was the shattering moment of my life. Probably, that, as much as any single incident, made me a storyteller. I grabbed 'em, and I tried to break 'em and found I couldn't. He looked at me and said, "Yes, Blue, those are slave chains, from the slave market in Richmond, Virginia. My great-grandfather got them when he was going through with the Union Army." And then I knew I had to break out of my dream and take care of business, 'cause there's work to do in this world. And then I knew the chains have not been broken yet. There are visible chains and invisible chains, chains of suffering, chains of hunger, chains of disease, and there are people locked behind prison doors. I decided I would spend my life breaking chains. Every place I go I carry these, with my balloons, my dragon, my teddy bear, my mouth harp, my bells— 'cause I mean business.[17]

Literally and metaphorically, the chains figure powerfully in Blue's storytelling. Groups of white listeners visibly squirm when he brings them out and puts them on. They're a deadly, hard object against the streamers and balloons, tough and impersonal elements on the flesh of this most gentle and personal of men. Dramatically they achieve a potent effect, reminding Blue, as well as his audiences, of the ongoing struggle of all humanity to free itself. Sometimes he slams the chains down on the floor and challenges members of the audience to come forward and pick them up. "What chains bind you?" he asks.

When he was performing for an all-black audience recently, he took a final request. Someone asked him to play something on his harmonica. Blue began to blow, sweetly, the melody of "America the Beautiful." After he had gotten through it, and his black audience was beginning to wonder

Photograph by Karen Wright Rohr

where he was taking them with the song, the chains appeared from their blue sack and, as though they had a mind of their own, settled on his slender wrists. Each time he tried to continue with the song (now he was singing it, with a cracking, falsetto voice, as he had as a schoolboy), the chains flew up into his mouth and gagged him. Slowly, the story spun out—of being hit by a racist's brick as a child; of his brother, Tommy, being urinated on in the schoolyard by white children; of his Great-Aunt Sat, who had been killed in bed by her master; of his own dormant dreaming at Harvard—until the awakening shock of the sound of the chains hitting the desk. The story then became a shout, a warning, an urging: "Put your life on the line, like Martin Luther King, put your life in a tree, like that Jesus cat from Galilee. Break chains or die."[18] Only *then*, he told his audience, could they sing the song again—as he did for them, in a clear, flawless voice—adding a verb to the title, which now became "America *Be* Beautiful."

By the end of the story/song the audience was galvanized, nodding and clapping its approval. None of us present had imagined this would be the result of that request simply to play some music. "America *Be* Beautiful" is the only one of his stories that Blue has been willing to preserve on a commercial recording.[19] He is reluctant to call the others finished or definitive and thus ready for print or record; he believes they should not be fixed and that they must be allowed to change every time he tells them. But this story and the way he did it, in one twelve-minute take with a back-up group of jazz musicians, never changes. It is, in a primal way, his naked song, his reality song, to jar back to their wide-open senses anyone who mistakes the playful side of ribbons and bells for the whole man. "America *Be* Beautiful" identifies at once the seriousness with which he treats everything about his "calling." Usually Blue will hold back from revealing this side of his person, especially around children or with an audience he routinely collects on the streets and with which he has not built the rapport that calls forth this story. He is worried about offending people and turning them away.

While it is the immediately recognizable sign of his profession, his costume also serves as a protection. In keeping with the traditional dress of many African storytellers, Blue has pinned objects to his clothing— rainbows, butterflies, bells, a saxophone—and carries sacks full of props with him whenever he is performing. Each object has a meaning, a story behind it; he or a child will point to one of these talismans and he will launch into its story. Yet he is ambivalent about the costume, at times wishing that he didn't have to wear it to reach an audience. He will often tell a group to forget about it altogether, to see through the mask. Frequently this barrier to understanding is difficult to remove immediately with groups of children or cautious adults who are "checking him out," uneasy about letting their kids or themselves stand too close to this unusual and unexpected character. After a story or two, though, the children tire of bopping his balloons and the adults relax; imperceptibly, the costume begins to dissolve and, finally, the words become more important than the outfit. On the other hand, Blue is aware of crowd dynamics and knows that he must first appear to be "a living Christmas tree"—flamboyant and "gotten up"—if he is ever to have a chance with them. And if he cannot sustain a mood, if the youngters continue to fidget or the adults get bored, he can return to the mask. He senses that many people will not want to look behind the contrivance. So he retreats back into it. They may think the costume "weird," but it won't offend.

Similarly, he shies away from discussing his feelings about children's television and its reigning personalities and programs or the stereotypical methods of storytelling passed down through the schools of education and library science, even though he feels very strongly about both subjects. Though he tries to be diplomatic and moderate his remarks about children's television programming, his voice rises and gathers steam, and he is obviously anything but the prancing figure in the park. After making a pilot and waiting for over a year to get a response from a network, he was told by a broadcasting executive that his network would not consider a show for children with a black man as the featured performer. He winces at the idea of librarians or teachers merely reading or memorizing stories from books. He bangs his fist on the table at what he calls the "idolatry" of such an accepted practice: "By the time you get through college, or even high school today, you have become convinced that every worthwhile thing is written in a book ... the idolatry of the written word."[20] He fumes about television and the unimaginative, dehumanized, and sometimes racist attitudes it fosters:

> We are becoming alienated from the human being. You know, technology is very seductive. We have a whole generation of children coming up, and adults, too, who worship technology and the image. They have forgotten what it is to be human ... to feel, to bleed. ... We must return to a one-to-one or a one-to-many sharing and telling of stories. We must come back to ourselves. It's easy to put on the technology—quick changes, bright colors, flash animation, all that stuff—but you ought to get someone on there to celebrate what WE can do as human beings. Find a live storyteller, and put him on regularly. Sure, I'd like to try it. I can DO that stuff. Say, "Hey, everybody, I'm gonna tell a story. All I'm gonna use is me, alright? I'll become a dragon for you ... just watch." To get up there without a book, using your face and voice and body to hold 'em. That's what a storyteller is.
>
> You should get a black man on there. A black fusion of the best of Captain Kangaroo, Mister Rogers, and Sesame Street, a black male who has dimension and who can get to a lot of people no one else can reach in this country. A man who's not always clowning, but who can do it all.
>
> In being trained as educators, we are conditioned to behave in a certain way. For instance, how do I look? How many teachers would dare step out the door like this? And children are looking at this. So can't we play a little bit? Can't we get OFF it, now and then?
>
> I ask the kids why they think I wear this rainbow pin. The human race is a rainbow. We're all different colors. I just happen to be blue. There are all different colors of skin, but there's something within the skin. It's something like a butterfly, but you can't name it. There's something in each of us that's beautiful. You've just gotta see it through the eyes of love.
>
> Get THAT on television. It's worth a hundred of those car-

toons. Teaching kids the ABC's is fine, but you have to transform the heart. Then you can transform the quality of their lives.

Kids have to find that each of us has a value and a worth. You have to dream out loud and tell your story. Tell a story that is playful, but one that will help a child, or an adult, to discover his own particular self. His unique butterfly.[21]

In the late 1960s and 1970s Blue's SOUL THEATRE had moved into the prisons around Boston, where he had been giving classes in poetry and working with the inmates for a number of years, in addition to maintaining his increasingly more active role in the community. He was struck by the prisoners' attitudes: "They came to my class for one thing. They wanted something beautiful." So he began to formulate a project involving them that would be "a very serious work in alternative ways of teaching, of evoking, of educating. Something nonverbal for those who are not into reading, because, even if you can't read or write, you can still apprehend and communicate great beauty and wisdom."[22] The prisoners asked him to do their Christmas service. They told him they did not want any "jive" in the program, and this once again led him to create an experience that joined worship with dance, music, drama, and storytelling. Eventually the project took the name of "Soul Shout," and it earned him his Ph.D. in 1973 with Union Graduate School (Harvard was the sponsoring institution).

The prison experience and the completion of the doctoral project seem to have been a watershed for Blue. Since the early 1970s he has been the "storytellin' fool" of New England. Further afield, he is often asked to be the resident storyteller or one of the featured participants at conferences and festivals, such as the Canadian Library Association Annual Conference in Winnipeg in 1974, the New Age Congress in Florence in 1978, and the Spoleto Festival in Charleston, South Carolina, in 1978, 1979, and 1980. In 1976 his story "Malcolm X" received an award from the Walt Whitman International Competition for Poetry on Sound Tape. In 1977 he told stories for seventy-two hours to draw attention to those who were starving throughout the world. His 1977 version of *Hamlet*, "Hamlet's Got the Blues," was performed with a twenty-seven piece orchestra for the Christmas concert at the Berklee College of Music. In 1978 he told stories for the opening ceremonies of the New York City Marathon. In order to help remove some racial barriers, he and Ruth spent a week in 1978 in several small towns in the coalmining region of Virginia, living, eating, and storytelling with the miners and their families. Blue has given numerous storytelling workshops in the Boston area, for educators, students, parents, and children. Since 1975 he has served as a Field Education

Supervisor for seminarians at the Harvard Divinity School, offering regular seminars in "The Art of Storytelling."

The pace of Blue's schedule would exhaust or unnerve anyone less consumed by his art and sense of purpose. A recent trip to Gainesville, Florida, is typical. During the course of a five-day stay, he gave half a dozen radio, television, and newspaper interviews—several of them lengthy, all of them personal interactions with the interviewer. On one particular day, he began by telling "The Three Bears" to a group of preschoolers in the local public library, shifted gears and told a completely different, hip version of the same story to college students after lunch, and made a guest appearance in a class later in the afternoon, telling another two hours' worth of different stories centered on the theme of education, including "Miss Wunderlich." Then he held forth at a cocktail party (he doesn't smoke or drink) for several more hours about his theories and techniques, seasoning his nonstop remarks with brief examples from other stories. In the evening he gave another program of stories for an adult, largely academic audience to demonstrate his various styles of storytelling, from the get-acquainted, "Peek-a-Boo" piece he does with young children, to his "Po' Caterpillar" for a slightly older audience, to his "Ugly Duckling Number Two," revved up to full-throttle for a street-wise group, to his rendering of *Othello* for a mature (and, this time, literary) gathering. After the break and after most of the audience had left, he settled in for another two hours with a Buddhist tale, "The King of the Golden Deer," told with minimal gestures and improvisation; followed by "Once I had a Brother," which left several in the small group openly weeping; and, to end the evening, his story of the Creation, told for laughs and for a deeper feeling of wonder and joy. He has each of God's creations complain, as he is brought individually into the earth, that God has forgotten to provide him with something or someone to play with. Blue's God, who is absent-minded and repeats after each of the animals' demands, "I should have thought of that!", is nonetheless majestic when he realizes each animal's need and summons up his magical powers to help them all out of their loneliness.

At this point Blue stopped so as not to "wear out" his audience, but he made the group promise that the next time he was in town they would organize a night-long storytelling session to "wake up the sun." After another half-hour of conversation, he left to go back to his hotel room. But he could not sleep and began to sketch out, in writing, another group of stories he wanted to tell. Dragons are his current passion. The gift of a hand-made, blue calico dragon from two children he met on a long train journey has prompted this new series of tales. He promised the children he would take the androgynous dragon, Almara (who is about the size of a medicine ball, with a droopy snout and a long, spikey tail) everywhere with him and unlock the creature's stories. By the end of the weekend, he has added another character to his collection of "props"—a finger-puppet mouse, again hand-made, whom he immediately dubbed "Just-One-of-Those-Things, the Third." Blue imagined him as an aristocratic English mouse with a hyphenated name who suffered from a broken heart and became a blues singer in the barrooms of St. Louis.

In the car on the way to the airport the next day he was still playing with "Just-One-of-Those-Things, the Third" (it's the whole name or nothing) and imagining a life's scenario for him. Ruth reminded him that he needed to write some postcards, which both he and Ruth had been too busy to buy or write for the last five days, and which had to be mailed at the airport for the Florida postmark before they took their flight back to Boston.

It is neither a casually lived nor an easy life. Ruth tries to keep a modicum of order in it, handling all of the daily details of correspondence (which can be voluminous), bookings, accommodations, and promises—for copies of tapes or articles, for a story that must be told for a certain person at a certain place and time, for making arrangements for performances at a hospital or a prison that wasn't included in the original itinerary. Sometimes Blue will make a dozen promises in the course of a single performance and its aftermath. He rarely turns down any request, and he will never disregard or patronize any interest he has awakened by his presence. A nine-year-old boy, David, decided that he wanted to become a storyteller, and he came to several of Blue's performances in Gainesville, staying late with his father to speak to Blue. Soon they were fast friends. David even produced a painted découpage plaque of a butterfly and created a story for Blue's last appearance in town—a service for the Unitarian Fellowship, early Sunday morning. He told one of the other boys that Blue was his father. "He's not your father, he's black," the friend objected. But David refused to budge. Blue called on him to assist with one of the stories in front of the congregation. David beamed, wearing an "I told you so" look on his face. He tucked a letter into Blue's hand as he and Ruth were leaving the church. They promised to correspond, and one knew that somehow, in the hectic swirl of Blue's life, the promise would be kept. His five days' stay and much of his life is full of moments like these—simple, personal breakthroughs that are, for the most part, his compensation.

Blue runs on very little sleep, often grabbing a catnap for a few minutes in a car or a dark corner of a room before a performance. He says he "lives on air," and, indeed, one rarely sees him eat very much of his strictly vegetarian diet. He is too busy talking, telling, moving. My

Russian mother-in-law prepared a fifteen-vegetable borscht for him, and she has to remind him several times during the course of the meal to "eat now, talk later." Ruth produced a high-protein drink for him from somewhere one afternoon because she knew he would not stop for food once he began his workshop. She often asked him if he had to go to the bathroom. She must ask because he might well forget to do that until it is nearly too late, and the car or the performance has to be brought to a screeching halt for nature's call.

All of these quirks are part of what he calls his "madness." And his obsession, his compulsion to be either telling stories or talking about storytelling, can often exhaust or exasperate those around him who aren't (and most aren't) as "crazy" as he is. (Huizinga would call him the *Vates*, the divinely "touched" mythopoetic creator.) Some adults hold their children back from him, as if an inner voice cried to them, "Beware," even though Blue tries to explain his mission in the most unthreatening of terms:

> I have my own kind of madness, a calling, you know? I do it for the same reason that rose bushes bloom. It's my calling. . . . I pray my stories out. That's why I was born. God put me in the world to do one thing, to tell stories. Stories open blind eyes and deaf ears and make the lame dance, to remind us that we all are supposed to be like angels.
>
> One of my jobs as a storyteller is to awaken us to our common humanity. We live in a rainbow world. We must be concerned for all people, and better than a lot of sermons and lectures is the work of art: the song, the dance, the piece of music, the story.
>
> I'm a walking story, the reason I go on the streets is, listen, they're hungry in the streets, everybody is saying, come on tell us a great story, give us bread, oh, something wonderful so we can make it, so we can fall in love with life.
>
> If enough stories are told, we'll have better lives. We are storytelling creatures. We are born storytellers, all the human race. A baby from the time it opens its mouth and cries, it's telling stories. . . . What I try to do is make my stories fit the world. . . . On the street there are people who are sad, who are troubled, who want to laugh.[23]

It must be a "madness" because Blue does not make or even expect to make a living at it. It must be given away. Ruth's professional work brings home the steady income that supports the storytelling. She has been a library director and archivist at Harvard and currently is the coordinator for a Rockefeller grant project on the oral history of older black women in America, which she administers through Radcliffe's Schlesinger Library. Blue's father was puzzled by the nature of Blue's work when he explained that he had become a storyteller. "Can't you do better than that?" his father asked. "Why I can tell stories, too, and I didn't go to no college."[24] Still Blue is convinced he is doing exactly what he was called to do, in his own "mad" way. And because he feels so much of his abilities rest on inspiration, he adamantly refuses to "package" his work, letting each story try to be the perfect story for that time and place. It is why he spends the first part of each performance invoking his muse, whom he names the "Poem-maker, Soul-shaker," for guidance. It is why he sometimes loses an audience merely looking for a show. It is why he will probably never be a fully commercialized and marketable product.

Of the hundreds of stories he has either created or adapted, there is one that many feel could make him famous, "Muddy Duddy." He first told the story in 1976 when he was the resident storyteller for the Habitat Forum of the United Nations Conference on Human Settlements in Vancouver, British Columbia. His task was to invent stories after each of the daily sessions of the conference that would somehow summarize the spirit of that day's topic of discussion. On this particular day, the subject had been crop rotation, erosion, and the most effective uses of the soil. He was to tell his story outdoors, as he generally did. It happened to be raining, and a child named "Muddy Duddy" just happened to be born that same day.

Like so many of Blue's other characters, Muddy Duddy is misunderstood. He loves to play in the mud, rolling in it, dancing on it, to the consternation of his mother. She "whups" him when he is sent home from school one day with a note from the teacher: Muddy Duddy has brought mud to Show-and-Tell and danced it all over the classroom—"only thing he's good at is fingerpainting." That night Muddy Duddy has a dream in which a friend appears to him—a deep-voiced worm named "Muddy Buddy," who asks him:

"What's happenin'? *Qué pasa?* What it is?
Dey messin wit' ya?"
Duddy say, "Yeah, I got a whuppin'.
Nobody loves mud but you and me,
my life's gonna be a muddy tragedy."
Muddy Buddy say, "You mean in the Aristotelean sense of the
    unities or what?"
He say, "No, mama jus' give me a whuppin'."
He say, "If you can't lick 'em, join 'em. Join the establishment.
Become a gardener. Don't buy no rake, no hoe, Cry po'.

Use your fingers, your toes, when nobody's looking, use your nose.
Put some water down there, tho."
Muddy Duddy cry, "Ho, ho, ho, ho!"
Next day he went to his mama.
He say, "Mama, Mama! I want a garden! I want a garden!"
She say, "Hold it. We're po'. Can't buy a rake or a hoe."
He say, "I know we're po'—can't buy a rake or a hoe;
I'll use my finger and my toe.
When nobody's lookin' I'll use my nose."
She say, "We can't buy any seeds."
He say, "Give me a nickel, that's all I need."
With this nickel he got the loose radish and carrot seeds layin'
   around.
He scraped them up—for a nickel.
He come home, bam, he didn't want to lose 'em, you know.
Guess what he did?
Got a bucket of water,
threw it on the ground.
He got down, people.
With fingers, his toes, and his nose,
he planted rows on rows
of carrots and radishes.
And guess what?
Things sure grows.
He became famous for that, you know.
Never learned nothing in school.
They said he's hopeless—can't read or write.
But when it comes to growing carrots and radishes—DYNOMITE![25]

Muddy Duddy grows up to be the town's oddball, still tending his
vegetables in his unorthodox way. Again Muddy Buddy the worm visits
him in his dream. This time he tells him to "make his move" and instructs
him to fashion a bird out the mud of the next day's rainfall. Muddy Duddy
sculpts the creature and joyfully puts it to his ear. The bird sings to him.
The townspeople are struck with wonder over the bird and want to know
who taught Muddy Duddy to make it. He tells them, "Guess what?
Somebody loves mud more than me. Guess what it be? The one that made
that bird singing, the one that made this tree, this earth—that's all mud,
you know. A great Muddy Duddy made it, showed me what to do." They
ask him, "Muddy Duddy, where'd you get that sound?" He replies, "The
one that put the sound in that bird showed me."
   Soon Muddy Duddy becomes world-renowned for his earthy, musical

sculptures, though the establishment that celebrates his work does not quite understand its source and mistakes the medium for the message. Muddy Duddy grows old and dies, and that day it rains again. When the people gather to mourn him, they hear a music coming from the earth. Muddy Duddy is singing to them, and they throw themselves on the ground, Muddy Duddys all, to listen. Blue ends the story:

> No such thing as common ground or common sound.
> Hey, everybody, get down, dig that ground!
> You better fall in love with it.
> Get down. Groove on the sound.
> Cause guess what?
> One day it's going to keep you, sleep you, lullabye you,
> with the mole singing' his soul,
> and the worm in his turn.
> Dust to dust.
> And when the rain falls,
> It's mud to mud.
> Papa, Mama, Brother, Daughter,
> we ain't nothing—but dust and water.[26]

Whenever Blue does the story, he finds some mud to dig his hands into and smear on his face, his nose, and his toes. Thus, he becomes Muddy Duddy, too, in the same way that he transforms himself into the essence of all his stories. They may be about a destitute wolf or a bowl of home-made soup, but the hundreds of stories that Blue already knows or will continue to create are the mask for the same theme—revealing the cosmic in the insignificant or, as Blue is likely to quote Blake on the matter, "seeing the world in a grain of sand."

> I tell people you don't have to pray, don't try to be clever or smart. What stories do you tell those who can't follow the plot? Well, listen, you can do it! That's the point. You have to become the instrument of love. So you walk in there and before you open your mouth, they got the feeling. You have to see the perfect inside the broken.[27]

One interviewer asked Blue if he ever thought he would some day run out of stories. Blue thought for a moment. Then he turned the question around and mused, "does a rose ever run out of red?" He certainly means more, though, than to tantalize with Zen-like turns of phrase, more beneath his joking and riddling and being "gotten-up." He points to his costume and insists, "People think I'm a gotten-up thing. I'm not gotten-up. This is me, more than the other me." He goes on:

I'm saying it's a bad scene in this world. One thing I have to watch very carefully when I'm going 'round is not lettin' the kids find out how tough this world is. I have to fight my own cynicism.

We're human beings out there. We're not always clowns ... or we don't always stay clowns. But what are we going to do to salvage all these lives? Bring the youngsters stories that'll make their hearts open.

Storytelling is no particular people's art ... but I think it's the greatest of the human arts. And the most difficult. Most articles on me, they're just a waste of time. They say, "he's charming, he wears balloons, he tells stories, be sure and see him." It ain't nothing! Here's a man with a passion. What can we do? How do we get the dream?[28]

I think we know the answer! We keep on breaking chains.

Notes

1. Doris Johnson, "Butterflies are Free inside Brother Blue," *Boston Herald American*, July 31, 1976, p. 7.

2. Taped interview with Brother Blue, Gainesville, FL, January 30, 1980. I have tried to transcribe, in this and other taped interviews or performances, Brother Blue's unique speech patterns in order to preserve the flavor of his presence for the reader. All taped interviews, performances, and workshops are used with permission of Brother Blue.

3. Doris Johnson, "Butterflies."

4. Connie Bloom, *"Singing the Blues," Akron Beacon Journal*, October 4, 1976, p. A-8.

5. Taped recording of a storytelling workshop with Brother Blue, Thomas Cultural Center, Gainesville, FL, February 2, 1980.

6. Taped interview with Brother Blue, January 30, 1980.

7. Fatima Cortez El-Mohammed, "Visit from Planet Blue," in the newsletter of the Afro-American Cultural Center, University of Connecticut, Storrs, October 1976, p. 5.

8. Taped recording of a storytelling performance at the J. Wayne Reitz Student Union, University of Florida, Gainesville, January 31, 1980. This is an abbreviated version of the complete story, which took about twenty minutes to tell that evening.

9. Doris Johnson, "Butterflies."

10. John Marion, "A Spoleto Retrospective," *Osceola*, Columbia, SC, June 22, 1978, p. 16.

11. Doris Johnson, "Butterflies."

12. Timothy Noah, "Brother Blue," *Harvard Magazine*, January-February 1979, p. 87.

13. Ibid.

14. Taped recording of a storytelling workshop with Brother Blue, February 2, 1980.

15. Diane Chun, "You Can Call Me Blue," *The Gainesville Sun, Scene Magazine*, February 1, 1980, p. 23.

16. Xeroxed statement, "Brother Blue's SOUL THEATRE."

17. Taped recording of a storytelling workshop, February 2, 1980.

18. Taped recording of a storytelling performance by Brother Blue at the Neighborhood Center, Gainesville, FL, February 2, 1980.

19. Brother Blue, "America *Be* Beautiful," included on *Getting It All Together*, with Phil Wilson, Mae Arnette, et al. (Summerville, MA: Outrageous Records, 1977).

20. Dick Pothier, "Let Brother Blue Put a Story on You," *Philadelphia Inquirer*, May 18, 1979, p. 4.

21. Diane Chun, "You Can Call Me Blue."

22. John Marion, "A Spoleto Retrospective."

23. An anonymous, untitled, unpaged article in the *Boston Sunday Globe*, Aug. 13, 1978.

24. Taped recording of a storytelling workshop, February 2, 1980.

25. Taped recording of the story "Muddy Duddy," presented for the Unitarian Fellowship, Gainesville, FL, February 3, 1980.

26. Ibid.

27. Joseph S. Precopio, "Brother Blue: His Own Story," *Berkeley Beacon*, September 27, 1978, p. 6.

28. Diane Chun, "You Can Call Me Blue," p. 23.

*Some Extraordinary Writers and
Their Characters*

15

Aesop as Litmus
The Acid Test of Children's Literature

ROBERT G. MINER, JR.

*"Ask now the beasts, and they shall teach thee;
and the fowls of the air, and they shall tell thee."*
Job, xii.[7]

The basic English children's edition of *Aesop's Fables* is by Sir Roger L'Estrange and came out in two volumes, 1692 and 1699. After establishing in his introduction that his book is "for the Use and Edification of Children," L'Estrange goes on to insist that

> Nothing spoils Young People, like Ill Example; and that the very Sufferance of it, within the Reach of their Ken, or Imitation, is but a more Artificial way of Teaching them to do Amiss ... Now this Medly, (such as it is) of Salutary Hints, and Councels, being Dedicated to the Use, and Benefit of Children, the Innocence of it must be preserved Sacred too, without the least Mixture of any Thing that's Prophane, Loose, or Scurrilous, or but so much as Bordering That way.

A normal enough sentiment, of course, but interesting in the light of some of the fables that follow it. On page 7, for example:

Socrates and Calisto

> There happen'd a Dispute betwixt Socrates and Calisto; the One, a Famous Philosopher, and the Other, as Famous a Prostitute. The Question was only This; which of the Two professions had the greater influence upon Mankind. Calisto appeals to Matter of Fact, and Experiment: for Socrates, says she, I have Proselyted Ten times as many of Your People, as ever you did of Mine. Right,

says Socrates, for Your Proselytes, as you call them follow their Inclinations, whereas Mine are forc'd to work against the Grain. Well well! says Lais (Another of the same Trade,) the Doctors may talk their Pleasure, of the force of Virtue and Wisdom, but I never found any Difference yet, in all my practice, betwixt the Flesh and Bloud of a Fornicator, and that of a Philosopher; and the One Knocks at my Door every jot as often as the Other.

No philosophers and fewer fornicators knock on children's doors these days. The difference in attitude that this suggests may be significant.

The L'Estrange edition of *Aesop* set me thinking about other editions of *Aesop*, before and after 1699. What were they like? Where did they come from? Perhaps, there was more to Aesop and his fables than I remembered from my childhood—after all, that courtesan had a point, didn't she? And if only I had heard of it when young; as it was, I had had to wait for High School and Freud to discover what any well-bred eighteenth century tot would have known from his nursery days.

Even the briefest of histories of *Aesop's Fables* is complicated. There were, for instance, several *hundred* editions and variations of *Aesop* before L'Estrange, beginning, sometime in the sixth century, B.C., and in at least a score of basic languages. None of these editions were for children (children, of course, were not invented until the seventeenth century); but much of the content of these editions came to be considered particularly suitable for children (which is an interesting fact in itself: must certain kinds of great basic literature eventually end up the exclusive property of children—folk tales, ballads, fables, myth, the Bible?).

It seems likely that a man named Aesop did exist in Greece in the sixth century, B.C. Joseph Jacobs, the eminent Aesop scholar, argues that Aesop did not invent the "beast-tale with a moral" (as he calls it) but rather invented a new use for it. Before Aesop it was used to amuse children; Aesop used it to convince men, to make political points in the age of the tyrants when direct speech could be unhealthy. Even indirect, metaphorical stories seem to have been unhealthy for Aesop, however, and for one reason or another he was killed in 671 B.C. by outraged citizens of Delphi—perhaps for making a point too well.

After his death fables continued to be attributed to him and his influence can be traced through references in Plato, Aristotle, Xenophon, Herodotus, Aristophanes. Socrates is even said to have turned some *Aesop* into verse while awaiting death. After the founding of the democracies in Greece, fables became part of the rhetorical tradition and continued to grow as a form: they were considered the exclusive property of the well-educated and a sophisticated way to make a point. In 300 B.C. Demetrius

Phalereus, who founded the Alexandria Library, collected all the available fables in his *Assemblies of Aesopic Tales*. Then a first century A.D. Latin version in verse appeared. This was by Phaedrus, like Aesop a slave from Greece, who seems to have added some fables of his own and whose *Aesop* is the first we know of intended to be read as literature rather than a mere collection of folk wisdom. The earliest extant Greek collection is in prose and was written about the second century A.D. It is known in the trade as the *Augustana*. Also in the second century Babrius produced a Greek *Aesop* in verse upon which many of the later versions came to be based. The Latin verse *Aesop* of Avianus in the late fourth century, A.D. continued the tradition of *Aesop* as literature that culminates in the seventeenth century with the work of Jean de La Fontaine.

The Middle Ages drew their versions of *Aesop* chiefly from prose paraphrases of Phaedrus and Avianus that appeared from the fifth century onward. In the ninth century a prose collection of fables appeared under the name of "Romulus." Sometime before 1030 Ademar of Chabannes produced a prose collection, too. Collections appeared in France from then on, the most important before La Fontaine being one by Marie of France which she claimed was translated from the English—of King Alfred.

The history of English editions of *Aesop's Fables* begins with Marie of France's assertion about [King] Alfred's version. Whether or not he actually produced one is questionable (there is an *Aesop* by *an* Alfred in the 1170's—some years after King Alfred's death), but the story ought to be true. It would be appropriate that Alfred, attempting to revitalize his ravaged society, should have chosen to translate *Aesop* into the vernacular as a basic text for popular education. Nothing is really known about "King Alfred's" *Aesop*, but the idea of there having been one then, and for that reason, helps emphasize the very real connection between *Aesop* and education (and, therefore, children) that developed in England several centuries later.

England was the home of *Aesop* in the centuries following King Alfred, and the popularity of the fables with the Normans led to numerous French versions (done in England) and to the inclusion of several fables in the Bayeux Tapestry of the twelfth century. The fables then show up in the popular literature of anecdote—and in sermons—of the thirteenth and fourteenth centuries. Collections of fables appropriate for use in sermons (one wonders what *they* include) were made by Holkot, Bromyard and others. And of course Chaucer, Lydgate and Gower all used some fables in their works.

It was not until the fifteenth century that another complete English collection of *Aesop* appears. That was Caxton's edition of 1484 and one of the very first books printed in English. Interesting enough in itself, this fact takes on added significance when you realize that Caxton took the time to translate, as well as print, it: all this for *Aesop* while Caxton was engaged in his frenetic attempt to print everything of importance to his time. *Aesop*, then, was important (and popular: Caxton was sensitive to popular needs) in the fifteenth century. With Caxton's help it became more so. Because from this time onward a surprising number of important men begin to mention Aesop in their writing, usually with the same particular focus: learning and children.

In *The Book Named the Governor*, printed in 1531, Sir Thomas Elyot was quick to grasp the potential of *Aesop* for the education of children. Elyot develops a theme that is echoed again and again in the years leading up to L'Estrange's *Aesop* of 1692:

> After a fewe and quicke rules of grammar, immediately, or inter-lasyge it therwith, wolde he redde to the childe Esopes fables in greke: in which argument children moche do delite. And surely it is a moche pleasant lesson and also profitable, as well for that it is elegant and brefe, (and not withstanding it hath moche varietie in wordes, and ther wis moche helpeth to the understandinge of greke) as also in those fables is included moche morall and politike wysedome.

In Elyot's view, *Aesop* should be the very first book a child reads. His argument for *Aesop* is little changed by the time it is used by L'Estrange:

> For as the Foundations of a Virtuous and a Happy Life, are all laid in the very Arms of our Nurses, so 'tis but Natural, and Reasonable, that our Cares, and Applications toward the Forming, and Cultivating of our Manners, should Begin There too. And in Order to Those Ends, I thought I could not do better, than to Advance That Service under the Veyle of Emblem, and Figure, after the Practice, and the Methods of the Antients. . . For Children must be Ply'd with Idle Tales, and Twittle-Twattles; and betwixt Jeast and Earnestness, Flatter'd, and Cajol'd, into a Sense, and Love of their Duty. A Childs lesson, must be fitted to a Childs Talent and Humour . . .

Between Elyot and L'Estrange several prominent men talk about *Aesop*, among them Sir Philip Sidney, Francis Bacon, and John Locke. Before them, however, and just after Elyot, comes an illuminating event in the history of *Aesop* and its connection with learning. *Aesop* was such a popular and influential book, apparently, that William Bullockar used it as the best way to make his point. In 1585 he brought out his *Aesopz*

Fablez in tru Ortography, spelled new, to convince his fellow countrymen of the excellence of his method of spelling.

Both Sidney and Bacon make essentially the same comment about *Aesop*. They are primarily interested in how *Aesop* works, both emphasize its power to instruct and delight at the same time: through indirection and entertainment the fables elevate the human mind. Locke's emphasis is different. He is interested in the proper reading for children and what influence it can have. He suggests that what is needed in England is an edition of the fables specifically for children. Which is where L'Estrange got the idea.

By the time L'Estrange's version begins to come out in 1692, *Aesop* is not only one of the basic books in Western culture, but also a vitally important book for children.

Children's books are beginning to exist in response to discovery that children exist and what they first read could be a matter of first importance.

The eighteenth century experienced a great expansion of books for children under the energetic John Newbery and others of his business-like mien. Not unexpectedly, *Aesop* figured prominently in this development. It is not that there were so many different versions, but rather that unrecorded numbers of bits and pieces of Aesop appeared as chapbooks and pamphlets. These appeared continually—and promptly disappeared, from overwork. This, too, is in the proper Aesopic tradition: scholars note for example that only three copies of Caxton's *Aesop* survive today and only one of them in decent shape. The rest have been thumbed out of existence. Two major new versions of *Aesop* did appear during the eighteenth century, one by the Reverend Samuel Croxall in 1722 and another by (of all people) Samuel Richardson. Croxall's *Aesop* was a translation, not merely a revision of L'Estrange or Caxton, and it is less extravagant—and less earthy—than L'Estrange's. At the same time it is livelier than Caxton's. Croxall, too, had children in mind when he did his edition. Each fable was supplied with a drawn conclusion, and the book ends:

> It is not expected that they who are versed and hackneyed in the paths of life should trouble themselves to pursue these little loose sketches of morality; such may do well enough without them. They are written for the benefit of the young and inexperienced; if they do but relish the contents of this book, so as to think it worth reading over two or three times, it will have attained its end; and should it meet with such a reception, the several authors originally concerned in these fables, and the present compiler of the whole,

may be allowed not altogether to have misapplied their time, in preparing such a collation for their entertainment.

Richardson's version is entitled *Aesop's Fables, With Instructive Morals and Reflections, Abstracted From All Party Considerations, Adapted to all Capacities*. It does not seem to have been popular and may serve as a lesson to those who try to purge literature for children of all living and breathing blemishes.

The point about these eighteenth century editions is that they reflect the attitudes and prejudices of their times towards children and literature for children. Aesop might prove a quick and convenient indicator of the basic attitudes of various different ages toward its children and what they read. The idea deserves a thorough look. It also suggests related questions that may have some light shed on them in the process.

What for example, gives Aesop its longevity, its almost universal appeal? Among the better known languages *Aesop* has appeared in Chinese, Basque, Bengali, Breton, Catalan, Esperanto, Estonian, Gascon, Hindustani, Icelandic, Marathi, Hyanja, Pushto, Sanskrit, Serbo-croat, Swahili, Tonga, Turkish, Welsh. Is it that animal stories appeal somehow to that ancient human wish to belong? Maybe to hear of animals making our mistakes, proving our points is somehow comforting in an anthropomorphically primitive way. Or maybe the necessary impersonality of an animal fable tickles the fancy: objective and simple that way, life seems subject to solid, comfortable, consistent laws. No ifs and buts about what an animal does.

Another question that arises is related to changes in moral values. Which of the fables is consistently repeated in every age? Which for children? Which not? And why? Is it still fashionable, for instance, to be happy with one's lot? To emulate the tortoise in a nuclear age? And how did the eighteenth century react to a fable chastising the monkey for wanting to cover and decorate his private parts?

And what of American *Aesops*? It would not be surprising to see them take on different shape from English ones—or would it? Is there anything of the pioneer in, say, the boy who cried wolf, or the wolf in sheep's clothing? The dog in the manger? Is sour grapes a tale to suit post-colonial tastes?

Of course the psychological, scientific, and sociological claims on *Aesop* cannot be neglected. Anne Caldwell, author of *Origins of Psychopharmacology from CPZ to LSD*, has suggested that the connection between fables and hallucinogens needs exploring (any child prone to nightmares can verify that, I bet). And what about some sort of statistical-sociological study of the relationship between the number of editions of *Aesop* in any age and its intensity of feeling for its children? The possibilities, like the versions of *Aesop*, seem endless.

Perhaps after all this we shall discover that *Aesop* is one of those books that future millennia (if there are any) will say were vital to our civilization (look, after all, at the sheer numbers) but which we never noticed because it was so thoroughly basic. I cannot remember when I first heard of the hare and the tortoise, but I can distinctly remember yawning ostentatiously when it was used by my second grade teacher to make a point about (my lack of) diligence. I wonder which version *I* had read?

16

Pinocchio
Archetype of the Motherless Child

James W. Heisig

Carlo Collodi's *The Adventures of Pinocchio* has to stand, along with Lewis Carroll's *Alice's Adventures in Wonderland*, L. Frank Baum's *The Wonderful World of Oz* and J.M. Barrie's *Peter Pan*, as one of the few truly classic pieces of children's literature. For whatever the fate of these authors has been in academic circles—where Carroll has understandably proved the most exciting of the lot—many of the characters they created have become independent entities with lives of their own, free of the vagaries of literary taste and opinion. They seem to have escaped the written page, disowned their makers and become part of the very fabric of twentieth century civilization, in much the same way as the fairies, heroes and ogres found in the folktales of the brothers Grimm, Perrault, Basile and Hans Christian Andersen have returned to the hearths, the taverns and the nurseries from which they were originally gleaned. To some extent theatrical productions, films, cartoon animations and the vast market of children's books have contributed to this process. Yet the resultant success could not have occurred were it not also for a certain profound and universal psychological appeal, transcending the powers of commercialism. A study of *Pinocchio* may, I think, shed some light on the dark forces of enchantment at work in such tales.

Carlo Lorenzini was born in Florence in 1826, the first of nine children. His father was employed as a cook by the Marchesi Garzoni. His mother, a cultured woman of rich sensitivities, worked as a seamstress and chambermaid to the same household. At sixteen years of age Carlo entered the seminary at Val d'Elsa, probably with the financial aid of the marchese since his parents were short of funds at the time.[1] There he studied Latin, scholastic philosophy and theology, graduating with honors four years later. Feeling unsuited to an ecclesiastical career, however, he left the seminary and turned to journalism, a profession in which he was to exploit his biting but inoffensive wit to earn himself a place of respect as a critic and political commentator.[2]

Lorenzini interrupted his apprenticeship with the *Rivista di Firenze* in 1848 to fight alongside his fellow Tuscans in the war against the Hapsburg Empire. Upon his return he was made secretary of the Tuscan Senate and shortly thereafter founded a journal of political satire, *Il Lampione*. In 1849 he was promoted to secretary first class in the provisional government of Tuscany, a post which he resigned after the restoration of Austrian rule. Not surprisingly his journal was soon suppressed. In 1853 he initiated another journal, *Lo Scaramuccia*, devoted to the dramatic arts. What little political comment he could work into its pages had to be carefully disguised to avoid the ubiquitous eye of the censors.

In April, 1859, Piedmont again declared war against Austria and Lorenzini abandoned his flourishing career—between 1850 and 1859 he had published a number of books on a wide variety of subjects—to fight as a volunteer on the plains of Lombardy. He returned after the Peace of Villafranca and was named secretary of the Prefecture of Florence. There he remained until 1881, inaugurating a number of significant educational reforms during his term of office. In 1860 he reopened *Il Lampione*, picking up where he had left off eleven years before. In that same year he published a little book in defense of the unification of Italy, *Il sig. Albèri ha ragione*, which carried for the first time the pseudonym of Collodi—the name of a small town near Pescia where his mother had been born and where he had spent so many happy holidays as a young child.

What turned Collodi to children's books was, ironically, the pressure of gambling debts. With his creditors growing impatient and his usual income too meagre to meet their demands, he contracted to translate three of Perrault's *contes* and a selection of fables from de Beaumont and d'Aulnoy. The collection appeared in 1875 as *I racconti delle Fate*. Soon afterwards he put his pedagogical skills to use to update a well known children's reader, which he published in 1876 under the title of *Giannettino*. The success of these ventures led Collodi, now over fifty years old, to write a number of other textbooks for children on reading, geometry, grammar and arithmetic. The last of these appeared in 1890; in October of that year, while preparing an outline for yet another children's book, Collodi died suddenly and without warning.

It was during these last years of his life, in which Collodi had dedicated his talents almost exclusively to children's literature, that the figure of Pinocchio was born. In 1881 Ferdinando Martini, an established publisher and author, began a children's magazine called *Giornale per i bambini*, which had immediate success, reaching a subscription of some 25,000. Collodi, who had recently retired from public office, was among the first to be invited to write for it. His need for money and the solicitations of the editor, Guido Biagi, prompted him to overcome his habitual laziness and put pen to paper. Some time later Biagi received a packet in the mail with a manuscript bearing the title "La storia di un burattino" and the following message: "I am sending you this childishness to do with as you see fit. But if you print it, pay me well so that I have a good reason to continue with it." In fact it took a good deal more coaxing both from the editor and from children who had grown fond of the little wooden puppet and his adventures, before Collodi agreed to see the project to the end.[3] Two years later it appeared as a complete book whose sales quickly soared to a million copies in Italy alone.[4]

It is difficult to know just how to classify *Pinocchio* in terms of literary genre. Strictly speaking we cannot treat it as a folktale since it was not handed down from tradition but rather originated in the creative mind of its author. On the other hand, it would be equally unfair simply to class it as a piece of imaginative fantasy for children, since the little wooden marionette who wanted to become a real boy has *become* something of a folktale tradition over the years. What is more, there is much in Collodi's style which betrays a close affinity with the household tale and the apologue. And the problem of classification is further complicated by Collodi's introduction of certain social and political criticisms into the text which add an element of contextual reality foreign to the folktale. In short, *Pinocchio* seems to fall on the borderlands between a number of literary forms and therefore lends itself to a variety of interpretations, no one of which can be taken as exhaustive.

The unusual blend of fantasy and reality which so many critics have observed in *Pinocchio* stems in part, I think, from Collodi's intention to recover in imagination his lost childhood. The course of his careeer having been run, he now seeks in his mature years to relive his past creatively and thereby to pass judgment on it, to evaluate its influence on his personality. Indeed the very fact that he chose the role of a storyteller to achieve this anamnesis supports such a view, for already as a lad Collodi was beloved for his ability to fascinate other children with his stories. His brother Ippolito tells us that "he did it so well and with such mimicry that half the world took delight and the children listened to him with their mouths agape."[5] Moreover Collodi knew well enough that other character traits which had established themselves in his youth continued to mark him throughout life and into old age. His nephew writes that Carlo's career in government was distinguished "neither by zeal nor by punctuality nor by subordination" (P. Lorenzini, p. 986). He was an individual bordering on eccentricity, largely self-taught and always distrustful of status and rank. A true Florentine in spirit, Collodi was ever ready to mock what he saw about him, though always with affection and good humor (Biagi, p. 97, Morganti, pp. 12f). These same qualities, by his own admission, were dominant in his childhood. The picture he paints of his early days at school as prankster and clown leave little doubt on the matter: eating cherries in class and stuffing the pits in his neighbor's pockets; catching flies and putting them into someone else's ears; painting figures on the trousers of the lad in front of him; and in general causing frustration to his would-be teachers.[6] The fact that this short autobiographical sketch was done in Collodi's last years after the completion of *Pinocchio* maintains our thesis that the book was an introspective venture. It does not take much effort to see in the puppet a mirror-image of the independent, indolent and self-reliant little Carlino who refused to listen to his elders.[7] Yet there is something suspicious about Collodi's conclusion in that sketch, namely that he abandoned his impish ways and became a good boy, obedient and respectful toward his teachers. To some purpose imagination seems to have distorted memory so that his own life story might turn out as Pinocchio's had.

Unlike the adventures of Wendy Darling, Alice and Dorothy, the adventures of Pinocchio do not begin in the real world and progress to the fanciful. From the very outset we move in a land without time or geography. The color of Collodi's landscapes is of course unmistakably Tuscan, as Baldini has pointed out;[8] but it is so *typically* depicted that it is meant to be "everywhere and nowhere." Likewise there is an apparent disregard for season and time. It snows and rains to fit the occasion; fireflies appear months ahead of their season; the muscatel grapes are ripe in the middle of winter (see Ch. 20, 21).[9] The spoken idiom and certain details of social structure and fashion belong to the lower and middle bourgeoisie of nineteenth-century Italy. Yet the story and its principal themes belong to that universal time which its opening words recall: "Once upon a time . . ."[10]

Further, unlike Alice's "wonderland," the "wonderful world" of Oz and "Neverland," there is no dream-like quality to Pinocchio's world. The fantastical elements are always kept in check by the realistic environment. The miracle of a living puppet is balanced by Pinocchio's subservience to the nature of a little boy, just as the anthropomorphisms of the animal characters must submit to the laws of nature. Even the Blue Fairy, who works some splendid feats of disappearance and transformation, is nevertheless powerless against the superior force of Pinocchio's free will and susceptible to sickness. Indeed every trace of magic or surrealism is set against a backdrop of reality where magic is the exception and not the rule (Fanciulli and Monaci, pp. 216-218).

At the same time the book is full of factual inconsistencies of the sort frequent in fairy-tales but uncommon in authored children's books.[11] For example, since Pinocchio does not go to school as he should he is unable to read the simple signs at the carnival, and yet somehow he succeeds in deciphering the more difficult text on the tombstone of the beautiful child. He has no ears, having escaped Geppetto's workshop before they could be added, and yet hears perfectly well. (It is conceivable, let it be noted, that Collodi may have intended a bit of irony here, because it is Pinocchio's inability to "listen" which causes him so much trouble.) Or again, Collodi seems to have forgotten that he gave his puppet a bread-crust hat and paper jacket for all the weather that meagre wardrobe is made to suffer. That such slips are due merely to the carelessness of the author, who could after all have later corrected them, is unlikely. Even without their help the blend of the realistic and the fantastic would be dominant in the story.

Perhaps no aspect of *Pinocchio* is more striking than the role which animals play in the story. In the words of one commentator, it is "a veritable Noah's ark . . . with the typical apologal function of betraying and translating the various dispositions of mankind" (Bernabei, p. 593; Baldini, p. 120). Crickets, rabbits, dogs, apes, donkeys, birds and fish of various sorts; not to mention the fox, the cat, the eel, the snake, the snail, the fire-fly, the crab, the marmot, the calf and the little goat—all these characters and more figure in the world of Pinocchio as naturally and unpretentiously as if they were human. It may be the case that by means of such animal projections the child is led to recognize traits of personality and signs of virtue and vice which are as yet indistinguishable to him, or at least only vaguely discernible, in the adult world about him.[12] If this is so, then from the very outset *Pinocchio* is a didactic venture, and the blend of fantasy and reality serves the higher purposes of a moral fable.

If *Pinocchio* is a fable in narrative, it seems to be one with a fundamentally conflicting moral to it, and this for reasons again of the mixture of fantasy and reality. The lesson for children is clear and forthright. Hardly is Pinocchio taught to walk before he runs away in disobedience; as a result he burns his feet and has to be repaired. Repentance is short-lived, however, and he takes off self-reliantly again and again, piling up a history of lies and broken promises, and involving himself with shady characters who promise to fulfill all his desires without his having to go to school or do a stitch of work. In consequence of his misdeeds Pinocchio is nearly used for firewood, is hung by the neck on an oak tree, finds his nose grown to immense proportions, loses his money to the fox and the cat and goes to prison, is caught in a trap and tied up as a watchdog, is forced to beg for food, spends a second term in jail, is almost fried as a fish in a pan, is transformed into a donkey, is sold to a circus and then to a man who decides to make a drum of his hide after drowning him, and is finally swallowed by the great shark. The moral is obvious: evil comes to those who disobey their elders. "Woe to little boys who rebel against their parents. . . . They'll come to no good in this world and sooner or later will live to regret their actions bitterly." Both the episodic style of the moral and the underlying metaphysic (virtue rewards, vice punishes) are close to the thought-patterns of the young child. It is, as Chesterton has wisely noted in his autobiography, the most spontaneously appealing world to the child who knows too little of hypocrisy and cunning to reject such moralizing.[13] And perhaps the appeal of *Pinocchio* to older generations simply indicates a desire to return to that purity of ideals which one once enjoyed as a child at play in imagination.

Together with this unambiguous advice to children to obey authority we find Collodi's lighthearted but subtler mockery of civil authority. Three times it happens that innocent parties are cast into prison: Geppetto for chasing after Pinocchio, Pinocchio for being robbed of his money and again later for staying to help a wounded friend. In the town of Fools' Trap,[14] the judge is a giant gorilla wearing gold-rimmed glasses without lenses and his police are great bulldogs. When a general amnesty is proclaimed by the mayor, Pinocchio manages to escape prison with the others only by admitting that he is a criminal, since the jailer wants to keep him locked up because of his innocence. Such parody works deceptively to undermine trust in lawful authority on the part of the young child, and hence stands in contradiction to the surface moral of the story. More importantly, it seems to suggest that in the *real* world there is no justice; that only in the world of *fantasy* does good come of good, evil of evil. On our earlier hypothesis this tension can be traced back to Collodi's intention to recapture his youth and its ideals as a means of reflecting on his past life with its political concerns. But the conflict is not Collodi's own; it is a paradigm of our very human condition.

We are compelled, therefore, to see in Pinocchio more than merely the ghost-image of Collodi. In the same way that Pinocchio learns the harsh truths of life through experience by leaving his father-creator behind and venturing out into the world alone, so also does he escape the control of Collodi himself. It is a phenomenon familiar to the writer. John Fowles, for example, pauses in Chapter 13 of his brilliant study of Victorian England, *The French Lieutenant's Woman*, to reflect on the autonomy his characters had achieved: "Perhaps you suppose that a novelist has only to pull the right strings and his puppets will behave in a lifelike manner. . . . It is only when our characters and events begin to disobey us that they begin to live." In the case of Pinocchio this lifelikeness means, however, not the concretization of an individual figure, but rather his universalization. Pinocchio represents man, *homo viator*. In the suggestive phrase of Benedetto Croce, "The wood of which Pinocchio is carved is our very own humanity."[15] This insight needs to be understood in turn on two levels.

On the first level, Pinocchio appears to us, in the words of one commentator, as "the personification of our very own natural tendencies" (Bernabei, p. 595; cf. Morganti, pp. 26, 29) and, more importantly, as the personification of a life-myth which brings those tendencies into harmony one with another. This Collodi achieves by depicting Pinocchio's progress as a quasi-Socratic version of the way to virtue. He learns the lessons of life not from abstract classroom theories, but from direct experience, the frequent repetition of which ends in true conversion. His latent sentiments of loyalty and altruism surface only as he slowly learns the need to trim his frenzied passions for independence and the sweet life. He is victimized by wicked and evil men not because of any real wickedness on his own part, but because of ignorance; and he disobeys his elders since he does not yet know any better. In short, Pinocchio's travels lead him from an ignorance of ignorance to a knowledge of ignorance and thence to a self-conscious trust in the wisdom of age and tradition. In contrast to the cat and the fox whose hypocritical masquerade brings them finally to misfortune, Pinocchio's innocence is educated by his adventures in a world (unlike that of Voltaire's *Candide*) where happiness is ultimately guaranteed to the pure of heart.

Of all the animals who assist in Pinocchio's self-education, the Talking Cricket merits special attention. As every schoolboy knows, he represents "conscience," the wee inner voice of warning, the bond between law and responsibility. At their first encounter Pinocchio falls into a rage with the "patient little philosopher" and flattens him to the wall with a wooden hammer from Geppetto's workbench. But the Cricket cannot be so easily disposed of and his ghost appears later in the story to haunt Pinocchio, though his advice is again ignored. Still later the Cricket is called in by the Blue Fairy for his opinion on the ailing puppet, whether he be dead or alive. And here, true to his function as a *psychic* censor, he refuses to say anything about Pinocchio's *physical* well being, but simply denounces him as a disobedient little rogue who is going to be the death of his good father by and by. It is only at their final meeting that Pinocchio addresses him as "my dear little Cricket" and follows his counsel. Thus Collodi embodies in the figure of the Talking Cricket the imperative to trust in those inner promptings of the mind which curtail and yet finally protect one's independence.

Morganti summarizes the paradigmatic role of Pinocchio on what I have called this first level simply and accurately: "Collodi gives a place of value to the basic human goodness of the child and to his or her right to self-determination in the process of education. To adults, the child seems but a puppet ... without a will, who must follow blindly the will of his educators."[16] The conflict in the moral of *Pinocchio* which was pointed up earlier, therefore, cloaks a deeper irony in the book. It is not merely the case that children seem to be required to have faith in an older generation which often turns out to be corrupt; but also that true maturity is a function of individual insight which cannot be learned except through personal experience and reflection. Likewise, when Collodi concludes his sketch of school memories with the advice that students should obey their teachers, we can only presume that he is writing tongue-in-cheek, perhaps somewhat fearful of enunciating his own life-myth into a general principle.[17] In *Pinocchio* its signs are more apparent, though many have overlooked them and consequently have not understood the reasons (however mistaken) for which the book was condemned as immoral (Morganti, pp. 25, 50f).

Pinocchio stands before us as a reflection of our human condition on another level—one is tempted to say a "deeper" level to stress its greater distance from consciousness, though not necessarily to imply a greater importance as well—which complements and balances the level of moral self-affirmation. To appreciate this we may consider the figure of the Blue Fairy, who can serve as a sort of psychopomp into the nether world of primordial, archetypal images. To ignore her, or to dismiss her as a mere *dea ex machina* who directs the fate of Pinocchio to a happy ending in typical fairytale fashion,[18] is in my view radically mistaken and a distortion of the textual evidence of Collodi's finished tale.

The Blue Fairy, it will be remembered, first makes her appearance as a beautiful child with blue hair who lives in the mysterious House of the Dead, where she awaits the funeral bier to carry her off. She speaks without moving her lips and watches helplessly as the murderers abduct Pinocchio. In the following episode we discover that the beautiful child is really a Fairy who has lived in the woods for a thousand years and commands an assembly of animals to do her bidding. It is she who makes Pinocchio's nose to grow, in order to teach him a lesson about telling lies. Then, having grown fond of him, offers the proposition: "If you want to stay with me, you can be my little brother and I your good little sister."

Pinocchio agrees but only on condition that he can be with his father as well. The Fairy explains that she has already made arrangements for Geppetto to join them; and that if Pinocchio is really anxious to meet him, he need only take the path through the forest and he will find him on his way. Of course, things turn out otherwise; and when Pinocchio eventually returns to look for the Fairy he finds only a tombstone whose epitaph tells him that she died meantime of sorrow, abandoned by her little brother Pinocchio. Shortly thereafter he encounters the Fairy again, this time mysteriously grown into a good peasant woman. At first she tries to hide her identity, but when she sees the depth of his affection for her, reveals to him that whereas she had been his little sister previously, now she is "a woman who could almost be your mother." Whereupon Pinocchio begins to call her "mamma." His mischievous ways part them a third time, after which he returns with his usual fervent purpose of amendment. But before long Pinocchio's foolheartedness gets him in further trouble, and this time their separation is final. He sees her for the last time, though only for a brief moment, in the audience of a circus where he is performing as a donkey. She appears later in the form of a beautiful little goat with blue-colored wool who tries, in vain, to save him from the giant shark. The next news that comes to Pinocchio is that she is lying sick in bed, "gravely ill, struck down by a thousand misfortunes and without so much as enough to buy a crumb of bread." In his grief he vows to work double-time to help her, to which purpose he stays up half the night at work. When he falls asleep the Fairy appears to him in a dream and tells him that as a reward for his goodness she is going to make him a real boy. And with this miracle the adventures of Pinocchio come to a close.

Now there can be little doubt about the central role which the Blue Fairy enjoys in Pinocchio's life-story. As soon as he meets the beautiful child, his aimless wanderings begin to have an object: he wants to be with her. She proves inspiration and goal enough temporarily to conquer his innate distaste for school and even to forget about his father. For it is she who promises to make him a real boy, something Geppetto could not do. As Collodi himself suggests, she is something *like* a little sister; or later, something *like* a mother. More than that he does not seem to know. Indeed one feels that as the story progresses, the author does little more than *record* the activities of the Blue Fairy, who spontaneously suggests the part she will play in Pinocchio's process of development.

At this point we are obliged further to clarify our original hypothesis and to see *Pinocchio* as an involuntary autobiography which covers not only Collodi's childhood and his public career, but his private adult life as well. He never married, though it seems he sired a "secret" daughter (Morganti, p. 16), who would thus have been, for all practical purposes of reputation, "dead" like the beautiful child who could not communicate by word of mouth. But note the immediate transformation which the symbol undergoes once it has been introduced into the story. The child returns Pinocchio from the threat of death which he had incurred by choking on the money he refused to give up; and then she teaches him a lesson about lies, those with short legs (which do not carry one very far) and those with long noses (which are apparent for all to see). The connection with Collodi's gambling habits and the daughter he tried to keep hidden by deceit could not be clearer. The symbol becomes his savior both financially (the writing of the story provided him with an income) and psychologically (by reflecting him to himself).

The transformation continues and the child soon becomes the idealization of Collodi's own mother, for whom his respect seems to have been constant and unfailing, as hers had been for him.[19] The link between the images of child and mother can only be guessed at. Perhaps, because rumor has left us little or no information about the mother of Collodi's daughter, it is the filial love—in the one case given, in the other received—which was more important to him than matrimonial love. In any event, the final import of the story is clear: Geppetto gives Pinocchio his body, but the puppet must search elsewhere for his soul, which he eventually finds in the healing power of a mother's love.

Here again *Pinocchio* as the story of man-writ-small rises to the stature of man-writ-large. Willy-nilly Collodi has fallen into a world of symbols whose psychic roots touch more than the personal history which occasioned them in the first instance, and even more than the typical human problems of ethical maturation considered earlier. In a word, Pinocchio has now to be understood as *archetype of the motherless child*.

Pinocchio's own description of the Blue Fairy—"She is my mamma, who is like all those good mothers who love their children deeply and never lose sight of them . . . "—tells only half the tale. Bernabei intimates the double entendre by referring to her description as the *Blue* Fairy: the color of her hair makes her as unmistakable to the puppet as each mother is to her children; but it is also the color of heaven, the seat of Providence, the mother of all. Thus Bernabei finds it natural that she disappears at the end of the story "since the rightful place of *that* mother is in heaven rather than on earth" (p. 599; Fanciulli and Monaci-Guidotti, p. 220). The point is well taken, though others less familiar with feminine forms of the divinity in the history of religions and myth, and in particular within the Judeo-Christian tradition, might object to the inference.

To characterize Pinocchio mythologically as an archetypal motherless child is to classify his adventures psychologically as a quest for that which can transform a man from within, heal his divided self, and restore him to a state of primordial wholeness. For as the ego emerges from its embryonic identity with the mother's womb, it finds itself in a state of ambivalence. On the one hand the expansion of consciousness and the affirmation of autonomy are highly desirable; on the other, the comforts of unconsciousness and the bliss of ignorance are less threatening.[20] Pinocchio's search for a mother is a symbol of this fundamental dividedness. At one moment we see him stubbornly following his own will in deliberate disobedience of the Blue Fairy; at the next, eschewing all temptation to freedom in a frantic flight to her protecting arms. He is a puppet of contrary forces not yet integrated into his nascent ego. It is only after his final adventure with the giant shark, in which he successfully demonstrates mastery over himself, that Pinocchio assumes the form of a hero and the Blue Fairy disappears as an external reality. He ceases to be a puppet and becomes a real boy; she ceases to be a projection and becomes a dream-figure of the *scintilla divinitatis* dwelling within. The solution to the moral conflict met on the first level is therefore confirmed here on the second: personal consciousness and social obligation are harmonized through self-reflection, through union with but not absorption into the place of one's origins, the Great Mother, the realm of the unconscious.

Numerous other images and motifs in *Pinocchio* suggest similar mythological and psychological parallels which would add support to this interpretation of the tale. I would like briefly to consider two of them by way of illustration.

Let us first look at the unusual circumstances surrounding Pinocchio's birth. Master Cherry the carpenter wants to make a table-leg from an ordinary piece of wood, when he hears a voice crying out from it in protest. "Can it be that someone is hidden inside?" he asks himself, and hastens over to the house of his friend Geppetto, who has coincidentally been dreaming up a plan to make a puppet of wood and travel about with it to earn a living. Cherry parts with his log and Geppetto sets to work to carve himself a little marionette, with no further objections from the wood.

The scene immediately brings to mind Michelangelo's neo-Platonic *concetto* theory of art. According to this theory the true artist is one who discovers. He sees in a block of stone, for instance, an inner form which is hidden to the non-artist. His handiwork consists merely in chipping away what is extraneous in order that that form become visible to all. This theory is incarnated in Michelangelo's famous *Prigioni* in Florence's Academy of Fine Arts, figures struggling to get free of the rock which seems to hold them fast. This is also the image which Collodi creates—perhaps wittingly, being a Florentine himself and well acquainted with the art and theories of Michelangelo—in having the puppet *in potentia* (i.e., in a state of relative unconsciousness) cry out from a simple piece of wood, "a log like all the rest." From the very outset, then, the principle of self-realization, according to which everything must develop after its own ideal, not as a *product* of environmental tools and forces but as a *project* of consciously exercized free will, is articulated in mythopoetic imagery.

The creation of man out of wood is a theme found in a number of mythical traditions. For example, we read in the *Popul Vuh* of the Quiché tribes of southern Guatemala of the gods first creating man out of clay and, finding them blind and stupid, sending a flood to destroy them. Next they carved manikins out of wood; but these creatures had no heart, lacked insight and were forgetful of their creators. They too were destroyed by flood. And so on, until a satisfactory man was made.[21] The parallel is striking (all the more so in that it is nearly impossible that Collodi could have known of it) and shows us the other side of the coin in Pinocchio's creation.

Both in *Pinocchio* and in the Quiché myth the relationship between creature and creator is so symbolized as to accentuate a broken rapport and its eventual restoration. If the wooden manikins turn out contrary to the expectations of the gods, so does Pinocchio show his independence in a manner which brings grief to his poor father. And just as the gods need to experiment with the work of creation in order to achieve success, so does Collodi, dissatisfied with what he has made of his own life, need to recreate himself in the figure of Pinocchio, who in turn has to be cast aside like dead wood to give way to a real boy. In each case the creature, intended as a *reflection* of its creator's best qualities, reveals itself rather as a *distortion*. Its freedom, or capacity for self-formation, frustrates the plans of the gods and requires the redemptive work of a new creation.[22] In other words, if we may dissolve the relationship between Pinocchio and Geppetto into psychological language, man must acknowledge the relativity of consciousness vis-à-vis the accumulated wisdom of tradition if he is to achieve true self-realization; and conversely the keepers of tradition must beware fashioning a society which does not respect the essential freedoms of its individual members.

Secondly, let us consider the figure of the giant shark who swallows first Geppetto and then Pinocchio. Geppetto, we recall, has set off in a little skiff to look for his son. Meantime Pinocchio has nearly succeeded in catching his father up, but arrives at the seashore only in time to see him hopelessly out to sea. He dives in after him and swims to exhaustion until the waves cast him ashore on a sandy island beach. When he awakens a friendly dolphin tells him of the terrible shark who roams these waters and who has probably swallowed good Geppetto. Much later in the story, Pinocchio, now a donkey, is thrown into the sea to be drowned, but miraculously emerges his former self. "It must have been the sea water," he exclaims. "The sea works such extraordinary changes." (Later he tells how the Blue Fairy had sent a school of fish to eat away his donkey's flesh and set him free again.) Pinocchio then swims away to escape the farmer who had purchased him as a donkey, and is soon swallowed by the sea monster, "the Attila of fish and fishermen." When he awakens from the shock he finds himself in "a darkness so black and thick that it seemed to him that he had been dipped head first into an inkwell." Seeing a faint light in the distance, Pinocchio follows it and finds his father, who had been living in the shark for two years. That night they escape through the open mouth of the shark who sleeps with his jaws ajar because he suffers from asthma and heart murmurs. Lifting Geppetto onto his shoulders, Pinocchio swims ashore, with some final help from a passing tuna. He then labors day and night for five months to support his failing father, at the end of which time he becomes a real boy and Geppetto is restored to good health.

The religious and mythical motifs at work here are immediately evident to the reader. Pinocchio's adventure with the giant shark calls to mind stories like that of the Hebrew prophet Jonah or the Algonquin warrior Hiawatha, both swallowed by sea monsters, from whose bowels they emerge as heroes.[23] This same motif is re-enacted ritually, with remarkable similarity of detail, among certain New Guinea tribes in their ceremonies of initiation.[24] In addition various structural parallels are to be found in baptismal and penitential rites from a wide variety of religious traditions too numerous to mention. Pinocchio's transformation into a real boy takes the form of a double cleansing. First, the outer animal shell, the weaknesses of the flesh, is eaten away by a school of fishes. Second, the "old man" is devoured by the sea monsters and is replaced by a "new man" spiritually reborn. In each instance the change occurs through the dark forces which dwell beneath the waters, the realm where the Blue Fairy is in command. It is she who sends the fish and who lures Pinocchio into the mouth of the giant shark in sirenic fashion by appearing as a little goat on a white rock. In other words, the imagery must be seen as a further elaboration of Pinocchio's archetypal character. By confronting the unconscious the ego is confirmed and enabled to embrace social tradition and personal freedom in one saving act of self-realization. Thus the whole magic lantern of adventures is swept up into this one final heroic gesture of Pinocchio carrying the aged Geppetto on his back across the sea to dry land.

If we are moved and enchanted by the story of Pinocchio it can only be in virtue of some underlying affinity with the material upon which the author has drawn for his tale. In struggling to recover his lost childhood through the symbols of imagination, Collodi refracts the reader's gaze inwards to the often faint and nearly imperceptible truths of his own nature. This process takes three forms, as we have seen. First, it plays fantasy against reality, giving us an insight into the loss of idealism through continued contact with the bitter truth of man's injustice to man. Second, it plays the deeds of desire against the deeds of duty, giving us an insight into the contrary forces out of which responsible self-realization is forged. And third, it plays security against transformation, which gives an insight into man's need to yoke himself to a rhythm transcending the superficialities of the present moment. We are all of us, motherless children, whose task is to integrate our becoming with our origins.*

Notes

1. This information is provided by Carlo's nephew, Paolo Lorenzini, who incidentally denies the rumor that it was Carlo's mother who made the decision to place him in the seminary ("Il Collodi," *La Lettura*, November 1930, p. 985).

Unless otherwise indicated, the remainder of the biographical data was drawn from the following sources: Torindo Morganti, *Carlo Collodi* (Florence: Marzocco-Bemporad, 1952); Luigi Santucci, *Collodi* (Brescia: La Scuola, 1961); G. Fanciulli and E. Monaci, *La letteratura per l'infanzia* (Turin: S.E.I., 1949), pp. 209-21.

2. The best of his journalistic writings have been collected by Giuseppe Rigutini in two volumes, *Note Gaie* and *Divagazioni critico-umoristiche* (Florence: Bemporad, 1892).

3. Cf. Guido Biagi, *Passatis ti* (Florence: La Voce, 1923), pp. 112-14.

4. Numerous "sequels" to the story appeared later, including one by Collodi's nephew Paolo, though none of them ever achieved the renown of the original *Pinocchio*. Morganti lists the most important in Italian (p. 44). The first English edition, translated by M. A. Murray, appeared in 1892 and remains the best in print. Due to certain inadequacies and omissions, however, I have provided my own translations throughout this essay.

5. Lorenzini, "Collodi," *Il Giornalino della Domenica*, I, 23 November 1906.

6. Cf. "C. Collodi" in Stanley J. Kunitz and Howard Haycraft, *The Junior Book of Authors* (New York: H. W. Wilson, 1951), pp. 74-76.

7. P. Lorenzini, pp. 985-6. Note also that Collodi makes Pinocchio a confirmed story-teller who recounts his adventures, though not always very accurately, to any willing listener.

---

*Several weeks after my text was written, Glauco Cambon's "*Pinocchio* and the Problem of Children's Literature" (published in this journal, Vol. 2, 1973, pp. 50-60) came into my hands. If I understand Dr. Cambon correctly, I can only register amazement that our distinct points of view have yielded such similar conclusions. The question of literary genre which I have handled summarily he deals with at length; and most of the psychological themes which I have tried to describe in detail he condenses marvellously *en passant*.

8. Antonio Baldini, *Fine Ottocento* (Florence: Le Monnier, 1947), pp. 120f. Baldini's theory, developed in his essay 'La ragion politica di 'Pinocchio'," is that Collodi wanted to create a utopic Tuscany, cleansed of all moral and political strife, an ideal for which he had long struggled as a journalist (pp. 118f, 122-124). That Collodi had such visions is possible, even likely; but that he was expressing them in *Pinocchio* is a notion that overlooks too much of the non-political character of the book.

9. Cf. Mario Bernabei, "Commento a Pinocchio," *Rivista pedagogica*, 30 (1937), p. 597.

10. Cf. Max Lüthi, *Once Upon a Time* (New York: F. Ungar, 1970), pp. 47f.

11. Amerindo Cammilli, who edited the critical edition of *Pinocchio* (Florence: Sansoni, 1946), notes in his introduction nearly twenty such inconsistencies.

12. To my knowledge, Santucci has been the only commentator to sense this deeper psychological significance of these projections. See his *La letteratura infantile* (Milan: Fabbri, 1958), p. 32; and his *Collodi*, p. 54.

13. *The Autobiography of G. K. Chesterton* (New York: Sheed and Ward, 1936), p. 40. It is this truth which the late Professor Tolkien has raised to epic proportions in *The Lord of the Rings*.

14. It is difficult to find an English equivalent to the Italian *Acchiappacitrulli*. Literally it means "where the innocent (both legally and mentally) are caught red-handed."

15. "Pinocchio," *La letteratura della nuova Italia* (Bari: Laterza, 1939), Vol. V.

16. Morganti, p. 25. This I also take to be the reason for Pietro Mignosi's conclusion that *Pinocchio* represents in children's literature what Kant's *Critique of Practical Reason* does in the literature of philosophy. "Il pregiudizio della letteratura per l'infanzia," *L'educazione nazionale* 6:2 (October 1924), pp. 25-26. Cf. A. Michieli, *Commento a Pinocchio* (Turin: Bocca, 1933), pp. 156-158.

17. It is interesting that Colloci is reported by Ermenegildo Pistelli to have forgotten whether or not he wrote the concluding sentence to *Pinocchio* ("What a fool I was when I was a puppet . . . "and how happy I am now that I have become a real little boy!"). Pistelli suggests that these words may have been added by the editor, Biagi, at the suggestion of Felice Paggi, general editor of all children's literature dealing with moral themes. See Pistelli, *Eroi, uomini e ragazzi* (Florence: Sansoni, 1927), p. 250.

18. This is, for example, the view of Santucci (pp. 53, 59), who stresses her concreteness and lack of similarity with the fairies of Perrault. Morganti (p. 39) also denies the Blue Fairy any symbolic value.

19. Cf. P. Lorenzini, p. 986. I have not been able to determine the date of her death, in connection with his assumption of "Collodi' as a pen-name in 1860.

20. In this regard, see Erich Neumann, *The Origins and History of Consciousness* (Princeton University Press, 1954), pp. 39ff.

21. *Mythology of All Races*, ed. J. A. MacCullock (Boston: Marshall Jones Co., 1916-1932), 11.163f. An almost identical version of the same creation myth is found among the Dyaks of Borneo (9. 174-175).

22. P. Bargellini has argued that the main characters of the story can best be understood in terms of Christian theology: Geppetto = God; Pinocchio = man; the Blue Fairy = the Virgin Mary. The movement of the story is then seen to progress along the lines of salvation history: fall, covenant, messianic

hopes, redemption, resurrection. *La verità di Pinocchio* (Brescia: Morcelliana, 1942).

Such a theory is not without its supporting evidence, both in the grander themes of the book and in certain specific details. It seems more likely, however, that Collodi has fallen into a mythopoetic genre more basic than that of Christian theology. Then too, Collodi himself was not a church-going Catholic and even showed certain signs of outright impiety on occasion, a fact which caused his mother not a little grief (see P. Lorenzini, p. 986). This should not lead us to conclude as Michieli has (pp. 158f) that the absence of deliberate religious beliefs renders *Pinocchio* somehow imperfect and incomplete.

23. Walt Disney's famous animation of *Pinocchio* (probably the most successful of all the folktales and children's stories he has brought to the screen) depicts the giant shark as a whale named Monstro, thus recalling the widespread mistranslation of the biblical sea monster (*tannin*) in the story of Jonah. The escape scene in the Disney version is also of great interest. Pinocchio builds a fire which produces so much smoke that Monstro is forced to cough up his prisoners. An exact parallel occurs in a Maori myth where the hero, Nganaoa, finds his parents in the belly of a whale and builds a fire to set them free. *Mythology of All Races*, 9.69. See also Stith Thompson, *Motif-Index of Folk-Literature* (Bloomington: Indiana University Press, 1966), F.911.4.

For an interesting commentary on the profound personal repercussions of *Pinocchio* for Disney himself and their effects on the finished product, see Richard Schickel, *The Disney Version* (New York: Simon and Schuster, 1968), pp. 225-27.

24. James George Frazer, *Balder the Beautiful* (London: Macmillan, 1966), 2.239-241.

17

An Unpublished Children's Story
by George MacDonald

GLENN EDWARD SADLER

There is hardly a nineteenth-century writer of fairytales and stories for children and adults who has undergone a greater eclipse of popular reputation than has George MacDonald (1824-1905), praised in 1924 by G. K. Chesterton as being "a Saint Francis of Aberdeen" and by his son Dr. Greville MacDonald as having a "spiritual genius whose art was so rare that, had he confined himself to poetry and purely imaginative story-telling, he could not have been almost forgotten." MacDonald's "fairy-tales and allegorical fantasies were epoch-making," claims his son, "in the lives of multitudes, children and parents alike, and still are widely read."[1] For all of this, MacDonald has been neglected but not entirely forgotten. At least half a dozen or so of his stories have gained free entrance into the Palace of Classics: *At the Back of the North Wind*, 1871 (possibly his most famous); *The Princess and the Goblin*, 1872, and *The Princess and Curdie*, 1883, which have assured his fame; *The Wise Woman*, 1875; and his two adult faerie romances, *Phantastes*, 1858, and *Lilith*, 1895, fairytales, parables and fantasies which are currently in print.[2] (A first edition copy of his classic collection, *Dealings with the Fairies*, illustrated by Arthur Hughes, 1867, commands an extremely high price, even in worn condition.) In the midst of a revived interest in the ancient art of myth-making, and of symbolic literature, particularly folklore and fairy-tales, there is reason to believe that the general reader will be joining again the literary critic—as C. S. Lewis and W. H. Auden have done—in pursuing more of Mac-Donald's "working genius," his canny ability to cross successfully over the hazardous modern age barriers into Faerie and to spin wonder out of a night in the woods. "I do not write for children," insisted George MacDonald, "but for the childlike, whether of five, or fifty, or seventy-five."[3] No dictum about the intention of writing (or enjoying) books for children could be more necessary, demanding or rewarding than MacDonald's.

As a lifelong poet and novelist, MacDonald nearly exhausted his genius. Forced by financial stress and a rapidly growing family (eleven plus two adopted) to become a novelist and critic, MacDonald economically published almost everything he wrote, reissuing his stories and poems in varied forms. Meticulously he revised his lyrics and translations of Novalis, at times to the point of literal rigidity. Fairytales like the English Märchen, "The Fairy Fleet" (renamed in its longer form "The Carasoyn") or, for example, the highland romance of Second Sight, *The Portent*, he altered, unfortunately without an increase in power or structure.

A study of MacDonald's manuscripts, drafts and revisions reveals the painstaking care which he took with details (one can hardly read the text of *Sir Gibbie* because of corrections), and we see something of his mode of composition. One notes at once how MacDonald's visual and musical senses—faculties not uncommon among Scottish writers—[4] influenced and often activated him verbally, when he wrote poems as a first expression (frequently when confined to his bed during illness), poetic beginnings which later went into longer pieces or were placed in novels when he felt better. An example of this is his use of juvenile verse. Almost every reader of children's verse had read MacDonald's classic couplet "Baby"—

> Where did you come from, baby dear?
> Out of the everywhere into here—

which he embedded in *At the Back of the North Wind* as a poetic key to its meaning; thus making the tale of Diamond and Mistress North Wind a fanciful adventure into the spiritual maturation of the child or child-likeness (as he called it), rather than simply an instructional story which ends in death. Critics of MacDonald's stories have yet to fully appreciate the relationship of his poetry to his fiction in spite of their repeated comments on his "mythopoeic" imagination.

MacDonald did not ordinarily leave stories unfinished, as he did poems. His manuscripts, scattered widely throughout Britain and the United States,[5] show how frugal he really was. There survive only two short unpublished prose sketches of any consequence, both included in a sort of author's commonplace book compiled by MacDonald's son, of his father's "First-Fruits and Fragments," now at Houghton Library, Harvard. Contained in this large notebook are early poetic drafts, printer's proofs, some unfinished and obscure poems (for instance MacDonald's curious ballad fragment, "The Slave Ship," which was supposedly published in reaction to his views on slavery during his visit to America), and an additional chapter of *Robert Falconer*, largely in verse. In the notebook, the holograph, are also two stories: "The little girl that had no tongue" and "Robin Redbreast's or The Clergyman's Story," a dialogue of fowls based on the biblical story of the "tax-collector," Zacchaeus.

Of the two stories, "The little girl that had no tongue" is the best and no doubt the earlier, written nearly without revisions, and one should say, probably not intended for publication in its present form. It notably reflects, however, MacDonald's lifelong interest in the existential worth of childhood and his favorite theme, namely, forgetting one's self as the means of achieving the greater gift of knowing one's self and duty better. We find this theme, sometimes in paradoxical form, in almost every fairy-tale and story which MacDonald wrote: the Light Princess, for example, who has her sense of gravity restored when she surrenders herself for the life of her prince, or the Lost Princess who must learn from the Wise Woman daily submission to the task of tidying up her magical hut in the forest of trials and rewards. Like the story of *Sir Gibbie* (which is perhaps the end product of "The little girl that had no tongue"), Elsie must go down into the dungeon of self-forgetfulness before she can regain her speech. Throughout Elsie's story we discover MacDonald, the moralist and parablemaker, at work. Even a small child can understand what it means to escape from Old Ironhand, as the children do in MacDonald's well-known tale, "The Giant's Heart," another parable of retribution, confession, and restoration.

While reading "The little girl that had no tongue," one is reminded of MacDonald's gift of story-telling spontaneity, his fatherly awareness of the child's responses. It is a tale, in fact, which could have been written for his own children, as so many were; because of its strong treatment of damnation, he may have decided not to publish it. In type it belongs with his parable "The Castle," that strange tale of sibling rivalry and restored brotherhood, and with "Papa's Story," of the Scottish child-shepherdess Nelly, who is sent on a mission to rescue her wayward brother Willie— another fine example of MacDonald's overwhelming concern for the final triumph of goodness.

But what of the harshness in it? Like most writers of parables MacDonald wrote in the tradition of Bunyan; ugliness was as *real* to him as beauty. There runs throughout MacDonald's (and Bunyan's) stories the allegorical paradox of choices: encounters which result in instructions which, if obeyed, bring deep satisfaction. This is not unusual; however, MacDonald's expression of life's contrasts is cloaked in a reversal of joining parts—the key without a door and the door without a key, or the little girl without a tongue and the giant without a heart. The act of Exchange, especially when performed by a child, puts something more than doors and keys or physical organs and bodies together; MacDonald wants us to understand that giving is *actually* better than receiving. "The little girl that had no tongue" illustrates, finally, that George MacDonald could not have written the kind of stories which he did if he had not held strong views on human nature and relationships. Self-insight comes not by looking for it but, as Elsie learns, by forgetting one's own afflictions and giving to others: "She did not know whether anyone else could find a voice as she had done, she only knew it was when she had forgotten all about it, that it came to her."

Notes

1. Introduction to *George MacDonald and His Wife* (London: George Allen & Unwin, 1924), p. 14; Foreword by Greville MacDonald, p. 1. In a recent study of *George MacDonald* (New York: Twayne's English Authors Series, 1972), Richard H. Reis surveys MacDonald's "rediscovery."

2. *The Gifts of the Child Christ: Fairytales and Stories for All Ages*, ed. Glenn Edward Sadler, is a centennial, complete edition of MacDonald's fairytales and stories, in honor of his visit in 1872-73 to America. Published in two volumes in 1973, by W. B. Eerdmans Publishing Company, Grand Rapids, Michigan.

3. "The Fantastic Imagination," in *A Dish of Orts*, enlarged edition (London: Sampson Low, 1893), p. 317; reprinted in the edition of MacDonald's stories.

4. For example David Lindsay's *A Voyage to Arcturus* (1920), which belongs in the same genre with MacDonald's *Phantastes* and *Lilith*.

5. See the "Index to MSS Located and Consulted," in Glenn Edward Sadler, "The Cosmic Vision: A Study of the Poetry of George MacDonald," Ph.D. thesis, University of Aberdeen, 1966. Recently a correspondence between Mrs. MacDonald, her children, and Lewis Carroll has been discovered which demonstrates how vital the MacDonald-Dodgson friendship was to both writers. The full story of MacDonald's many famous friendships has yet to be told completely. (See *George MacDonald and His Wife*, pp. 342-346, regarding the origins of the MacDonald-Carroll friendship.)

The Little Girl That Had No Tongue

There was once a little girl that had no tongue—She could not speak a single word, even the shortest or simplest,—all day long she had to be silent. But she could hear wonderfully well, and she was always listening,—

Printed by permission of Houghton Library, Harvard University. Copyright reserved by the Executors of the Estate of George MacDonald. Squared brackets are used for the author's insertions; deletions are shown as they occur.

listening to her brothers and sisters,—listening to the wind, the brooks, the bees, the birds and the grasshoppers, and the more she listened, the more she wanted to speak. It seemed as if she were the only one in the whole world that could say nothing at all. At last when the spring days came, she said to herself "I *must* speak, I *must* find a tongue somehow"— She thought if she could only hear some new grand sound, perhaps it would fill her so full, that she would be obliged to speak—So one fine morning she set out.—She listened to the sea as it plashed on the black stones, but no voice came to her.—She listened to the music of the great cathedral organ, but that only made her feel more and more how very dumb she was, and she ran away from it as fast as she could go. She never looked about, till she found herself in a great forest, trees were all around, everything was still and quiet, not a footstep to be heard.—She did not know where she was going, but still she went on—The path grew narrow, the sky which had been blue, became grey and cloudy. The trees were thicker, and instead of oaks and beeches, firs and yews lifted up their dark branches—Stoats and weasles ran across the path; once, Elsie almost trod on a viper, that slipt into a long tuft of grass, flat toads sometimes crawled into a wet ditch, and blind worms crept under the hollow trees—There were a good many smoothly-folded leaves of the deadly nightshade, but no flowers. Thrushes and swallows did not seem to live there, only great black nests were in the fir-branches, the sun had gone in, the wind sighed, rooks cawed, and sometimes a raven flew by—

Dark grey walls now came through the trees. Elsie saw before her a long, lofty square building—It had small grated windows, iron doors, and broken chimneys. She could not tell why, but she felt frightened as she looked at it—She came closer—under the shadow of the moss-grown wall, she saw an iron grating; she looked down,—two or three of the rails were broken away—and underneath was a dungeon,—a dungeon full of men, women, boys, girls and children. Every one was bound down to the damp earth with strong ropes or rusty iron chains—Elsie could see what red blood shot eyes they had, what pale hungry faces, and what raw ugly wounds the rusty iron had eaten into their flesh. When any one moved hand or foot, how the chains did clack and rattle!—

"What o'clock is it?" asked a hoarse voice.

"It must be the afternoon," answered another, "the shadows are getting longer and longer. It must be nearly three o'clock. Old Ironhand has gone away. Oh! if we could only get out;—but we can't,—we can't get out"—Ever so many voices took up the cry, the wind sighed in the trees, and the rooks cawed, and flapped their black wings—

Not get out! thought Elsie,—not get out,—they must get out—If only there was a strong grown-up man or woman there, or even if she had a voice,—the voice that would not come,—she might rush off and tell people to be quick and help them out; but this she couldn't do—Still it was impossible to go away, she must stay there for a little longer—She thought no more now about looking for a voice, but crouched down close by the wall, to watch what would come next, and who the deliverer would be— Surely, someone would come—A tall bony woman now rushed through the trees, and stopped before the grating. "Aha! there you are," she cried. "It serves you quite right, and I don't pity you a bit. A nice way you are in, the chains pinch you firmly I daresay, and the ground is damp, and you don't get too much of Old Ironhand's bread and water. What a set of fools you are not to get out, of course you could, if you tried"—She had hardly gone, when a man with a large black book in his hand, and a pale grave face came up—

"Just what I expected," he began—"I always said how it would be,—You needn't think Giant Ironhand will keep you where you are. He has worse dungeons than these, dungeons where you won't be able to see the sun, and chains that are twice as heavy as these. Get out, poor unhappy creatures, get out, if you can, before you are worse off than you are now"—

And then he too went away. The wind sighed more than ever, and how these rooks did flap their black wings, and caw among the dark branches. Louder and louder came the cry. "We can't get out, we can't get out"—

Elsie could stand it no longer. [There was nothing else for it,—] she must go down into the dungeon herself—The bars were broken, she could easily squeeze through the hole, but first of all she began to hunt about in a heap of dust and rubbish—She rummaged there, till at last she dragged out an old iron bar, and then she pounced upon a worn out pocket knife, which somebody must have thrown away long before. Once it had had three or four blades, now it had only one, and that was tarnished jagged and blunt. . . . Still she thought it a great prize. And now she caught tight hold of the grating, squeezed through, and let herself drop—She slipped on the wet ground,—in the long narrow dungeon the air felt damp, mouldy and close, and then how dark it was! she could just see, and that was all—Here, close by, was somebody doubled up into a heap, groaning terribly; there was another with tangled dark hair, and deep red scars on both arms—"Oh! dear, Oh! dear, Oh! dear," cried one, "will it ever be night?"—"What good will night do?" answered a gruff voice, and then the chains clanked again.

Elsie felt ever so many blood-shot eyes fixed on her, and hoarse voices called out, "What is she here for?"—She could not answer, her heart now beat fast, she stumbled over a bruised ankle, she nearly fell over a bit of rusty chain—Just then, she heard some one say "I wouldn't be such a fool as to go on rubbing any more, Peter it's no use"—"I know it isn't," was the answer—These voices came from the end of the dungeon. Peter must be that boy in the corner with light hair, just like Elsie's brother Ralph's, he had let the chain fall, and his head was resting on his hands—She took courage, went over to him and knelt down: some links in the chain were worn very thin, and she began to hammer away with her iron bar,—still she found them much too strong for her, they would never break. But every second link had a join, and if the link was thin, and the join open, it might be just possible to slip it through—Peter began to help, they pulled till they were red in the face, they pulled till they were covered with rust, they pulled till their hands were sore and bleeding, but still they pulled on—The sun was going towards the west, the cawing of the rooks grew fainter and fainter, in another hour or two, the owls would begin to think of coming out,—and what if the giant should come home?— On they pulled in good earnest,—one more—two—three—four—five— six—seven—eight—nine—ten—eleven—There! there! at last it had come,—that jerk had done it. Peter was free, was free indeed!—

"I'm out! I'm out!" he screamed. He jumped up, stretched his numbed arms and legs, caught hold of Elsie, iron bar and all, and squeezed her, till she cried with pain and joy—A bit of rusty chain was still dangling at one of his feet, but that was nothing—The groaning had all stopped, every one turned round to look on; and backwards and forwards, the cry went, "Only think, Peter is actually out."—If Elsie had had any idea she would have succeeded as well, it would have seemed quite enough, but now she began to think she must have another out, only one more. Presently a voice behind her said, "Little girl, little girl"—she turned about; [and] there was a white hollow face, with wild staring eyes—It belonged to [was] a boy a good deal older than Peter who spoke—"I saw it all," he said, "every bit. Look here:—my name is Robert, and I'm tied with ropes— I've been hard at work trying to undo the knots, but I think there must be some charm in them, they won't come undone. As for the rope itself, it's as thick as a cable—if I only had a knife I could cut it, but there isn't such a thing in the place"—

At the word "knife" Elsie fumbled in her pocket, and drew out her prize—Robert's eyes glistened, but no sooner had he tried it w [against] his thumb, than his face fell again—"It's the bluntest old thing I ever saw," he grumbled, "it wouldn't cut anything. Here, take it back." But Elsie wouldn't take it back, she was trying it on the rope already. Now After great sawing, the tiniest bit in the world gave way, then They bit it with their teeth, they tore it open with their nails, and again the old blunt blade came in, and sawed it a little more. Slowly—very slowly it was beginning to loosen. You might have heard a pin drop in the dungeon, all strained their necks to look on, and there was nothing but [now the] whispers on every side [were] "Will it ever give way?" Another cut,—it was giving,—certainly it was giving.—it was giving more,—it was giving still more ... It had given! Down fell Robert, but up he was in a trice— He shook himself out from the broken cord, and shouted till the dungeon rang again—as for Peter, he capered about like a wild thing—

"Come, come," said he, catching hold of Elsie, "there are two of us now—let us be off while we can, or old Ironhand will be coming home, and then there will be a row"—

"And you are going to leave us behind," said a miserable little voice in the corner. But the creature that it came from, was even more miserable than the voice—He was all wizened and shrivelled up just like an old, old man, and this was little Johnny, the youngest in the whole place—It would be impossible not to try and take him—So the hammering and filing began again, his chains were not strong, and they were eaten with rust, they would soon give way—Before the last red gleam had faded out of the sky, they did fall rattling to the ground, while Johnny crept out, trembling from head to foot; for he could hardly believe such a good thing could be true—

And now they must go indeed. Hark! there is the great watch-dog. Giant Ironhand is on his way home, and will be at the door in no time— Robert, the tallest, must stand up, and let the others mount on his shoulders, then they must catch hold of the bars, and squeeze themselves through as best they can—Up, Peter, up Elsie, up, little Johnny, and now Robert himself must give a tremendous jump, and they must hold out their hands and help to drag him through. A tight squeeze, a good many bruises, and it is done—And now, Once out of the dungeon, there is nothing to be thought of but running—not through the thick part of the forest, they would only get entangled in trees and perhaps fall into gins and traps, but out into the open country, through the fir plantation, that must be their way—There! listen to the hoofs of the giant's black horse. Old Ironhand is riding up to the castle door, he is getting down, his spurs clank on the stone steps, and how sharp the crack of his great whip sounds!—He will be after them in a minute, soon the tread of his heavy boots that can take twenty-seven steps to their one, will be heard coming closer and closer. Their hearts beat quick, hand in hand they dart along the thick grass, and scramble over the deep ditch, Peter's bit of rusty chain dragging all the time in the damp earth, and now and then rattling against a sharp stone. On, on, on,—over roots of trees—over briars—over brambles,—over yellow gorse,—over ant hills—over bracken fern,—over tangled heath, over great rabbit holes—Hark! the castle door has shut with a loud bang, the giant smacks his whip, he scolds his servants, he whistles to his fierce wolf-dogs, he stamps on the ground, he is after them indeed. On, on, on, up the hill, out of the plantation, over the ploughed field. There! Peter is down, he has caught his rusty chain [has caught] on one of the deep furrows. Up, again, Peter, run for your life, catch [take] hold of Elsie's hand, never mind the rusty iron, never mind your trembling knees or your panting breath. If you stop for an instant, the giant will have his grip on you. He is coming nearer, and how the wolf-dogs bark! Over the hedge, jump the ditch the thorns are sharp, but once beyond the dip of the hill, once through the sparkling water, and you are safe, and can snap your fingers at any giant. How the great boughs crash, as Ironhand knocks his head against them! What a heavy tread he plants on the damp earth, and now it is coming nearer. And nearer, the ground shakes under it, they feel his breath blow like a cold wind on their cheeks,— it stirs their hair,—his big hand almost clutches their shoulders, but,— [they are too quick for him,] they are scrambling down the bank, they are in the water [he can't touch them there]—It is nearly up to their necks, they have enough to do to keep little Johnny's chin above it, but the middle is reached at last, the worst is over, they are getting near the opposite bank, they clutch hold of great bunches of willow-weed, and up with them. The slippery bank is climbed,—they are safe!—Giant Ironhand must go home without them. He shakes his big head with its long matted red hair, he doubles up his giant fist as much as to say "I would if I could," and then he stamps frowning away. They don't care a straw for him now—They are panting, they are ragged, they are muddy, they are bleeding, but they are free,—Hurrah!—and Peter, Robert, and little Johnny throw up their tattered caps, and cry Hurrah! with all their might—

Now it was very strange that whoever went through those waters, which were known in that country by the name of Peace, always had a wish to sing. It was more perhaps than a wish, people felt that sing they must and should. So the three boys all began to think of singing. They had known many songs once, but some they had forgotten, and some they did not care for just then. What, at last, they did remember was a verse, they had heard long before on Sunday afternoons, when the sun shone warm and bright and the bells rang out for church—I daresay you all know it very well—

> "Rejoice, the Lord is King
> Your God and King adore
> Children, give thanks and sing
> And praise him Evermore.
> Lift up your hearts, lift up your Voice
> Rejoice! again I say Rejoice!"—

Whether it was gladness made their voices sweet, I can't tell, but in the silent evening air, they sounded as fresh and bright as a thrush's song— Tears of quiet joy came into Elsie's clear blue eyes—Just then, soft, and very close to her, something said "Rejoice!" It was not one of the three boys, for they were singing on in front, it was not a little tomtit that had forgotten to go to bed, or a starling that was out late at night,—no—the word was said far too plainly for that. Neither was it someone hidden behind the hedge, it was much too near and close—There it was again! "Rejoice! rejoice! rejoice!"—What could it be? and how very near it was to Elsie, it almost seemed to be in her—Why, it *was* in her—it was her!—

"It's me! it's me!" she cried. "I said Rejoice,—Peter, Robert, Johnny,—Listen, listen,—I said Rejoice—Elsie can speak, Elsie has found a tongue"—They turned round,—Johnny's eyes grew wider and wider—What was this about speaking and finding tongues?—They certainly had never heard the little girl say anything before, but then they [had] all thought that she was not quite 'canny':—not exactly like themselves. But, when they heard how she [had] gone to look for a voice, and had found none, and that now, listening to their singing in the quiet night air, it had come to her, they were nearly as glad as she was, and all began to shout. "Elsie can speak, Elsie has found a tongue!"—The echo went over the still dewy fields, over the hedges where the glow worms glistened, over the leafy woods where the winds were at rest, and over the silvery waters of the river of Peace. And some of the birds raised their heads from under their wings, and gave a sleepy twitter in their dreams—

Past the city, and by the rushing sea, they went, and now they came in sight of the little cottage where Elsie lived—Through the trees, the rushlights gleamed in the upstairs windows,—Everyone was going to bed—

"Who's there?" cried a voice in answer to the loud knocking.

"It's me, it's Elsie!—Father, mother, everybody, get up and come down. Only think, I can speak I have found a tongue"—

What a great cry of joy there was then!—The bolts were unfastened, the doors were unbarred. Elsie had been given up as lost, and now that she had come back with a voice, they could not be half glad enough—Of course there was a great deal of kissing and hugging, and you may be sure the boys came in for a share—A fire was lighted, the kettle was put on, tea was laid out—Peter, Robert and little Johnny were famishing, and looked on with delight. Soon, great bunches of bread and butter began to disappear, one after another, like lightning, but that night no one ever once thought of the baker's bill—

Elsie had to tell her story a great many times—over and over again she had to say how she had stumbled on the forest, and what old Ironhand's castle was like—she did not know whether any one else could find a voice as she had done; she only knew it was when she had forgotten all about it, that it came to her.

18

Mr. Ruskin and Miss Greenway

MICHAEL PATRICK HEARN

In 1879, with the publication of her unpretentious collection of verses and pictures titled *Under the Window*, Kate Greenaway became a household name. As her chief rival Walter Crane explained, "The grace and charm of her children and young girls were quickly recognized, and her treatment of quaint early nineteenth-century costume, prim gardens, and the child-like spirit of her designs in an old-world atmosphere, though touched with conscious modern 'aestheticism,' captivated the public in a remarkable way."[1] This reclusive spinster suddenly became the confidante of poets and princesses. She was lionized and parodied in the press. Greenaway boys and girls appeared (often without the artist's permission) on porcelain and pewter, on toys and wallpaper. Her simple style of dress, derived in part from the Empire period, became the rage in the late Victorian age, and for once Paris in coining the term *Greenawayisme* looked to London for inspiration in fashion. Being as popular in the New as in the Old World, Kate Greenaway was credited with dressing the children of two continents.

This illustrator had no greater champion that John Ruskin, the most influential English art critic of the day. He was enchanted by *Under the Window*, and he at once wrote her an eccentric letter of great praise: "I lay awake half (no, a quarter) of last night thinking of the hundred things I want to say to you—and never shall get said!—and I'm giddy and weary, and now can't say even half or a quarter of one out of the hundred. They're about you,—and your gifts—and your graces, and your fancies, and your— yes, perhaps one or two little—tiny faults."[2] He wanted to know if she believed in fairies, in ghosts, in principalities or powers, in Heaven. "Do you only draw pretty children out of your head?" he persisted. "In my parish school there are at least twenty prettier than any in your book ... they are like—very ill-dressed Angeli. Could you draw groups of these as they *are*?" She was touched by this enthusiasm and treasured the opinions, both the good and the bad. They soon became fast friends, discussing possible collaborations, perhaps a new edition of *Beauty and the Beast* or a book on botany (he sent her "sods" for nature studies). Most of these suggestions, however, came to nothing. He invited her to visit him in his country home, where she found much to admire: "Such wild wide stretches of country and then such mountains—such mossy trees and stones—such a lake—such a shore—such pictures—such books—my mind was entirely content and satisfied."[3]

Why did the great defender of Turner and the Pre-Raphaelites devote so much time and energy toward the promotion of Kate Greenaway's humble art? Her appeal was in part nostalgic; she knew him when he was recalling his childhood, during the writing of his autobiography *Praeterita*. Clearly the author of *Modern Painters* had altered his aesthetics. He who once defended Turner against accusations that the landscape painter had hurled "handfuls of white, and blue, and red, at the canvas, letting what chanced to stick, stick," now attacked Whistler's nocturnes as "flinging a pot of paint in the public's face."[4] Ruskin had long been known for his unorthodox opinions of art; for example, he argued that George Cruikshank's illustrations for *German Popular Stories* (1823 and 1826) of the Brothers Grimm "are the finest things, next to Rembrandt's, that ... have been done since etching was invented."[5] Ruskin was now growing old. To many of his colleagues he had become, as the American expatriate called him, "the Peter Parley of Painting."[6] In these later years, Ruskin suffered from recurrent bouts of madness. His mind had never fully accepted his loss of faith and the renunciation of narrow Puritanism for humanism. More significantly he had fallen in love with a girl thirty years his junior.

Rose LaTouche was only nine years old when she first met Ruskin. He grew to love this strange, sensitive child, and as they corresponded over many years, she learned to love him in return. He was repeating the pattern of his failed marriage. Effie Gray, his former wife, was only twelve when she and the writer were first introduced. As a token of his affection, he wrote his famous fairy tale *The King of the Golden River*. His letters suggest that he grew less infatuated with Effie as she matured; yet he married her and then later divorced her (the marriage never having been consummated) so that she might become the wife of John Everett Millais, the Pre-Raphaelite artist who had painted Ruskin's portrait. The difference between Ruskin's love for Effie and that for Rose was that as the latter grew older, he desired her more. Judiciously, the middle-aged suitor waited until Rose reached eighteen to propose marriage. Her parents discouraged the match and went so far as to have Effie Millais warn their daughter that Ruskin was "utterly incapable of making a woman happy."[7] Ruskin chose as his confidante in this sad affair George MacDonald, the author of *At the Back of the North Wind* and a friend of the LaTouches; and after much intrigue, Rose agreed to marry Ruskin within three years. Unfortunately she died; hers was a death from which the author never recovered.

Ruskin discovered *Under the Window* only a few years after Rose's death. In the picture book's simplicity and purity he found comfort and hope. "Holbein lives for all time with his grim and ugly 'Dance of Death,' " he confided to his new protégé; "a not dissimilar and more beautiful immortality may be in store for you if you worthily apply yourself to produce a 'Dance of Life.' "[8] Greenaway was one of several female artists whom Ruskin championed. One may wonder what his Oxford audiences thought of his lectures devoted to this strange group. "You are fast becoming," he reassured the creator of *Under the Window*, "the helpfullest, in showing me that there are yet living souls on earth who can see beauty and peace, and Good-will among men—and rejoice in them."[9] Such praise offered with an almost religious fervor now seems excessive. "Your proper work would be in glass painting . . . seen, in sacred places, by multitudes," he wrote her. "You have the radiance and innocence of reinstated infant divinity showered again among the flowers of English meadows."[10]

What charmed him most about her work was her depiction of innocent girlhood. His affection for the young was not restricted to the children Effie and Rose. In maturity he confessed no sweeter pleasure than to join in the sports and gambols of the students of a private girls' academy which he supported. He even proposed that Greenaway be the headmistress of a drawing school in London "where nice young girls can go—and find no disagreeable people or ugly pictures."[11] In Greenaway, this "mixed child and woman," he found the medium through which to express his image of the young. "*My* knowledge of people is extremely limited," he once confessed to her, "continually mistaken—and what is founded on experience, chiefly of young girls."[12] When asked which one he preferred from a group of little girls that she had drawn, he became as coy as a prospective suitor: "Of course the Queen of them all is the little one in front—but she's just a month or six weeks too young for *me*. Then there's the staff bearer . . . but she's just three days and a minute or two too *old* for me. Then there's the divine one with the dark hair, and the beatific one with the brown—but I think they've *both* got lovers already, and have only come to please the rest, and wouldn't be mine, if I prayed them ever so. Then there's the little red beauty who is ruby and diamond in one, but—

but—not quite tall enough, again. I think the wisest choice will be the pale one between the beatific and the divine!"[13]

Ruskin's enthusiasm for Greenaway's subjects was matched by his persistence that she improve her drawing. In his desire that she perfect her art, he becomes obsessed with improving the feet of her figures. His letters, even to the last one he sent her just before his final breakdown, abound with demands that she sketch the bare feet of children: "And—you should go to some watering—place in August with fine sands, and draw no end of bare feet,—and—what else the Graces unveil in the train of the Sea Goddesses."[14] Perhaps there was nothing perverse in this insistence on improvement (she never did perfect the depiction of that part of the anatomy), but his persistence in his letters that she draw the naked figure is often embarrassing. She told him she had had enough anatomy when at art school, and she refused to work from the nude. Still he teasingly tried to get her to reveal the form beneath the frock: "As we've got so far as taking off hats, I trust we may in time get to taking off just a little more—say, mittens—and then—perhaps—even—shoes!—and (for fairies) even—stockings—And—then . . . *Will* you—(it's for your own good!) make her stand up, and then draw her for me without her hat—and, without her shoes . . . and without her mittens, and without her—frock and its frill? And let me see exactly how tall she is—and how—round. It will be *so* good of—and for—you—And to, and for—

me."[15] He even tried to get her to work in the classical manner, admonishing "you *must* draw figures now undraped for a while—Nobody wants anatomy,—but you can't get on without Form."[16] In spite of her refusals, he remained firm, and he could be brutal. When he objected to one maiden with "a perfect coalheaver's leg," he told her, "I'll send her back to have her gown taken off as soon as you're able to work again."[17] Such remarks suggest those made by that other Oxford don, Lewis Carroll, to another artist, E. Gertrude Thomson, from whom he commissioned a series of nymphet drawings, the "fairyfancies" of the posthumous *Three Sunsets and Other Poems* (1898).[18]

Kate Greenaway admitted that she had difficulty drawing from life.

She could not merely hold up a mirror to the visible world; her realm in which Ruskin found refuge was the creation of her own fancy. She preferred to offer an idealized portrayal of childhood. "Children," she argued, "like to know about other things—or what other children did—but not about children in an abstract sort of way. That belongs to older people."[19] Ruskin insisted on her "exquisite feeling given to teach—not merely to amuse."[20] Teach she did—not only in William Mavor's textbook *The English Spelling-Book* (1884) but also in the volumes she both wrote and illustrated. In each she offered examples of good behavior. Her world is free of conflict and everyday nuisances. Her delicate girls never tear their frocks while shinnying up trees; her roses rarely bear thorns. Her *Book of Games* (1889) avoids rough schoolyard sports; instead she selects word games and conundrums which require no strenuous participation. It is doubtful her two combatants in "F Fought for It" of *A Apple Pie* (1886) will ever come to blows; in *Little Ann* (1882), her dirty Jim is never so dirty and the little girl who beat her sister is never so vicious as the characters suggested by the verses of Ann and Jane Taylor. She could not bear such children. "I don't feel near strong enough for the strain of it," she wrote of painting children's portraits. "I know what the children are like—quite unaccustomed to sitting still.... I prefer the little girls and boys that live in that nice land, that come as you call them, fair or dark, in green ribbons or blue. I like making cowslip fields grow and apple trees bloom at a moment's notice. This is what it is ... to have gone through life with an enchanted land ever beside you."[21] In her "enchanted land," children act as they should and not as they do.

Perhaps she perfected her vision in *Marigold Garden* (1885), a companion volume to *Under the Window* but without the brown witch and other "mere ugly nonsense" which Ruskin had objected to in the earlier picture book. In the new volume of her own verses, her drawings were never prettier. When a child herself, she used to plan "out delightful places just close and unexpected" where her fancy might roam freely. "My bedroom window used to look out over red roofs and chimney-pots," she once wrote Ruskin, "and I made steps up to a lovely garden up there with nasturtiums growing and brilliant flowers so near to the sky. There were some old houses joined ours at the side, and I made a secret door into long lines of old rooms, all so delightful, leading into an old garden. I imagined it so often that I knew its look so well; it got to be very real."[22] This private world is "Somewhere Town" of *Under the Window*, "Over the tiles and the chimney-pots ... up in the morning early." Through her picture books this child-woman was able to take other children through that secret door to an enchanted marigold garden.

Although boys may accompany her girls, men rarely invade this sanctuary. Those who do appear are actually tall maidens in false mustaches. She could not draw the male form. She never married, and there is no evidence she had suitors. It was once rumored that she was actually Mrs. Randolph Caldecott, a possibility Caldecott did not find amusing. One contemporary described her as "short and dumpy, with hair turning grey and very unruly. Bright brown eyes, one with a slight droop of the lid. A kind, merry face, a flow of brisk talk, laughter for the obvious things, no complexities about art, matter of fact, easy, simple, and natural ... not pretty hands."[23] Her plainness distressed her. Once she warned a correspondent, "Please, you are not to make so much of me, for I am not in the least a frog Princess. Wouldn't it be nice if I were, to emerge suddenly, brilliant and splendid?" It hurt her that she was not the creature her art suggested: "I was given quite the wrong sort of body to live in, I am sure. I ought to have been taller, slimmer, and at any rate passably good-looking, so that my soul might have taken flights, my fancy might have expanded."[24] Suffering from a lisp, she was shy and felt ill at ease with men. Ironically, her staunchest defenders were gentlemen.

Her lack of sympathy for certain aspects of human character influenced her attitude towards Nature. "I could never understand," Edmund Evans, her printer, noted in his memoirs, "her liking only calm-weather skies, blue and white; she utterly disagreed with me when I told her of the pleasure stormy-weather skies gave me, such skies as Constable evidently loved."[25] Perhaps her rheumatism affected this opinion, but more likely it was because she could not undersand why anyone preferred the ugly to the beautiful. "People laugh at me," she once told a friend, "I am so delighted and pleased with things, and say I see with rose-coloured spectacles. What do you think—is it not a beautiful world?"[26]

Unlike Evans, Ruskin would have nothing but sunny days and golden sunsets from her. He sought in her world an alternative to Victorian technocracy. "There are no railroads in it, to carry the children away with," he wrote in "Fairy Land," his Oxford lecture devoted to her art; "no tunnel or pit mouths to swallow them up, no league-long viaducts— no blinkered iron bridges? There are only winding brooks, wooden footbridges, and grassy hills without any holes cut into them!" Her books supported his quarrel with the Industrial Revolution, a fight he had waged since he wrote *The King of the Golden River*.

In choosing her texts, Greenaway was careful to remain within the pre-industrial England of the late eighteenth and early nineteenth centuries. Mavor, the Taylors, *Mother Goose*, *A Apple Pie*, *Dame Wiggins of Lee and Her Seven Wonderful Cats*, belonged to the age of John Newbery and John Harris when there were "no gasworks! no waterworks, no mowing machines, no sewing machines, no telegraph poles, no vestige, in fact, of science, civilization, economical arrangements, or commercial enter-prise!!!" There was no trace in her work of what Ruskin called the "plague-cloud," that nineteenth-century phenomenon that polluted his contem-poraries' landscape paintings. This pollution of Nature by materialism increased Ruskin's disenchantment with the modern world. His protégé's vision remained uncorrupted; he knew she would be the perfect collab-orator for his projected "story about perpetual spring." Her spirit was an eighteenth-century sensibility akin to that of Mrs. Barbauld, whose ar-gument of Divine instruction in Nature, in *Hymns in Prose for Children* (1781), was shared by Ruskin in his *Modern Painters*. "Every field," Mrs. Barbauld wrote, "is like an open book; every painted flower hath a lesson written on its leaves. Every murmuring brook hath a tongue; a voice is in every whispering wind. They all speak of him who made them; they all tell us, he is very good." Mrs. Barbauld's vision of Paradise could easily be a description of the world in Kate Greenaway's picture books. "There is a land," her *Hymns in Prose* concludes, "where the roses are without thorns, where the flowers are not mixed with brambles. In that land, there is eternal spring, and light without any cloud . . .; rivers of pleasure are there, and flowers that never fade. . . . This country is Heaven: it is the country of those that are good; and nothing that is wicked must inhabit there."

Not surprisingly Ruskin saw much in his friend's drawings to soothe his troubled soul. In these children's books the weary teacher could retire like Robert Browning's Pied Piper of Hamelin to that "joyous land, / Joining the town and just at hand, / Where waters gushed and fruit-trees grew, / And flowers put forth a fairer hue, / And everything was strange and new." Ruskin characteristically did not fully approve of Greenaway's vision of Paradise in her 1888 edition of the Browning poem. "A *real* view of Hampstead ponds in spring," he wrote, "would have been more celestial to me than this customary flat of yours with trees stuck into it at regular distances. And not a Peacock! nor a flying horse!!" Yet he acknowledged the comfort her *Pied Piper of Hamelin* gave him: "I feel as if he had piped me back out of the hill again, and would give some spring times yet to rejoice in your lovely work and its witness to them."[27]

Her simple work invigorated him for a time, and under his tutelage she improved as an artist. He frequently played Svengali to her Trilby. He often scolded her like a naughty pupil. "Now be a good girl," he wrote, "and draw some flowers that won't look as if their leaves had been in curlpapers all night—and some more chairs than that one chair—with the shade all right and the legs all square—and then I'll tell you what you must do next."[28] He could be irritable, but his criticisms were always affectionate. He wished her shoes "weren't quite so like mussel-shells," her "roses like truffles," her "suns and moons like straw hats," her "lillies crumpled like pocket-handkerchiefs." He told her which painters to admire and which to avoid. He even advised her on literature. The Brontës, he stressed, were not for her; all she should read was Shakespeare.

His letters were not filled solely with art instruction; he could be intimate. Once he described a miracle performed by his beloved Rose, "a saint in her way," in reviving a dying friend through prayer.[29] He also confided in her on "the sadness of deliberately preparing for the close of life." "A great deal of the time I have lost in the mere friction of life," he wrote her, "scarcely any sense of Peace—And no hope of any life to come. I forget it all more in the theatre than anywhere—cathedrals are no good any more."[30] She knew that he cared deeply for her, and she for him. She wrote him almost daily, filling her letters with impromptu sketches; and even during the last, silent decade of his life, she carried on an affectionate monologue with him. Typical of her concern was her birthday greeting: "I wish I was going to be there to see all the lovely flowers you are going to have. If I were there you should ask me to tea—I think—yes, I think you ought to ask me to tea—and we'd have raspberry jam for tea—a muffin, some violets—and a Turner to look at—oh, yes, I think you should ask me to tea."[31] She was not an intellectual, and Ruskin must have been amused by her opinions on art; but her simple, childlike interest comforted him in his old age. She found in his words and thought a "holiness," an inspiration for her work.

During his final illness, she produced only a few books, primarily her annual almanac. She experimented with children's portraits in oil, a medium she never mastered; and she occasionally exhibited watercolors and designed book-plates and magazine illustrations. His death in 1900 left her deeply grieved. "It was a great shock," she wrote a colleague. "I feel it very much for he was a great friend—and there is no one else like him."[32] She now tried to revive her career, by proposing many new projects such as editions of Andersen's *The Snow Queen* and Blake's *Song of Innocence*. Her vogue, however, had passed. Her heart seemed no longer in her work, and she suffered from breast cancer. She died in November 1901, at age forty-five, only a little over a year after the death of Ruskin.

Notes

The illustrations in the text are from Kate Greenaway's *Under the Window: Pictures and Rhymes for Children*, reproduced by permission of Frederick Warne & Co., Inc.

1. Quoted by M. H. Spielmann and G. S. Layard, *Kate Greenway* (London: Adam and Charles Black, 1905), p. 71.

2. Letter to Kate Greenaway, Jan. 6, 1880, *The Letters of John Ruskin, The Works of John Ruskin*, vol. 37, ed. E. T. Cook and Alexander Wedderburn (New York: Longmans, Green, and Co., 1909), p. 307.

3. Quoted by Spielmann and Layard, p. 113.

4. See John D. Rosenberg, *The Darkening Glass* (New York: Columbia University Press, 1961), p. 207.

5. "Appendix," *The Elements of Drawing, The Works of John Ruskin*, vol. 15 (1904), p. 222.

6. Quoted by Rosenberg, p. 208.

7. Quoted by Rosenberg, p. 202.

8. Quoted by Spielmann and Layard, p. 5.

9. Letter to KG, Christmas Day 1881, p. 383.

10. Letter to KG, Dec. 7, 1880, p. 331; and "Fairyland," *The Art of England*, quoted by Spielmann and Layard, p. 5.

11. Letter to KG, Nov. 2, 1886, quoted by Spielmann and Layard, p. 155.

12. Letter to KG, Jan. 15, 1885, p. 508.

13. Letter to KG, Feb. 11, 1884, p. 474.

14. Letter to KG, July 10, 1883, p. 460.

15. Letter to KG, July 6, 1883, p. 459.

16. Letter to KG, April 20, 1884, quoted by Spielmann and Layard, p. 133.

17. Letter to KG, Jan. 28, 1884, p. 473.

18. It should be noted that Ruskin was the drawing instructor of Alice Liddell, the little girl for whom Carroll wrote *Alice's Adventures in Wonderland*.

19. Quoted by Spielman and Layard, p. 124.

20. Letter to KG, June 15, 1883, p. 454.

21. Quoted by Spielmann and Layard, pp. 239-40.

22. Quoted by Spielmann and Layard, p. 218.

23. Quoted by Esther Hallam Meynell, *A Woman Talking* (London: Chapman & Hall, 1940), p. 29.

24. Quoted by Spielmann and Layard, pp. 112 and 208.

25. *Edmund Evans' Reminiscences*, ed. and introduced by Ruari McLean (Oxford: The Clarendon Press, 1967), p. 63.

26. Quoted by Spielmann and Layard, p. 266.

27. Letters to KG, Feb. 23, 1888, p. 601; and May-day, 1889, p. 608.

28. Letter to KG, June 7, 1883, p. 453.

29. Letter to KG, Jan. 23, 1884, pp. 472-73.

30. Letter to KG, March 20, 1884, p. 478.

31. Quoted by Spielmann and Layard, p. 166.

32. Quoted by Spielmann and Layard, p. 248.

19

Reflections on *Little Women*

ANNE HOLLANDER

Little Women has been a justly famous children's classic for a century, even though none of the characters is really a child when the story begins. Amy, the youngest, is already twelve, well beyond the age at which girls first read the book. In consequence, this novel, like many great childhood books, must serve as a pattern and a model, a mold for goals and aspirations rather than an accurate mirror of known experience. The little girls who read *Little Women* can learn what it might be like to be older; but, most important, they can see with reassurance in Alcott's pages how the feelings familiar in childhood are preserved in later days, and how individual character abides through life.

A satisfying continuity informs all the lives in *Little Women*. Alcott creates a world where a deep "natural piety" indeed effortlessly binds the child to the woman she becomes. The novel shows that as a young girl grows up, she may rely with comfort on being the same person, whatever mysterious and difficult changes must be undergone in order to become an older and wiser one. Readers can turn again and again to Alcott's book solely for a gratifying taste of her simple, stable vision of feminine completeness.

Unscholarly but devoted readers of *Little Women* have often insisted that the book is good only because of the character of Jo. Most modern response to the novel consists of irritation at the death of Beth and annoyance at Amy's final marital success, accompanied by universal sympathy for Jo's impatience with ladylike decorum and her ambitions for a career. In current perception these last two of Jo's qualities have appeared to overshadow all the struggles undergone by the other sisters, in a narrative to which Alcott herself tried to give an even-handed symmetry.

The character of Jo is the one identified with Alcott, not only on the biographical evidence but through the more obvious interest the author takes and the keener liking she feels for this particular one of her four heroines. For many readers the memory of Jo's struggles remains the strongest later on. This enduring impression, along with dislike of Amy and impatience with bashful, dying Beth, may reflect the force of the author's own intractable preferences, not quite thoroughly transmuted into art.

But art there certainly is; and among those readers not themselves so averse to ladyhood as Jo or Alcott herself, or so literary in their own personal ambitions, there are other problems and conflicts in *Little Women* that vibrate in the memory. Alcott's acuteness and considerable talent were variously deployed among her heroines; and by using a whole family of sisters for her subject, she succeeded better than many authors have since in rendering some of the complex truth about American female consciousness.

It remains true that among the sisters Beth receives somewhat summary treatment and the least emotional attention. She is there to be hallowed by the others, and for that she is in fact better dead, since her actual personal experiences are not very interesting even to her creator. Her goodness serves as a foil to the moral problems of the others; we really cannot care what her life is like for her. None of us, like none of them, is quite good enough. Beth's mortal illness, moreover, is accepted with no advice whatsoever from medical science. She seems to die a moral death, to retire voluntarily from life's scene so that the stage will be more spacious for the other actors.

The badness of the three other sisters, however, like their virtues, is more interestingly distributed than is usually remembered. If one can set aside the pervasive memory of impulsive tomboy Jo, whose only fault now seems to have been being ahead of her time, we can see Alcott's moral scheme more clearly. The novel is not just Jo's story; it is the tale of four Pilgrim's Progresses—admittedly with Beth fairly early out of the race, having won in advance. The three others have all got thoroughly realistic "bosom enemies," personal failings that each must try to conquer before their author can let them have their rewards. It is clear enough that certain of these failings privately seemed worse to Alcott than others, but she gives them all a serious look, keen enough to carry across generations into modern awareness.

As the book transparently shows, Alcott cared a great deal about troublesome anger and rebelliousness and nothing whatever about shyness; but she does give a lot of thought to vanity, envy, selfishness, and pride. She likes literature and music much better than painting and sculpture;

but she has a strong understanding of frustrated artistic ambition and the pain of not being very good at what you love best to do. Meg, for example, is the only sister with no talent, except a fleeting one for acting in childhood dramatics. Her chief struggle is with envy, and it is manifestly a harder one for a girl with no intrinisically satisfying and valuable gifts. She has only personal beauty, in a period of American cultural history when fine clothes really mattered.

In the second half of the nineteenth century feminine dress made strong visual demands, and the elements of conspicuous consumption had a vigorously gaudy flavor and an imposing social importance. Modest simplicity in dress and furnishing was unfashionable and socially degrading; and Meg is keenly aware that her own good looks would have more absolute current worth if they might always be framed and set off by the elaborate and costly appurtenances of contemporary taste. Fortunately, she is not only beautiful but also basically good and so able to respond spontaneously to true love in simple garb without any mercenary qualms when the moment arrives. Later, however, as a matron of slender means, she has some very instructive struggles with her unconquered demons. Alcott is careful to demonstrate that such inward problems are not solved by love, however true it may be.

Meg, in any case, has no trouble being "womanly"; her rebellion is entirely against not having the riches that she rightly believes would show her purely passive, feminine qualities to better advantage. Motherhood, wifehood, and daughterhood are her aptitudes, and she has to learn to accept the virtuous practice of them without the scope and visibility that money would make possible.

Jo is famous for hating feminine trappings and for wanting to get rich by her own efforts, and thus apparently has no real faults by modern standards. "Womanliness" is not for her, because she is afraid it will require idiotic small-talk and tight shoes. The roughness of manner for which Jo suffered was called "unladylike" at the time, and thus the character earns a deal of sympathy in the present, when "lady" is a derogatory word, and most nineteenth-century views of middle-class female behavior are under general condemnation. In fact, despite the red-flag term, Jo is never condemned by her family, or by her author, except for what we still believe is bad in either sex: quickness of temper and impatience, lack of consideration and rage. Otherwise, her physical gracelessness is lamented but not chastised, and the only prohibition that seems really strange is against her *running*. This requires explanantion.

The nineteenth-century stricture against running for ladies seems to have been an aspect of sexual modesty, not simply a matter of general decorum. In an age before brassières, when corseting constricted only the thorax below the breasts, a well-behaved lady might not indulge in "any form of motion more rapid than walking," for fear of betraying somewhere below her neck the "portion of the general system which gives to woman her peculiar prerogative as well as her distinctive character."[1] Bouncing breasts were apparently unacceptable to the respectable eye, and at the time only the restriction of bodily movement could ensure their stability.

Freedom-loving Jo is not loath to accept male instruction and domination; she is delighted to submit to her father, just as the others are. She is afraid only of sex, as she demonstrates whenever Laurie tries to approach her at all amorously. Jo's fear of sex, like her impatience, is one of the forms her immaturity takes, well past the age when an interest in sex might seem natural. Her fear erupts most noticeably during the period when Meg, who is only a year older, is tremulously succumbing to John Brooke's attractions. Jo, far from feeling any sympathetic excitement about this, or any envy of the delights of love, is filled with a fury and a misery born of terror. She is not just afraid of losing Meg; she fears Meg's emergent sexual being and, more deeply, her own. Later, she is shown as preferring literary romantic heroes to live ones, who might try to arouse her own responses. Very posssibly many young girls who read about this particular aspect of Jo's late adolescence may find that this, too, is a sympathetic trait, along with Jo's hatred of the restrictive feminine "sphere."

The three older "little women" all have faults of a fairly minor character—feminine vanity, impulsiveness, shyness—which are often objectively endearing and are also apparently so to the author herself. These weaknesses are shown to be incidental to truly generous natures: Meg, Jo, and Beth are all unquestionably loving and good-hearted girls. Amy, the youngest, is basically different and (to this reader at least) much more interesting.

Amy is undoubtedly the Bad Sister throughout the early parts of the book. Alcott seems to have very little sympathy for her shortcomings, which are painted as both more irritating and more serious than those of the other girls. She is the one who is actually bad, whereas the others are only flawed, thus:

Meg—pleasure-loving and vain
Jo—quick-tempered and tomboyish } *generous*
Beth—shy and timid

Amy—conceited, affected, and *selfish*

One is tempted to believe that Alcott detests Amy for those same traits that George Eliot seems to hate in certain of her own characters: blond hair, blue eyes, physical grace, and personal charm. And Amy's faults are not at all endearing. This sister, judging from her behavior in the beginning, at least, is really both nasty and pretentious—a true brat; and not only that, she is the only one seriously committed to high standards of visual appearance, that well-known moral pitfall.

I have heard Amy described as "insipid," as if literary blondness must always guarantee a corresponding pallidness of character; but in fact her inward conflicts are harder than those of her sisters, since she has much graver faults to overcome. And she is successful, not only in conquering her selfishness but in turning her love of beauty to good spiritual account. It is not for nothing that Alcott has given her a "determined chin," wide mouth, and "keen blue eyes," along with the charm and blond curls that seem to blind all eyes to her real strength and to inhibit the interests of most readers. Amy has a hard time being good—all the harder because she has an easy time being pleasing—and gets hated for it into the bargain, even by her author. But Alcott is nothing if not fair, and she is scrupulous in her portrayal of Amy's trials, especially her efforts to be a serious artist, even though she writes of "artistic attempts" with considerable condescension. Alcott seems to find visual art somewhat ridiculous, whereas literature is *de facto* serious.

Unlike Jo, Amy aims for the highest with a pure ambition. Jo simply wants to be successful and to make money, but Amy says: "I want to be great or nothing."[2] She refuses to be "a commonplace dauber." Her desire to be great is only finally and correctly deterred by the sight of true greatness during her visit to Rome; and so she gives up trying. This particular renunciation can also clearly be seen as part of Amy's refinement of character, a praiseworthy if symbolic subjugation of her overt sexuality. It may be pointed out, incidentally, that we hear nothing of any humility on the part of Jo in the face of great writing, since success, not creative excellence, is her standard.

On the face of it, Amy is a frivolous, failed artist, while Jo is a serious, successful one. But in fact Amy's creative talent can be seen as more authentic that Jo's, because Amy does recognize and accept and even enjoy her own sexuality, which is the core of the creative self. Alcott demonstrates this through the mature Amy's straightforward, uncoy ease in attracting men and her effortless skill at self-presentation, which are emblems of her commitment to the combined truths of sex and art. Her childhood selfishness and affectation are conquered quite early; she fights hard to grow up, so that her love of beauty, her personal allure, and her artistic talent may all be purely expressed, undistorted by vanity or hope of gain. Nevertheless, the too-explicit erotic drive in Amy must be suppressed, and this can be symbolically accomplished by the transmutation of her serious artistic aims into the endowments of a lady.

Jo's literary talent, on the other hand, is qualified in the earlier part of the book, even as her sexuality remains willfully neutralized. Her writing is not yet an authentic channel for the basic erotic force behind all art, as Amy's talent clearly is. Jo's writing rather is the agent of her retreat from sex—she uses it to make herself more like a man. Alcott expresses the slightly compromised quality of Jo's literary ambition (and of her sexuality) by having her primarily desire fame and financial gain, along publicly accepted lines of masculine accomplishment. She writes for newspapers in order to get paid, for instance, instead of struggling to write great poems, which might never sell. Jo can write as a true artist only later, when she finally comes to terms with her own sexual self and thus rather belatedly grows up in her own turn.

In the end, after Amy gives up art, Alcott permits her to use her taste and her esthetic skill for the embellishment of life with no loss of integrity or diminution in her strength of character. It is Amy, the lover of material beauty, not Jo, the lover of freedom, who gets to escape and go traveling in Europe, but only after she has earned the regard of all concerned for her successful conquering of self. Jo finally says, after Amy does the right thing in a compromising social situation: "You've a deal more principle and generosity and nobleness of character than I ever gave you credit for, Amy. You've behaved sweetly and I respect you with all my heart." And Amy repeats what she has already said a bit earlier in a different way: "You laugh at me when I say I want to be a lady, but I mean a true gentlewoman in mind and manners. ... I want to be above the little meannesses and follies and faults that spoil so many women" (p. 279). Amy actively and painfully resists being spoiled, and so she wins—at first the trip to Europe and at last the one rich and handsome husband on the scene, not because of her blond beauty but rather in spite of it. She proves a true March daughter (and she, at least, is certainly not afraid of sex), and thus Laurie may love her at last.

Laurie, the neighboring, rich young man, finds his most important function in the novel not as a possible husband for any sister but as a student of The March Way of Life. Born to riches and idleness and personally neglected as a child, this youth is clearly destined for depravity, especially since he is half-Italian, and we must know what that means. Alcott lets this fact, plus a talent for music, stand (as she lets Amy's talent for art stand) for sexuality itself, the whole erotic and artistically creative dimension in life. Laurie, like Amy, seems always to be an acknowledged sexual being. Alcott shows this quality in him, as she shows it in Amy, by making him a lover of beauty who reveals his commitment to it through a natural, unsought creative talent—in his case, inherited directly from his Italian musical mother—and not in detached or cultivated appreciation. In both characters, their own physical beauty represents the fusion of art and sex.

This youthful and passionate male neighbor, an obvious candidate for the dissolute life, comes under the variously superior moral influences of all the females next door—Amy at this point, however, being still a nasty child of little account. We are given a good, old-fashioned demonstration of the redeeming power of love in the persons of virtuous women. But it is, and course, love minus sex, an American protestant love without unhealthy and uncomfortable Italian overtones, love which uses music to calm the fevered spirit of Saul and uplift the soul in German fashion, rather than to stir the senses or the passions in Italian operatic style. An energetic American lack of cynical European prurience, which Henry James often so tellingly describes, is emphasized by Alcott in her account of Laurie's relations with the Marches. Fellowship, insisted on by Jo, appears here as an American ideal for governing the conduct between the sexes. Passion had better be quiet; and perhaps it will be if no one insists on it too much in advance. Later on, Laurie tears up the opera he had tried to write about Jo. In doing this, he seems to accept the incompatibility of sex and art with love and virtue; and, like Amy in Rome, he renounces the former and thus proves worthy to regain them—suitably transformed, or course, by the latter.

The passionate, creative element—frightening, powerful, and laden with danger—is set forth disapprovingly in both Amy and Laurie as an aspect of selfishness, laziness, and generally reprehensible narcissism entirely lacking in all the book's "good" characters, however imperfect they otherwise are. The action of the book in part consists in the taming of this dangerous force in both Amy and Laurie, a process which nevertheless then permits them to have one another and so cancel the threat they might otherwise represent to the rest of virtuous humanity. Amy, in an unusually explicit scene near the end of the book, after she is safely married to him, is shown stroking Laurie's nose and admiring his beauty, whereas Jo, during her long sway over him in the main part of the novel, had done nothing but tease and berate him and deflate his possible vanity and amorous temper. It is only after such harsh training for both these selfish and talented young beauties that they may marry; and it is also obvious that indeed they must. Laurie cannot marry Jo because he is immutably erotic, and she refuses to learn that lesson. Amy is saved from the "prostitution" of a wealthy, loveless marriage, Laurie is saved from "going to the devil" because the March morals have prevailed over them both, and they agree in unison to that domination.

But it is also very clear that they have been permitted to have no reciprocal influence, to teach nothing in return. In the course of *Little Women*, the creative strength and possible virtues of art and eroticism are gradually discredited, subdued and neutralized. Amy must give up art, Laurie must give up composing, and even Jo must abandon the sensational creations of her fantasy-life—her one such outlet—so that the negative and unworldly virtues may triumph: denial of the self; patience in suffering and, more important, in boredom; the willing abjuration of worldly pleasures. The two who have understood and acknowledged the creative, positive power of pleasure in physical beauty have got each other, and the rest can get on more comfortably without it and without wanting it.

At the core of all the interesting moral distributions in *Little Women* is not sex, however, but money. The riches of patience and self-denial are especially necessary to the self-respect of the women in this particular family because it has lost its material fortune, but not because it has always been poor. It is significant that the modest Marches are not "congenitally" poor at all, and they have very little understanding of the spiritual drain of that condition. Being really poor is very different from having lately become relatively poor, in an increasingly affluent society like that of later-nineteenth-century America. American wealth in Alcott's time was in the process of reaching the outrageous stage that was later to require antitrust legislation, income tax, and other basic socioeconomic adjustments suitable to a democratic nation. The unworldly girls in *Little Women* must hold fast to what they hope are immutable values and to the capacity for inner steadfastness in a shifting and increasingly materialistic society. They are people with Old Money now vanished—a situation that could bring with it those advantages that leisure offers, such as education, reflection, the luxury of moral scruples, and the cultivation of the feelings. Indeed, these are the Marches' only legacy, and they must use and enjoy and hope to rely on them, always asserting their superiority over material riches newly, mindlessly, and soullessly acquired.

All this provides a foundation for an enduring American moral tale, one which continues to register as authentic even in a world changed out of all recognition. A notable absence in modern life of irksome rules for female decorum still cannot cancel the validity of the view that money may come and likewise go; that the status it quickly confers may be as quickly removed; and that some other sources of satisfaction and self-esteem had better be found.

When the March girls are first introduced, the two oldest are already following the first steps to modern American female success by earning money. But they are not pursuing careers, they are simply augmenting the family income; and a particular message comes through very clearly in every page of *Little Women*. Whereas impoverished American men may make use of drive, intellect, ambition, personal force, and the resources of public endeavor in order to gain the basic honor due to self-respecting males, poor women have only the resources of traditionally private female power and passive virtue. And these, as suggested in the case of Meg's enviousness, are best cultivated in circumstances of material ease. Poor middle-class women may not simply cut loose and try to make their way by their wits and strength of mind, as poor men may do, to preserve their self-esteem in degraded circumstances. Impoverished women have to bear not only poverty but the shame of poverty, because they may not wipe it out through positive action. As Amy admonishes Jo, poor women cannot even wield their moral power so successfully as rich women can, smiling and frowning according to their approval and disapproval, affecting the behavior and presumably elevating the souls of their male friends. As Amy explains it, poor and thus insignificant women who express moral scruples and judgments may risk being thought of as prudes and cranks, while rich women can perhaps do some good. Excellent goals for impoverished women seem to be to observe life closely but to keep their own counsel, to refine their own private judgments, and to develop an independence of mind that requires no reassuring responses. The female self may thus develop in its own esteem without requiring either male or material support.

Wealth—inherited, married, or earned—can thus be incidental to female personal satisfaction and sense of worth, and so can marriage. No attitude about money must be taken that might cloud the judgment; and so the judgment must be continually strengthened, even while prudence may govern the scope of speech and action. Money may be thought of as an obviously desirable thing but clearly detachable from virtue, including one's own. One may marry a wealthy man or may inherit a fortune, or one may never do either; but one keeps one's personal integrity and freedom in all cases. Again, Alcott does not attempt to instruct the really poor, only the potentially impoverished. Being "a true gentlewoman" in this transcendent version of the American way is seen in part to consist of being supported only from within. Money and marriage are uncertain, especially for women: character lasts for life.

Alcott further demonstrates that to achieve a good character the practice of patience, kindness, discretion, and forbearance among one's fellows must totally absorb one's creative zeal. Such zeal may not be expended on the committed practice of any art, or any intellectual pursuit which might make the kind of demand that would promote the unseemly selfishness of the creative life. Alcott's little sermons against the seductions of serious art and abstract thought, at least for women, are peppered throughout *Little Women*, but she is most explicit in chapter thirty-four.

Jo has been present at a serious philosophical discussion in the city; she feels fascinated and "pleasurably excited" until Professor Bhaer defends Truth, God, Religion, and all the Old Values. Then she is corrected: "She began to see that character is a better possession than money, rank, intellect, or beauty" (p. 320), or indeed, *talent*, one might believe Alcott privately added, in case it, too, should fail the severer tests of life.

Thus does Alcott excuse herself for not being a genius and justify the minorness of her own gifts. The linked faculties of erotic, artistic, and intellectual scope—again, especially for women—are sweepingly dismissed in favor of the cardinal virtues. These, she shows us, not only bring their own rewards but deserve and sweeten all other kinds of success. She is careful to offer her pilgrims no serious and interesting external temptations—no quick artistic triumphs, no plausible and exciting seducers, no possibilities of easy luxury, no compelling pressure of any kind toward the compromise of honor. Therefore we get no vivid image of the bitter costs virtue may exact, the very real losses entailed by those lasting gains she so eloquently describes and advocates. She may perhaps have felt them too keenly for words.

Notes

1. Attributed to William A. Alcott, an influential educator and writer on educational subjects in the mid-nineteenth century. The phrase is quoted in Robert Palfrey Utter and Gwendolyn Bridges Needham, *Pamela's Daughters* (New York: Russell and Russell, 1936), p. 384, an extremely interesting survey of changing tastes in literary heroines.

2. Louisa May Alcott, *Little Women* (1868-69; rpt. Boston: Little, Brown and Company, Centennial ed. [1976]), p. 366. Subsequent references will appear in the text.

20

Tradition and the Talent of
Frances Hodgson Burnett

Little Lord Fauntleroy, A Little Princess, and

The Secret Garden

PHYLLIS BIXLER KOPPES

Frances Hodgson Burnett's lasting contribution to children's litera-ture consists of three books, *Little Lord Fauntleroy* (1886), *A Little Princess* (1905), and her best work, *The Secret Garden* (1911). This was Marghanita Laski's assessment in 1951, and subsequent critical opinion has usually agreed with her.[1] Burnett's individual achievement in these books can be described by placing them within the appropriate literary traditions. In *Little Lord Fauntleroy* and *A Little Princess* Burnett combined two genres she knew as a child: the fairy tale and the exemplum. In *The Secret Garden* she continued to use themes and motifs from these genres, but she gave symbolic enrichment and mythic enlargement to her poetic vision by add-ing tropes from pastoral tradition at least as old as Virgil's *Georgics*. Pre-vious descriptions of development in Burnett's three best known works have focused on the increasing depth and subtlety in the portrayal of her main child characters.[2] While this approach highlights a special strength of *The Secret Garden*, it fails to explain why *A Little Princess* and especially *Little Lord Fauntleroy* remain "curiously compelling"[3] now that beautiful, innocent children are not as fashionable as when Burnett was writing. The following analysis of Burnett's earlier works as fairy tale-exempla, on the other hand, avoids using standards of psychological credibility in char-acterization more appropriate to realistic novels of child life. Moreover, a discussion of Burnett's use of mythic and pastoral traditions in *The Secret Garden*, shows this work to be her masterpiece not just because its main child characters are multi-faceted but because the work as a whole is richer than its predecessors in thematic development and symbolic resonance.

Both the exemplum and the fairy tale made a deep impression on Burnett as a child. In *The One I Knew Best of All: A Memory of the Mind of a Child* (1893) Burnett was highly critical of the exempla she had read.

She described them as "horrible little books" given by "religious aunts," books "containing memoirs of dreadful children who died early of complicated diseases, whose lingering developments they enlivened by giving unlimited moral advice and instruction to their parents and immediate relatives."[4] In "Little Saint Elizabeth" (1890), the story of a child whose good instincts are warped by her aunt's religiosity and by the many "legends of saints and stories of martyrs" she has read, Burnett similarly scorned the excesses of the religious exempla as well as the attempts to imitate them too literally and self-consciously.[5] Despite such harsh criticism, however, Burnett returned to this genre repeatedly in her memoir; like Little Saint Elizabeth, she had been much affected by the religious stories she read. "There was nothing she would have been so thankful for as to find that she might attain being an Example," Burnett said of herself as a child; but self-examination had told her that she could not match the fictional children in their high standards of conduct or in their ability to effect instant conversions in others (*The One I Knew Best*, pp. 188-189). Fairy tales, on the hand, provided Burnett with more affectionate memories. As an adult, she had friends on two continents scouring old bookstores for a particular collection of tales which she had owned, memorized, and then lost when she was seven or eight years old. She was retelling the stories to children and was about to publish them when someone found her "Lost Fairy Book." In 1904 she wrote an appreciative preface to a new edition of this work, *Granny's Wonderful Chair* (1856) by Frances Browne.[6]

Browne's fairy tales — which are at the same time parables against greed and pride — could well have pointed Burnett toward the combination of fairy tale and exemplum she achieved in *Little Lord Fauntleroy* and *A Little Princess*.[7] From the religious exemplum she took the child paragon who has a beneficial influence on those around him; her narratives are secularizations of the story about a saintly child who converts others.[8] Cedric Fauntleroy and Sara Crewe become the agents of secular conversions or rebirths by bringing the socially alienated or insecure into the human family. Cedric effects this marvelous change in his irascible, misanthropic grandfather. Sara befriends two misfits and a servant in Miss Minchin's school, and she gives the wealthy recluse next door a reason to live. Burnett's exempla are secularized also in that her main child characters do not need to be converted themselves before they convert others — they are innocent. Cedric Fauntleroy especially typifies what Burnett called "the innocent friend of the whole world," the child "born without sense of the existence of any barrier between his own innocent heart and any other."[9] Cedric's innocence plays a key role in the "conversion" of his grandfather; the child brings out the good in the selfish old man simply by assuming that his grandfather is good.

Despite the absence of supernatural trappings beyond a series of marvelous coincidences, Burnett's stories are fairy tales as well as exempla. Most obviously, they are versions of the tale which also underlines much of Burnett's popular adult fiction about women, the Cinderella tale.[10] An examination of that tale's many variants reveals that Cinderella is not only worthy to be a princess but also a princess by nature. When she is a scullery-maid, she is enchanted, under a spell; at the end of the story she simply returns to her natural, disenchanted state as a princess.[11] Sara Crewe undergoes a parallel pattern of enchantment and disenchantment. When her wealthy father brings her to school, she is recognized as a princess by all because of her fine clothes and regal bearing. After word arrives that her father died penniless, she is treated as a servant by the "wicked stepmother," Miss Minchin, and some of the older "stepsisters" in the school. Sara's real identity is at last discovered by the recluse next door, who restores to her the vast fortune which her father mistakenly thought he had lost. Cedric Fauntleroy's case is similar; by receiving the title of "Lord" he is merely being restored to his rightful inheritance. Like the Cinderella tale, Burnett's stories do not emphasize a change within the main character but rather the recognition of that character's true nature. Cedric is "every inch a lord" and Sara is a "princess"[12] even when the world does not recognize them as such. The change comes within others, those who are influenced by the child's true nature.

In her portrayal of Cedric and Sara, therefore, Burnett's primary concern is not character change or development as might be expected in more realistic works, but rather character revelation. She reveals the true nature of her main characters in a manner peculiarly appropriate both to the fairy tale and exemplum: she presents Cedric and Sara with a series of tests. These tests are designed to demonstrate whether the children's conspicuous beauty, like Cinderella's, is a reliable sign of their nature, whether they are as inwardly noble and virtuous as their outward appearance would suggest. Cedric Fauntleroy, for example, must not allow his affections to be bought by his grandfather's wealth; he must not be sullen and angry because he is separated from his mother, his "Dearest"; he must face the threat of an impostor heir with grace and equanimity. Sara Crewe's test is to maintain the charitable nature and even temper of a princess while she is treated as a servant and beggar, and unlike Cedric she knows she is being tested. Before she loses her vast wealth, for example, Sara suggests that she may be "good tempered" simply because she has everything she wants and everyone is kind to her. She wonders how she will ever find out if she is "really a nice child or a horrid one": "Perhaps I'm a *hideous* child," she says, "and no one will ever know, just because I never have any trials."[13]

In *A Little Princess* Burnett's central themes of the testing of virtue and the relationship between appearance and reality are effectively amplified by the fact that recognition of Sara's true nature becomes a test for other characters in the story. Most of those we get to know well do pass this test—the pupils who visit Sara in her attic room, the servant Becky, the Indian servant of the recluse next door, and even Miss Minchin's sister, Miss Amelia. Like a family of children in the neighborhood, these characters recognize that Sara "is not a beggar, however shabby she looks" (p. 130). The headmistress, Miss Minchin, of course fails this test and therefore, unlike most of the adults in Burnett's stories, she is not "converted" by the exemplary child. Miss Minchin does not recognize Sara's true nature because there is a basic flaw in her vision: she judges only by superficial appearances. She thinks that Sara can be changed from a princess into a beggar simply by changing from a pink silk gauze dress to a tight black frock (pp. 85-86). To Miss Minchin scullerymaids are "not little girls" but rather "machines" for carrying coal-scuttles and making fires (p. 74). She looks at an old table, a soap dish, and colored tissue paper which Sara and her friends are using to make their attic snack a magic feast, and she sees only "rubbish" (p. 205).

The importance of a person's point of view is underscored also by Burnett's symbolic use of fairy tale magic, a concept she will develop further in *The Secret Garden*. In *A Little Princess* magic becomes a metaphor for the ability to see with the imagination, for example, Sara's ability to see her attic room as a dungeon or banquet hall in a romantic story and to see herself as a princess in a fairy tale. Like magic, this ability to see with the imagination is also a power—it helps Sara to endure her physical hardships and to maintain her sense of self-worth in the presence of Miss Minchin's insults. And finally, magic becomes a way of explaining the marvelous changes that come about in Sara's life as her true nature and identity are rediscovered by the world. This is "the Magic that won't let those worst things *ever* quite happen" (p. 212). It is the larger "Magic" which works throughout the kind of story Sara finds herself living in (pp. 218, 221). *A Little Princess* is a modern version of a familiar fairy tale, and it has gained thematic and symbolic richness in Burnett's retelling.

The frequent references to fairy tales and magic make it difficult to mistake *A Little Princess* for a realistic novel of child life. The clues in *Little Lord Fauntleroy* are less obvious, but they are there. The story does contain a few explicit comparisons to the world of the fairy tale; the Earl's castle is "like the palace in a fairy story" for example, and Little Lord

Fauntleroy is "rather like a small copy of the fairy prince."[14] But the primary clue to the kind of story Burnett offers is precisely that characteristic which makes it a failure as a piece of realistic fiction: its exaggeration. Cedric's change in station, like Sara's, is exaggerated to fairy tale proportions. He moves from considerable poverty in a New York City apartment to untold wealth in one of the most beautiful country estates in England. The main figures in Cedric's life are painted in broad strokes just as he is. His mother is a paragon of sacrificial parenthood, willing to deny herself her son's companionship for what she considers to be his good; like Fauntleroy, she is being tested, and the purity of her motives eventually becomes obvious even to the suspicious Earl. The Earl himself becomes a moral monster as Burnett increasingly darkens his outline; no one besides Cedric has been able to find anything good in this "cynical, worldly old man" (p. 110), a man who had neglected his own wife and had been indifferent to his own children (p. 147).

In the center of such a story, a hero of conspicuous beauty and incorruptible virtue is entirely appropriate. As a contemporary reviewer put it, Little Lord Fauntleroy is a "paladin in knickerbockers."[15] His nobility shines forth in any environment, in a tiny corner grocery store as in a vast banquet hall. As he rides forth he extends the arm of charity to the less fortunate; he sets up his bootblack friend in business and provides special physical comforts for an old apple woman who had been kind to him. Armed only with his innocence and goodness Fauntleroy tames the ogre in his castle—he changes a selfish old man into an affectionate grandfather and responsible landlord.

As is well known, this "paladin in knickerbockers" was not so successful in winning the affection of a generation of boys whose parents apparently believed, like Miss Minchin, that a change in children's clothes would effect a marvelous change in their nature. A justifiable sympathy for these real-life victims probably played a significant role in the unjustifiably negative criticism and reputation Burnett's book has sometimes received.[16] To defend Burnett's achievement in *Little Lord Fauntleroy*, however, critics need not just recite evidence that the fictional Cedric "is not really a sissy";[17] more important, it is necessary to recognize the kind of tale in which he figures. In *Little Lord Fauntleroy*, Burnett uses techniques of exaggerated characterization and plot to conjure up the spirit of heroic innocence. Both tales appropriately elicit our wonder: they have an evocative power precisely because their main characters as well as their situations are out of the ordinary—"too good to be true."[18]

Little Lord Fauntleroy, like *A Little Princess*, is a *märchen*, a "wonder tale." But it is also an exemplum. Its purpose, however, is not that of the religious exempla about dying child saints, that is, to frighten readers into an early conversion. Nor is its purpose that of so many secular exempla in children's literature, to demonstrate or inculcate specific modes of behavior. *Little Lord Fauntleroy* survives changing fashions because Burnett returned to an earlier and more enduring use of the exemplum form to make a symbolic statement about the testing and the power of virtue.

In *The Secret Garden* Burnett built on her earlier works by continuing to use themes and motifs from the exemplum and the fairy tale, but, as I indicated earlier, she gave symbolic enrichment and mythic enlargement to her poetic vision by adding tropes from a literary pastoral tradition at least as old as Virgil's *Georgics*. *The Secret Garden*, like *Little Lord Fauntleroy*, is an exemplum about power, the power to bring to human life the marvelous change of physical healing and psychological rebirth. As in *A Little Princess*, Burnett uses the concept of magic to describe the workings of this power, and as in both of her earlier works, she shows the saving effect of this power on a reclusive adult. In the climax of *The Secret Garden*, the embittered widower Archibald Craven embraces the son he has avoided and joins the human family again. In contrast to her earlier works, however, Burnett now dramatizes a marvelous change not just within adults but also within her main child characters. Much of her story depicts the gradual physical and psychological rebirth of the orphaned Mary Lennox and her hypochondriac cousin, Colin Craven. In this story marvelous change has its source not so much in the nature of a child as in nature itself. The magic power which brings change in human lives is the same divine power which is evidenced by the seasonal cycle and the earth's fertility. By choosing a garden rather than an innocent child as the symbolic center of her story, Burnett drew on an ancient pastoral tradition and made the transition from fairy tale to myth.

Burnett's mythic imagination and her use of a more modern pastoral tradition are illustrated in the childhood memoir she wrote eighteen years before *The Secret Garden* (1911). In *The One I Knew Best of All* (1893), which might well be subtitled "A Portrait of the Artist as a Child," Burnett discusses the books and magazines which shaped her imagination. But she also assigns a large role in her development to nature; she describes an "enchanted" garden she played in as a very young child (pp. 29-43). Later, in an episode which foreshadows her famous fictional garden, she depicts her delight in imagining a profusion of flowers and green shoots in a long-locked and abandoned garden she discovered near her home in Manchester, England (pp. 254-260).[19] She devotes a long chapter to the formative effect the forests and mountains of Tennessee had on her as an adolescent, just before she sold her first story (pp. 251-285). Burnett's memoir as well as *The Secret Garden* thus belong to a modern pastoral tradition which suggests that there is a special affinity between the child and nature and that the child can be beneficially educated by nature. This tradition was established primarily by Rousseau's *Emile* (1762) and Wordsworth's *Prelude* (1805, 1850), was continued in nineteenth-century classics such as Mark Twain's *Tom Sawyer* (1876) and *Huckleberry Finn* (1885), and was restated in Kenneth Grahame's *Golden Age* (1895), which had a significant influence on the portrayal of childhood in children's literature during the early decades of the twentieth century.[20]

The pastoral episodes in Burnett's memoir also provide a preview of the mythic imagination at work later in *The Secret Garden*. She describes the "enchanted" garden she played in as the "Garden of Eden" because it was the scene of "the first Crime of her infancy" (p. 31). In this episode Burnett uses a Judeo-Christian myth to enhance her poignant portrayal of an impressionable child's exaggerated sense of guilt for a small misdemeanor. In contrast Burnett evokes a Pagan mythological tradition to express her unalloyed pleasure in nature as an adolescent. These days in the Tennessee mountains and forests she calls her "Dryad Days." She speculates that she felt so much a part of nature "because ages before—dim, far-off beautiful ages before, she had been a little Faun or Dryad—or perhaps a swaying thing of boughs and leaves herself" (p. 264). Later, she compares her revels with those of the "Bacchantes of old" (p. 280). In any case, she feels that she has been "reincarnated" from the age "when there had been fair pagan gods and goddesses who found the fair earth beautiful enough for deity itself" (pp. 264-265).

The Secret Garden is consistent with the Edenic myth in that Burnett portrays a garden fallen from former glory and main child characters who are not innocent, especially as compared with those in her earlier works. More explicitly, however, *The Secret Garden* evokes the pagan mythological tradition, particularly through two of the Yorkshire folk who help initiate Mary and Colin into nature's mysteries. The first is Mother Sowerby who works largely behind the scenes on behalf of her adopted children in the garden. This "comfortable wonderful mother creature," who has twelve children of her own she has fattened on "th' air of th' moor" and "th' grass same as th' wild ponies," has the aura of that archetypical God Mother, the Earth Mother.[21] In addition Mother Sowerby's twelve-year-old son Dickon, an un-self-conscious nature child, is obviously meant to suggest Pan. When Mary first sees Dickon, he is sitting under a tree and playing a rude pipe for some attending animals. The children call him an "animal charmer" who can charm the "boy animal" Colin (p. 192). As a more local nature deity than Mother Sowerby, Dickon participates in the garden ceremonies instituted to make Colin well. Despite her evocation of these pagan nature deities, however, Burnett stops short of a deification of nature itself: the "Magic" which the children summon is the creative life force that works *through* nature as well as through themselves (pp. 300-301, 349-350). Moreover, Burnett means to be non-sectarian in her description of this power and its appropriate worship.[22] Her "Pan" sings the "Doxology" (p. 344), and Mother Sowerby tells Colin that "th' Magic listened . . . It would ha' listened to anything tha'd sung. It was the joy that mattered. Eh! lad, lad—what's names to th' Joy Maker" (p. 350).

In dramatizing the workings of this magic power, Burnett draws on an ancient literary as well as mythic tradition. Much of the symbolic richness and formal integrity of *The Secret Garden* can be explicated by demonstrating its place within the georgic pastoral tradition (so called because this tradition is typified by Virgil's *Georgics* which describe the farmer's life rather than his bucolic *Eclogues*, which depict shepherd life). One of the most important characteristics of the georgic pastoral is an emphasis on time and change, especially as these are experienced through nature's diurnal and seasonal cycles. The bucolic shepherd usually enjoys a suspension of time and change, an eternal summer afternoon under the trees. The life of the farmer, on the other hand, is determined by the seasonal cycle.[23] Like georgic pastoralists before her, Burnett found that the seasonal cycle, especially the new life spring brings after the death of winter, provides a mythic metaphor for human change, growth, rebirth. Like Thoreau in *Walden*, Burnett uses the seasonal cycle to give form to her work as well as to symbolically underscore the marvelous change within her characters. Mary arrives on the moors during a late-winter rain storm; it is early spring when she and Colin enter the secret garden; during the summer the garden and the two children fully recover from their various ills; and this harvest of health is ready when Colin's father returns in the fall.

The georgic emphasis on the seasonal cycle tends to present nature as ever changing, ever new; most often, Burnett's children are interested in the new changes which springtime brings moment by moment to the garden. But the realization that nature's diurnal and seasonal cycles are themselves unchanging can also bring a glimpse of what Spenser called the "eterne in mutabilitie" (*Faerie Queene*, III, vi. 4.5). There are moments when "one's heart stands still at the strange unchanging majesty of the rising sun—which has been happening every morning for thousands and thousands and thousands of years" (p. 268). It is thus that Burnett describes Colin's feelings when he first learned that he could walk, when his first experience of the changes of springtime in the garden elicited his cry, "I shall live forever and ever and ever!" (p. 267).

A second distinguishing characteristic of the georgic pastoral tradition is its emphasis on work. In bucolic poetry the shepherd's life is admired for its leisure, idleness, *otium*. The georgic farmer, on the other hand, is praised for his work. Nature may sometimes cause him to contemplate its beauty, but it also invites him to participate in its wonders, to assist through his own work in nature's ceaseless creation; the farmer thus has almost a demiurgic role. In Burnett's novel, Mary and Colin experience this georgic cooperation between man and nature most obviously through their work in the garden. They search for green shoots under the dead brown, they pull weeds and plant seeds, and they rejoice as spring brings the garden into bloom. Perhaps less obviously, Burnett underscores this georgic theme through her use of the children's magic experiments to make Colin well. By incanting, by sitting and processing in a "mystic circle" (p. 322), the children become participants in nature's song and dance,[24] they practice magic as they work in the garden. As Colin says, "The Magic works best when you work yourself" (p. 341). But the children are aware that the magic cannot be controlled entirely by their own acts; that is why they call it "Magic." The power that makes Colin well must also come from outside him: it is like the spring which is needed if their own work in the garden is to be rewarded with bloom. The children's magic experiments (like their work in the garden) are examples of the georgic reciprocity between man and nature which Wordsworth described as being both "willing to work and to be wrought upon," of being "creator and receiver both" (1805, XIII.100, II.271). This georgic combination creates the conditions under which human rebirth can occur even as the seasonal cycle gives form to the experience of rebirth.

The georgic reciprocity between man and nature is reflected in two stylistic characteristics of Burnett's narrative which help account for some of its literary power. The book is both lyrical and incantational; its language is thus both an expression of being and a tool for doing. The members of the secret garden community are constantly describing nature's beauty in paeans which seem involuntary expressions of joy. From the beginning Ben Weatherstaff, the gardener, and Dickon, the boy from the moors— the folk who have long been close to "the good rich earth"—are the songsters of nature. But Mary and Colin also find themselves singing as they discover that the spring in the garden is moving inside of them too. These descriptions become incantatory even before Colin establishes incantations as a formal part of his magic experiment; before Colin first enters the garden, Mary soothes him to sleep after one of his tantrums with a soft, droning description of spring's beginnings in the garden (pp. 227-228). The children's imitation of the folk dialect of Yorkshire as they work in the garden can also be seen as the incantatory use of an especially potent language. Moreover, the novel as a whole has an incantatory as well as lyrical quality not only because of the liberal use of dialect but also because key words such as "brown," "green," "Spring," "Magic," "awakening," "growing," and "alive" are repeated over and over. Language becomes a tool for doing in Burnett's story also through the proverbial wisdom which Hesiod and Virgil established as part of the georgic tradition. Language is a repository and transmitter of lore which can guide man in his work. In *The Secret Garden* Mary and Colin are guided by the lore of Ben Weatherstaff, Dickon, and especially Mother Sowerby, whose proverbial wisdom is quoted as authoritative by many characters throughout the narrative.

The inclusion of that social creation, proverbial wisdom, points to another important characteristic of the georgic pastoral tradition: it emphasizes cooperation not only between nature and man but also between man and man. Unlike Virgil's bucolic *Eclogues*, his *Georgics* give an important role to family and community life. In Burnett's story human cooperation is demonstrated through the secret garden society formed to make Colin well. The magic rituals in the garden suggest the importance of human effort, but they are also expressions of social identity—the ceremonies give form to the garden community. Finally, as in *Little Lord Fauntleroy*, family reconciliation provides the climax to *The Secret Garden*. Communities as well as individuals can experience the marvelous change of rebirth.

The secret garden is the central georgic trope, the unifying symbol of rebirth in Burnett's novel. A closer examination of her use of the garden demonstrates how well she was able to meld themes and motifs from fairy tale, exemplum, and pastoral tradition into a coherent mythic statement. First, the garden is the place where the children work and observe the magic of change and new life which the seasons bring in nature and in themselves. But the garden's symbolic meaning is intensified in a number of other ways. For example, the garden represents that which is dead or apparently dead in the past. The sickness of the garden clearly suggests the illness and ill-temper which the children put behind them. The garden is also associated with Colin's dead mother: it was her favorite place and the occasion of her death; Colin's father, Archibald Craven, had the garden locked up because it reminds him of the past. But the garden also represents the redemptive magic which can infuse the present and future. According to Mother Sowerby, Colin's mother is still watching over him, especially in the garden. It was Colin's mother who magically initiated the plan to bring him to the garden by sending the robin to show Mary the hidden key and door (pp. 273-274). Like Burnett's earlier works, *The Secret Garden* suggests motifs form the Cinderella story. In some of that tale's variants, the supernatural agency which helps Cinderella is associated with her dead mother. Perrault's fairy godmother, for example, can be seen as the spirit of Cinderella's dead mother. Other variants express the mother's magical help more clearly as Burnett does, through animals, birds, plants. Cinderella is helped by a calf her mother had given her or by a bird which perches in a hazel tree Cinderella had planted on her mother's grave.[25]

Burnett's garden becomes representative of redemptive forces in the present and future also because she identifies it with the children as well as with Colin's mother. Like Mary, the garden has suffered neglect because nobody wanted it—it too is an "orphan." Also, both children are ten years old, and the garden has been locked ten years, since Colin's mother died shortly after he was born. The children, like the garden, are gifts which the dead mother has given to the present and future. Archibald Craven must accept all of these gifts if he is to live joyfully in the present and future.

Finally, Burnett connects the garden with human rebirth by making it a georgic "landscape of the mind."[26] One character says that being inside the garden is like being in a dream (p. 127). A recurring metaphor for what happens to the garden as well as to the characters is "waking up" or "awakening." Details such as the garden's secrecy and its "wild" rather than "tidy" appearance (p. 134) further suggest the unconscious mind. Unfortunately, Burnett sometimes allows this part of her symbolism to become too conscious, especially in a chapter in which she describes the power of the mind, the dangers of locking it up, and the necessity of replacing the weeds of bad thoughts with the plants of beautiful thoughts (pp. 353-355). More often, however, Burnett allows her fictional garden to speak for itself so that in its apparent artlessness it seems less a "gardener's garden" than "a wilderness of growing things" (p. 208).

Because Burnett has invested the secret garden with so much symbolic meaning, she can use it to make the family reunion at the end of her exemplum about power something more than just a sentimental cliché. The garden gives her not only a setting for this scene but also a vivid image for what her story suggests about rebirth. As Archibald Craven gets near the walled garden in search of his son, he hears "the laughter of young things, the uncontrollable laughter of children who were trying not to be heard but who in a moment or so—as their excitement mounted— would burst forth." And the garden's secret does "burst forth" in the person of a healthy Colin followed by his playmates; through the door now "flung wide open," Colin makes an "unseeing dash" "full speed" toward his father (pp. 369-370). Throughout the novel, Burnett has stressed that the garden can come back to life not because of its secrecy, but because of that which can somehow find a way inside its locked walls: the powers of nature and the helpful work of human beings. Now Burnett uses the walled garden to show that the marvelous change of rebirth is a secret that cannot be kept, that a community of the reborn has the ability—indeed, the inner necessity—to expand and include the world outside.

Because it taps some of the oldest of folktale motifs, pastoral tropes, and mythic themes, Burnett's exemplum about power has a resonant complexity; but it also has an integrity, especially because of its unifying symbolic image, the secret garden. In *Little Lord Fauntleroy* and *A Little Princess* Frances Hodgson Burnett had made her own poetic contribution to two genres within the tradition of children's literature, the exemplum and the fairy tale. In *The Secret Garden* she used a variety of literary traditions to create a work of thematic and symbolic richness which well deserves to be regarded as a juvenile masterpiece.

Notes

1. Marghanita Laski, *Mrs. Ewing, Mrs. Molesworth, and Mrs. Hodgson Burnett* (New York: Oxford Univ. Press, 1951), pp. 81-91. For similar estimates of Burnett's achievement see, e.g., John Rowe Townsend, *Written for Children: An Outline of English-Language Children's Literature*, rev. ed. (Philadelphia: Lippincott, 1965, 1974), pp. 86-89; and Roger Lancelyn Green, "The Golden Age of Children's Books," *Only Connect: Reading on Children's Literature*, ed. Sheila Egoff et al. (Toronto: Oxford Univ. Press, 1969), pp. 10-11. Although it does not merit a place with Burnett's three best known books for children, *The Lost Prince* (1915) deserves more critical attention than it has received. This longer work is Burnett's contribution to the adventure romance, a popular children's genre not discussed in this article. Especially interesting is the fact that Burnett anticipated some of the main themes and plot interests of J.R.R. Tolkien's *Lord of the Rings*: the use of two apparently insignificant creatures, in Burnett's case children, to help bring about the return of a king in exile.

2. See, e.g., Laski, pp. 81-91; Townsend, pp. 86-89; Gillian Avery with the assistance of Augusta Bull, *Nineteenth Century Children: Heroes and Heroines in English Children's Stories 1790-1900* (London: Hodder and Stoughton, 1965), pp. 177-179; and Ann Thwaite, *Waiting for the Party: The Life of Frances Hodgson Burnett 1849-1924* (New York: Scribner's, 1974), pp. 220-22.

3. Gillian Avery discusses *Little Lord Fauntleroy* as an example of the cult of the innocent child in children's literature during the last decades of the nineteenth century. "In spite of the clouds of sentimentality, *Little Lord Fauntleroy* (1886) is curiously compelling," Avery declares, p. 178.

4. Illus. Reginald B. Birch (New York: Scribner's, 1893), p. 111; hereafter, references to this memoir will be made in the text.

5. *Little Saint Elizabeth and Other Stories*, illus. Reginald B. Birch (New York: Scribner's, 1890), pp. 15-55.

6. Vivian Burnett, *The Romantick Lady (Frances Hodgson Burnett): The Life Story of an Imagination* (New York: Scribner's, 1927), pp. 10-11; Ann Thwaite, *Waiting for the Party*, pp. 12, 256.

7. Browne's "Story of Childe Charity," in fact, has many of the fairy tale

and exemplum themes which this article discusses as central in Burnett's fiction; *Granny's Wonderful Chair* (rpt. New York: Macmillan, 1961), pp. 109-27.

8. See Avery, pp. 81-93, 170-74, for a comparison of the saintly child in evangelistic fiction with the secular innocent in late-nineteenth-century children's literature.

9. Burnett used these words to describe her son Vivian in "How Fauntleroy Occurred and a Very Real Little Boy Became an Ideal One," *Piccino and Other Child Stories* (New York: Scribner's, 1894), pp. 203, 163.

10. Burnett began her career by writing formula fiction for women's magazines. Her early stories and novels often contain the familiar love match between the beautiful or talented young woman and a man who is socially or intellectually her superior. Sometimes, as in "A Quiet Life" (1878), the love match ends tragically. Often, however, the young woman marries her "Prince Charming." See, e.g., "Pretty Polly Pemberton" (1877) and *Louisiana* (1880). In a 1901 version of this formula, *The Making of a Marchioness*, Burnett made explicit references to the Cinderella tale.

11. Iona and Peter Opie, *The Classic Fairy Tales* (London: Oxford Univ. Press, 1974), pp. 12-14.

12. In *Sara Crewe* (1888) Burnett's main character was somewhat spoiled and ill-tempered at the beginning of the story; in *A Little Princess* (1905) Burnett brought her story more in line with the Cinderella tale by immediately establishing Sara's noble nature.

13 *A Little Princess: Being the Whole Story of Sara Crewe Now Told for the First Time* (rpt. New York: Scribner's, 1938), p. 35; hereafter, references will be made in the text.

14. *Little Lord Fauntleroy*, illus. Reginald Birch (New York: Scribner's, 1886), p. 71; hereafter, references will be made in the text.

15. William Archer, London *World*, 23 May 1888; Archer's review of the play Burnett wrote based on her popular novel is quoted by Vivian Burnett, *Romantick Lady*, p. 168.

16. In 1932, e.g., F. J. Harvey Darton lamented that *Little Lord Fauntleroy* "ran through England like a sickly fever. Nine editions were published in as many months, and the odious little prig in the lace collar is not dead yet," *Children's Books in England: Five Centuries of Social Life* (Cambridge: University Press, 1932, 1966), p. 239; in this survey, Darton does not mention any of Burnett's other books.

17. As she is dressing up Fauntleroy in paperback for readers in the 1970's, Ann Thwaite says that Cedric got his reputation as "a prig and a sissy . . . partly because of the original illustrations by Reginald Birch" which "did the book a disservice, pretty and skilful as they were." The fictional Fauntleroy, Thwaite argues, "is not really a sissy. He is brave, thoughtful, enterprising, unaffected; he is, in fact, a likeable boy. Perhaps he is rather too good to be true," Introduction, *Little Lord Fauntleroy* (rpt. London: Collins, 1974), pp. 8-9.

18. Ann Thwaite, Introduction, *Little Lord Fauntleroy*, p. 8.

19. In *My Robin* (1912) Burnett described a robin and garden in Kent which also provided models for *The Secret Garden*. Near the end of her life she wrote *In the Garden* (1925) describing her years of experience as a gardener and exhorting her readers to have gardens. From 1898 until she died in 1924, according to her son (*Romantick Lady*, pp. 286-287), she was "the Passionate Gardener." Much of Burnett's portrayal of nature in *The Secret Garden*, therefore, was based on her

own observations. It was Burnett's lifelong habit, however, to transform her experience into the conventional forms of a story. "This has been my way of looking at life as it went by me," she said in the Preface to *Giovanni and the Other: Children Who Have Made Stories* (1892). Just as she earlier found a fairy tale in her love for her son Vivian, she now saw mythic significance in her experience as a gardener.

20. On the significance of Kenneth Grahame's *Golden Age*, see Roger Lancelyn Green, "The Golden Age of Children's Books," pp. 11-13. For a fuller discussion of this modern pastoral tradition and its expression in children's literature, see Phyllis Bixler Koppes, "The Child in Pastoral Myth: A Study in Rousseau and Wordsworth, Children's Literature and Literary Fantasy," Diss. Univ. of Kansas 1976, chs. III-VII.

21. *The Secret Garden* (New York: Frederick A. Stokes, 1911), pp. 316, 38; hereafter, references will be made in the text. Some of Mother Sowerby's folk wisdom is archetypically appropriate—it is a global wisdom:

> "When I was at school my jography told as th' world was shaped like a orange an' I found out before I was ten that th' whole orange doesn't belong to nobody. No one owns more than his bit of a quarter an' there's times it seems like there's not enow quarters to go around.
>
> "But don't you—none o' you—think as you own th' whole orange or you'll find out you're mistaken ... there's no sense in grabbin' at th' whole orange—peel an' all. If you do you'll likely not get even the pips, an' them's too bitter to eat" (pp. 244-45).

22. According to Vivian Burnett (*Romantick Lady*, pp. 376-77), Burnett was alternately interested in Theosophy, Spiritualism, Christian Science, and other forms of mind- or faith-healing. Except possibly in a discourse on the powers of the mind near the end of *The Secret Garden*, Burnett does not urge these sectarian ideas on her reader. They are more obviously on display in *The Lost Prince* (1915) and ecpially in *The Closed Room* (1904) and *The White People* (1917), both of which dramatize the belief that dead loved ones often stay close to one in some kind of afterlife.

23. As Virgil says in his *Georgics*, "The farmer's toil returns moving in a circle, as the year rolls back upon itself over its own footsteps," *Virgil, With an English Translation by H. Rushton Fairclough in Two Volumes*, rev. ed. (Cambridge: Harvard Univ. Press, 1957), Book II, p. 145. The distinctions between the bucolic and georgic pastoral traditions used in this article are developed more fully in Koppes, "The Child in Pastoral Myth," ch. I.

24. In the first book of his *Georgics*, p. 105, Virgil prescribes that country folk process around their fields calling on Ceres to bring fertilty.

25. Iona and Peter Opie, *The Classic Fairy Tales*, pp. 117-21.

26. A number of critics have noted the tendency for a pastoral landscape to become a picture of the mind. See, e.g., Bruno Snell, "Arcadia: The Discovery of a Spiritual Landscape," in *The Discovery of Mind: The Greek Origins of European Thought*, trans. T. G. Rosenmeyer (1953; rpt. New York: Harper, 1960), pp. 281-309; and Richard Cody, *The Landscape of the Mind: Pastoralism and Platonic Theory in Tasso's Aminta and Shakespeare's Early Comedies* (Oxford: Clarendon, 1969).

21

The Sea-Dream

Peter Pan and *Treasure Island*

KATHLEEN BLAKE

According to Robert Louis Stevenson's "A Gossip on Romance," romances "may be nourished with the realities of life, but their true mark is to satisfy the nameless longings of the reader, and to obey the ideal laws of the daydream. The right kind of thing should fall out in the right kind of place; the right kind of thing should follow; and not only the characters talk aptly and think naturally, but all the circumstances in the tale answer one to another like notes in music."[1]

Treasure Island (1883) is the fulfillment of the "sea-dreams" of its boy hero, Jim Hawkins, who broods over the treasure map before he even leaves England (*TI*, p. 49),[2] and of the sea-dreams of generations of boys like him, who knew what was the right thing to go with what, what should follow, what answered. There was a shape to the ideal, or a limited number of shapes. Stevenson says, "For my part, I like a story to begin with an old wayside inn where, 'toward the close of the year 17—,' several gentlemen in three-cocked hats were playing bowls. A friend of mine preferred the Malabar coast in a storm, with a ship beating to windward, and a scowling fellow of Herculean proportions striding along the beach."[3] In the verse addressed "To the Hesitating Purchaser" of *Treasure Island*, Stevenson names his models—Cooper, Ballantyne, and Kingston—promising the reader "the old romance, retold / Exactly in the ancient way." He had his followers too. The romance received another inspired casting. But whereas *Treasure Island* is the dream, *Peter Pan* (1911) is about dreaming, and waking.[4]

The dream, the music, the game, as Stevenson also calls it, had been available to boys since *Crusoe*, whose classic outlines define a tradition of juvenile literature, the Robinsonnade. *Robinson Crusoe* was published in 1719 and has never been out of print. It entered early into a career of adaptation, channeling towards the specifically juvenile in Johann Wyss's *Swiss Family Robinson* (English translation, 1814), which then itself prolifically spawned. Frederick Marryat's *Masterman Ready* (1841), James Fenimore Cooper's *The Crater* (1847), R. M. Ballantyne's *The Coral Island* (1853), Jules Verne's *Their Island Home or the Later Adventures of the Swiss Family Robinson* (1900) are only the most famous among many, which also include *The Island Home* (1851), *Canadian Crusoes* (1852), *Arctic Crusoe* (1854), *The Desert Home or English Family Robinson* (1858), two separate *Rival Crusoes* (1826, 1878), and many another account, as in W. H. G. Kingston's book *Shipwrecks and Disasters at Sea* (1873).[5] The hunger for stories of the South Seas and their lonely islands extended, yet insatiate, into the last third of the nineteenth century. It was shared by Robert Louis Stevenson, who at fifteen stopped Ballantyne in the street to express his admiration, and by J. M. Barrie, who wrote an introduction to *The Coral Island* in 1913 which began: "To be born is to be wrecked on an island" and for whom "R.L.S." were the sweetest initials in contemporary literature.[6]

The appetite was stimulated by novelties such as Ballantyne's *The Dog Crusoe* (1861), where the formula expands to render Crusoe a dog and to accommodate "redskins" and the prairies of the Far West. The prize of novelty must rest with W. Clark Russell's *The Frozen Pirate* (1887). Though an admixture of pirates is nothing new—Crusoe himself fought with mutineers–it is unusual for the island to be an iceberg. The castaway finds upon it a frozen pirate ship and frozen pirates. One of the pirates thaws to tell the tale of the pirate treasure, which opens the way to many a chilling adventure.

Stevenson has kind words for Russell's *A Sailor's Sweetheart* (1880): Russell excels in setting an incident and stops there. His books presumably belong to the category of the "amoral" in literature, of which Stevenson approves and which had been steadily gaining ground in the sea-adventure school. If Crusoe's shrewd practicality lay deeper than his religion, and the edifying passages in the *Swiss Family Robinson* served as overlay for a good adventure story, the trend toward the morally superficial is headlong in, for example, Marryat's *The Privateersman* (1846). Reflecting on his part in a bloody pirate attack off the coast of Hispaniola, the privateersman's mind misgives him—for a moment: "But employment prevented my thinking; the decks had to be cleaned, the bodies thrown overboard, the blood washed from the white planks." As Stevenson says, interest in such romances turns "not on the passionate slips and hesitations of the conscience, but on the problems of the body and of the practical intelligence, in clean, open-air adventure."[7]

Losing no time on edification, writers of penny dreadfuls made fast-moving medleys of the standard repertoire, as did Samuel Bracebridge Hemyng, creator of Jack Harkaway's countless and variegated adventures. One page of *Among the Pirates and On the Island of Palms* (c. 1890) moves the hero from the defeat of the pirates to the storm to the shipwreck to the island. Jack is a formidable boy. When the piratical black flag appears and the ship's captain is killed in the fray, Jack takes over: "It's the fortunes of war, men. I'll be your leader; don't despair."[8]

In Jack Harkaway we see the superboy of whom Stevenson's Jim Hawkins is a somewhat subtler example (he is responsible for every success on the island, benefiting from the lucky folly of a Crusoe) and to whom Peter Pan also owes his cockiness (on his island it is boy over man). By contrast, S. R. Crockett's *Sir Toady Crusoe* (1905) represents the type of the precious, small-boy, make-believe adventurer in the pirate and castaway mode—which had become by this time—less than a year after Barrie's play of *Peter Pan* appeared—just that, a mode. It is a short step from the let's-play-at-shipwrecks-and-islands sort of book to Neverland, and after a century of *Boy Voyagers* (1859) to every romantic fragment of land within the reach of the imagination, there was almost no interesting place left to send them to except the land of imagination itself.[9]

Treasure Island is the dream come true in the full-bodied glory of verisimilitude, which had belonged to tradition since Crusoe experienced the romance of his island in terms of common sense, a providential tally sheet, and the sound use of capital. This allows Jim Hawkins to dream his island and to go there, returning with real pieces of eight. "*Robinson Crusoe* is as realistic as it is romantic," says Stevenson, and that is the model for his own boys' book. We do not forget, he says, that we are reading. Our minds waver between consciousness that we are watching a performance and the fancy's active participation with the characters. In *Treasure Island* the pleasure of aesthetic distance—isn't this just the way things should have happened—is never quite lost in the gripping appeal of the verisimilar—what really happened is before your eyes. But for Stevenson, the latter is the triumph of the romance writer.[10]

Abandon realism, tip the mind toward consciousness of the story as a story, and you have the sea-dream as the Neverland. Stevenson says that the words of a good book "should run thenceforward in our ears like the noise of breakers."[11] *Treasure Island* is a good book. So is *Peter Pan*—but of a different sort utterly, for Barrie is concerned with showing how the palpable absolute conjured by such as Stevenson is both forever and never, and in particular, never again. "On these magic shores children at play are forever beaching their coracles. We too, have been there; we can still hear the sound of the surf, though we shall land no more" (*PP*. p. 44).

Robinson Crusoe built a canoe and set out to sea. He found himself caught in a current and his island of despair, as it receded, looking more and more desirable. Jim Hawkins sets out in the coracle built by the resident Crusoe of Treasure Island, the marooned wild man Ben Gunn.[12] An unexpected current turns his cruise into a fearful drift toward the open sea. Rocks and surf cut him off from the land, except that the currents of this island, like Crusoe's, run north, allowing the clever navigator to ride it out with the added aid of sail to a beachable northern inlet. Peter does not have this adventure; that is Barrie does not relate it, though perhaps he might had his narrative coin toss not come up for the lagoon. All that remains of this part of the dream are those children always beaching their coracles—of course they are coracles—on a shore familiarly surf-pounded. The surf and the coracles define Neverland. It isn't that what happens in Neverland never happened before, never would, and never could. Just about everything that happens there has happened before—in books.

In Neverland life falls into ideal shapes, "like in a book." Who is James Hook? He is the pirate captain, part history and part literary creation. Stevenson, writing *Treasure Island*, read up on pirates in one of the great source-books on the subject, the 1724 *Pyrates* by "Charles Johnson" (actually Defoe).[13] He uses Defoe's Blackbeard to define his own Flint: "Blackbeard was a child to Flint" (*TI*, p. 41). Barrie extends the system of piratical relations. James Hook was Blackbeard's bo'sun, and if Long John Silver (alias Barbeque, the Sea-Cook) is the only man who did not fear Flint or even the ghost of Flint, Hook is the only man "of whom Barbeque was afraid" and whom "the Sea-Cook feared" (*PP*, pp. 90, 99).

Captain Hook is also the Byronic hero in his boys' book manifestation. Like Byron's Corsair he is a "man of loneliness and mystery" (I., VIII).[14] "Where his frown of hatred darkly fell / Hope withering fled—and Mercy sigh'd farewell!" (I, IX). Hook's eyes express their balefulness in two glowing red spots. He suffers the "blighted bosom" of a Corsair (I, X), a self-torment as ineffable as Manfred's. Hardened by his thousand crimes, he yet harbors in his soul an unlooked-for reservoir of exquisite sensibility: "No little children love me!" (*PP*, p. 202). But no such inklings of humanity soften his relations with the general rout. Like the Corsair among his band on the pirate isle, "With these he mingles not but to command" (I, II). Hook is a "grand seigneur" (*PP*, p. 99).

Boys' book pirates are typically high-born like the Corsair and tend to be bigger than their men, better dressed, well-educated, and European. The pirate antagonist of Jack Harkaway is a "man of gigantic size ... wielding a large broad scimitar. ... But he was no Malay ... for he had a white, thoroughly European face." Ralph Rover of *The Coral Island* beholds "a man of immense stature and fierce aspect regarding me with

a smile of contempt [later a "Sardonic smile"]. He was a white man—
that is to say, he was a man of European blood." Marryat's *The Pirate
and the Three Cutters* (1836) offers a clear progenitor of Hook: "Superior
in talent, in knowledge of his profession, in courage, and moreover in
physical strength—which in him was almost Herculean. Unfortunately,
he was also superior in all villainy, in cruelty, and contempt of all in-
junctions, moral and Divine." Scion of a great border family (recall that
to reveal Hook's identity would have set the country in a blaze) and well-
educated (Hook never forgets that he has been at a famous public school),
this pirate, known as Cain, would have been handsome (like Hook) were
it not for his scars. And "strange to say, his eye was mild, and of a soft
blue" (the same color we find in the forget-me-not eyes of Hook, which
are blue with a profound melancholy when they are not lit up red with
murder).[15]

The pirate chief always exacts a shuddering respect, for his is a "not
wholly unheroic figure" (*PP*, p. 222). Above all he has class. Often born
an aristocrat, he possesses, even more importantly, the inner stuff of the
gentleman. Failing noble birth, the resource of the superior man is to
become the self-made "gentleman o' fortune," like Silver, who looks forward to retirement from the sea with money in the bank and a carriage
to ride in. Silver is always as spruce as possible in his fine broadcloth suit,
in contrast to his slovenly cohorts, while Hook cringes to observe Wendy's
eyes upon his soiled ruff. Silver despises his unruly, rum-sodden crew as
unworthy of the sea, a pack of low tailors, while Captain Hook is "fright-
fully *distingúe*," so superior to the rest that he "never felt more alone than
when surrounded by his dogs. They were socially so inferior to him" (*PP*,
pp. 186, 200). To be genteel is to inspire fear, according to the code of
Long John Silver. Hook too has the breeding to be most sinister when he
is most polite. The line of literary inheritance connects Hook to the at-
tractively wicked Silver; to Ballantyne's pirate, whose straightforward fe-
rocity of expression "rendered him less repulsive than his low-browed
associates";[16] to the Byronic hero, whose "name could sadden and his acts
surprise, / But they that feared him dared not to despise (I, XI)." Captain
James Hook draws his crew from Flint's *Walrus* (drawn by Stevenson from
the pages of Defoe), and his life's blood from printer's ink.

While life on any desert island goes by formulas, Neverland *is* formulas, and on it form is a way of life. The island is the land of dreams
(it is the landscape of a child's mind) and its presiding spirit, Peter, is
good form, a kind of embodiment of the play spirit, playing at islands.

There are moments when Jim Hawkins strides the thin line between
living his adventures and playing them, as for instance, when he enjoys
the confrontation between Captain Smollett and Silver—"It was as good

as the play to see them"—realizing at the same time that the issue is deadly earnest—"them that die'll be lucky ones" (*TI*, pp. 141, 143). The "air of adventure" (*TI*, p. 170) and elán in the doing take precedence over prudence or even utility. Why else would Jim sneak off the *Hispaniola* to go to the island, where he can expect nothing at all but trouble? The treasure map offers "the sport of the search" (*TI*, p. 42). As Squire Trelawney says, "Hang the treasure! It's the glory of the sea that has turned my head" (*TI*, p. 52). On this island a fusillade is no more to be minded than a game of cricket. The final treasure hunt seems "child's play" to Silver (*TI*, p. 232). Jim compares his desperate dodge and feint before the knife of Israel Hands to a game, a kind of sinister fulfillment of boy's sport back home.

But if there is a hint of the game player in Jim, it is outright in Peter. Make-believe and real are the same thing to him. He does nothing to simply get something done. He never just lives; he has adventures. And he organizes his life in order to have them. Even *not* having adventures, doing the sorts of things John and Michael have done all their lives, is something he plays at, "a new game that fascinated him enormously" (*PP*, p. 130). After saving Tiger Lily, Peter engages the forbidding Hook when he doesn't have to because he "could never resist a game" (*PP*, p. 145). The sport of the combat is the point, and the lines of opposition are arbitrary. For example, having once led his boys nearly to victory in battle with the redskins, he suddenly switches the sides; the encounter continues with boys as redskins, redskins as boys.

In Neverland the ideal displaces mere contingency:

> By all the unwritten laws of savage warfare it is always the redskin who attacks. . . . Through the long black night the savage scouts wriggle, snake-like, among the grass without stirring a blade. . . . Not a sound is to be heard, save when they give vent to a wonderful imitation of the lonely call of the coyote. The cry is answered by other braves; and some of them do it even better than the coyotes, who are not very good at it. . . . Every foot of ground between the spot where Hook had landed his forces and the home under the trees was stealthily examined by braves wearing their moccasins with the heels in front. . . . That this was the usual procedure was so well known to Hook that in disregarding it he cannot be excused on the plea of ignorance [*PP*, pp. 179–180].

Of course, the "unwritten laws," the "usual procedure" are formulas well established in literature. Cooper leaps to mind, or Twain on Cooper:

In his little box of stage-properties he kept six or eight cunning devices, tricks, artifices. . . . A favorite one was to make a moccasined person tread in the tracks of the moccasined enemy, and thus hide his own trail. Cooper wore out barrels and barrels of moccasins in working that trick. Another stage-property that he pulled out of his box pretty frequently was his broken twig. . . . Every time a Cooper person is in peril, and absolute silence is worth four dollars a minute, he is sure to step on a dry twig. There may be a hundred handier things to step on, but that wouldn't satisfy Cooper. Cooper requires him to turn out and find a dry twig; and if he can't do it, go and borrow one.[17]

The formula adventures that make up *Peter Pan* are presented in a style insistently "like in a book." It is as if the narrator (I call him Barrie for convenience) were saying: I tell it this way because this is what is needed for the sort of story I am telling. In Stevenson's words: "The right kind of thing should fall out in the right kind of place: the right kind of thing should follow." But it is a kind of cheating to reveal this principle of order within the story itself. Barrie's content is the content of romance, but his style subverts romantic illusion. He wants to establish the character of the terrible pirate captain; he proceeds as follows: "Let us now kill a pirate, to show Hook's method. Skylights will do" (*PP*, p. 100). He wants us to know that the pirate chief is not beyond all admiration; he stills the ticking of the crocodile as it waits below to receive Hook: "We purposely stopped the clock that this knowledge might be spared him: a little mark of respect from us at the end" (*PP*., p. 222). Things happen because the story requires them: "Will they [the children] reach the nursery in time? If so, how delightful for them, and we shall all breathe a sigh of relief, but there will be no story. On the other hand, if they are not on time . . . " (*PP*, p. 81).

Barrie has the power to lead his readers astray, as for example when he slips and writes the wrong ending. Two things are suggested here. One is that the narrator doesn't know everything and that something new has happened to change the plot since he heard the children's plans upon leaving Neverland; this implies the primacy of the story over its teller. Yet a second effect is just the reverse, for we have just read an ending as straightforwardly reported as any in the rest of the book, which then turns out to be a pure fiction, something that never "happened" at all. We are reminded of the narrative presence and power—not to mention caprice.

Barrie hovers in the background in the form of addresses to the reader, rhetorical questions, asides on mothers. He speaks to his characters and they talk back.

The narrative presence suggested by a line like "We now return to the nursery" (*PP*, p. 78) is conventional and unobtrusive in itself, but Barrie makes a point of obtruding conventions: "In the meantime, what of the boys? We have seen them at the first clang of weapons, turned as it were into stone figures, open-mouthed, all appealing with outstretched hands to Peter; and we return to them as their mouths close, and their arms fall to the sides" (*PP*, p. 184). The forward action of the characters and the plot comes to a dead stop when the narrator is not there to supervise it.

Such action is not the most important thing. Some passages have nothing to do with forwarding it. Barrie writes a conversation between himself and Mrs. Darling. He says he could spare her ten days of pain by announcing the children's return in advance. She replies that the cost would be too great in the children's loss of ten minutes of the happiness of surprising her. This interchange is curious because it takes place on some secondary (or is it primary?) plane, outside of "the story" and without effect on it. Mrs. Darling *is* surprised on the night of the children's return. Her foreknowledge is entirely hypothetical. In fact, the hypothetical is the presiding narrative attitude, which the reader is obliged to share: "Let us pretend to lie here among the sugar-cane and watch them [the boys] as they steal by in single file" (*PP*, p. 96).

Peter Pan never allows us to enter for long into the sea-dream because the story repeatedly reminds us that it is pure—dream, or game—arbitrary, conventional, made-up, literary. "Let us pretend." Art so overtakes nature in these woods that the coyotes come out second best at coyote calls. The Indians traverse every inch of ground between the lines of the boys and the pirates wearing their moccasins backwards because that is what they are supposed to do.

The true game player plays it straight, like the Indians, like Peter, like Stevenson. He may know that it is a game and enjoy its formal dimension, but he stays inside the frame so that its artificial limits do not impinge. In Barrie's work they impinge. He constantly reminds us of the frame. One might say that the narrator of *Peter Pan* is a dramatization of bad form. To rough out an equation: Hook is to Peter as Barrie is to Stevenson as adult is to child.

Peter remains a perpetual child because he does not remember things. In particular, he does not remember when he has been treated unfairly. He is fighting fair on the rock in the lagoon, and Hook bites him. This would undermine the faith of any other confiding boy by revealing the instability of the whole of idea of fair fight, precisely because it is just an idea. "No one gets over the first unfairness; no one except Peter. ... I suppose that was the real difference between him and all the rest" (*PP*,

p. 148). When Mr. Darling slips the medicine behind his back instead of taking it on the count of three as Michael does, Michael presumably begins to grow up. Adults cheat. They do not cut clean of the game. Mr. Darling wants to be admired by his children just as if he had taken the medicine, except that he happened to miss his mouth. And Hook has a passion for good form. The cheat upsets the system because he is both in it and out of it. One doesn't know where one is with him, and the game is demoralized.

Peter Pan, that "terrible masterpiece" as Peter Davies calls it, is a *tour de force* of literary demoralization.[18] Barrie presents himself as an adult forever banished from Neverland, a disgruntled onlooker cut off from his characters and doing maximum damage to their romantic world. His subversion is occasionally deliberate: "Nobody really wants us. So let us watch and say jaggy things, in the hope that some of them will hurt" (*PP*, p. 228). More often it comes of trying too hard to do the right thing. He goes through all the forms of the island narrative—in fact he hates to let any of them go and has to toss a coin to choose between them—but he is a fallen man because he perpetually shows that he knows they are forms. A narrator who writes, "Hook did not blanch, even at the gills" (*PP*, p. 144), is a fallen narrator. Good form is not to know one has it, like the childish Smee. Consciousness of form is bad form—a truth which is torture to Hook and, for Barrie, theme, style, and a last great desert-island book. (Let me not claim too much; it is just that to read *Peter Pan* is to feel that it *should* have been the last, as *Don Quixote* should have been the last knights-in-armor romance.)[19]

Barrie was a great admirer of Stevenson although he never met him. He thought of him as an inspired and lifelong boy, as "the spirit of boyhood tugging at the skirts of this old world of ours and compelling it to come back and play." Modern reclaimers of Stevenson's deteriorated fame are at pains to refute the much-worn biographical / critical judgment of his boyishness. It cannot be denied that Stevenson sometimes invites such a judgment, for example, when he draws a parallel between the writer of romance and the playful child. And it is worth noticing that even those who now argue his artistic maturation date it after *Treasure Island*. But whatever Stevenson's actual boyishness, the point is Barrie's opinion, for which he had his reasons. For example, in a letter of April 1893 from Vailima in Samoa, Stevenson gives Barrie a self-portrait: "general appearance of a blasted boy—or blighted youth— or ' . . . Child that has been in hell.'" So according to Barrie, Stevenson was Jim Hawkins in the apple barrel. On one occasion he cites a letter from Stevenson giving directions for Vailima; he makes them parallel the phrasing of Peter Pan's directions for Neverland. Apparently for Barrie, Stevenson was a kind of Peter Pan.[20]

He was immensely attracted by the boy in Stevenson and he loved his works. "Over *Treasure Island* I let my fire die in winter without knowing that I was freezing." Many would of course say that he was attracted to what he saw in Stevenson because he was himself the ultimate Peter Pan, an identification made for instance by Max Beerbohm and John Skinner in articles with the definitive titles, "The Child Barrie" and "James M. Barrie, or The Boy Who Wouldn't Grow Up." Yet Barrie did not altogether approve of the boyish insouciance of Stevenson. In a humorous sketch of how it might have been had the two ever met, Barrie describes his original inclination to suspect this man in a velvet suit and with a manner "doggedly debonair," though resistance eventually capitulated to his smile. Barrie wasn't happy with Stevenson's philosophy of life, which is, he says, "that we are but as the lighthearted birds. This is our moment of being; let us play the intoxicating game of life beautifully, artistically, before we fall dead from the tree." The philosopher could be Peter, who is youth and joy and "a little bird that has broken out of the egg" (*PP*, p. 221). Barrie says that the keynote of Stevenson's writing is an indifference to matters of life and death. He says he looks forward to a great book from Stevenson after all the wonderful "little" books, but "He will have to take existence a little more seriously."[21]

The curious thing is that *Peter Pan* is a more serious book than *Treasure Island*. Whereas, essentially, as Richard Aldington says, "an adult can get nothing more from *Treasure Island* than a boy does," *Peter Pan* is a boys' book not only for boys. Though Stevenson's book is "serious like a game properly and strenuously played," it is not a serious statement about "existence."[22] Neverland adventures are only pretend; yet Barrie's book is very much about matters of life and death because it is about the loss of the island and the loss of childhood. To grow up is to hear the clock ticking for you, like Hook; to be "dead and forgotten," like Mrs. Darling (*PP*, p. 246); to be replaced by your daughter in Peter's affection, like Wendy, and she by her daughter after her. Good form means absorption in the shape of the moment, taking it absolutely for granted as when playing or dreaming. Peter lives eternally because for him each moment is all there is. But Barrie calls him "heartless," and he calls him "tragic" (*PP*, p. 251) for the same reason. In notes for a never-written play (c. 1922) Barrie recalls the desperation that is part of Peter Pan's situation: "It is as if, long after writing P. Pan, its true meaning came back to me, desperate attempt to grow up but can't." Peter sneers at the "laws of nature" as figured by mothers (*PP*, p. 234), who represent the cycle of life that transforms a child into someone who has children into someone finished off altogether. Comparing the essays of Lamb and Stevenson, Barrie places Lamb higher because "he did not play at pretending that there is no cemetery around the corner." One cannot quite get away with being an eternal boy, it seems, for even Peter has mysterious bad dreams and cries in his sleep, and Stevenson writes books that are marvelous good form but "to those who want more than art for art's sake, never satisfying."[23]

In *Sir James Barrie* Harry M. Geduld sums up the prevailing modern reaction to Barrie's works: "serious critical interest in his novels and plays has recently been hostile, when it has not been negligible or non-existent." Since the waning of the tremendous popularity that he enjoyed in his lifetime, Barrie has been of interest, if at all, mainly biographically, for his pathology. His personal oddities were made for Freudian critics: his love for his mother; his short stature; his take-over of somebody else's children and the extravagance of his immersion in the games he created for them; his idealization of women, which kept him at safe arm's length from them; his probable impotence; his divorce. Because he himself was preoccupied with childhood (in some ways doubtless even arrested in childhood), a misleading simplification has been practiced on his most famous work: *Peter Pan* is taken as representing the charming fulfillment of the desire for perpetual childhood, being as such sentimental and even neurotic. Only very recently, with Alison Lurie's essay in *The New York Review of Books*, has a voice been raised contrary to the general chorus. Lurie attributes to Barrie a more self-conscious and even self-critical treatment of the theme of childhood than he has been given credit for before. She bases her analysis on *Tommy and Grizel* and *Mary Rose*. Her reading of *Peter Pan* is more conventional however since it stresses the attraction of eternal youth, whereas I think that here too the attraction (and surely it is attractive—we shouldn't be so bent on psychological well adjustment as to deny that) is explored in large part as a *dilemma*. It is worth dipping into the play version to illustrate Barrie's undercutting of a position like Peter's. Peter has no weight, he doesn't eat, and he can't be touched. There is pathos, even tragedy, in his isolation from the life force. When she leaves him, Wendy says she would like to give him a hug. He half understands, as the author tells us between the lines of dialogue: "If he could get the hang of the thing, his cry might become 'To live would be an awfully big adventure!' but he can never quite get the hang of it." There has been considerable distaste of Peter's line in both play and novel: "To die will be an awfully big adventure." It should be realized that no matter what his life—or maybe because of his life—Barrie was aware of and more than hints at the sterility, and even morbidity, of the ideal of perpetual youth.[24]

An index of the ambivalence, far from naive, of his attitude toward childishness as a way of life is the sophisticated self-reflexiveness—more possible in the novel than the play and thus giving the novel the fuller resonance—in his handling of boys'-book formulas a way of literature.[25] *Treasure Island* is the sea-dream pure and fine, its apotheosis. *Peter Pan* is the dream's deathblow, elegy, and obsessive half-life, artfully rendered in the medium of bad form. Just about everything that happens in Neverland has happened before in books. But these things can never happen again in the same way for the grown-up narrator and the grown-up reader. Barrie makes it all the harder for us to play the dream straight, to beach our coracles one more time.

Notes

1. Robert Louis Stevenson, "A Gossip on Romance" (1882), *The Works of Robert Louis Stevenson*, South Seas ed. (New York: Scribner's, 1925), XIII, p. 136.

2. *Stevenson's Works*, VI; this is the book version of 1883, slightly modified from the serial version appearing in *Young Folks*, 1881-1882. Page references appear in parentheses in the text, identified as *TI*.

3. "Gossip," *Stevenson's Works*, XIII, p. 132.

4. I use the novel version published in 1911 as *Peter Pan and Wendy* (*The Works of J. M. Barrie*, Peter Pan ed. [New York: Scribner's, 1930], IX (page references appear in the text identified as *PP*), more commonly known since as *Peter Pan*. The play first appeared in 1904, though it was not published until 1928, after a good deal of modification. In the novel version, there is the very substantial addition of a narrative voice, which would not figure on stage, and which complicates the story's character and especially its implied audience. As Roger Lancelyn Green says in *Fifty Years of Peter Pan* (London: Peter Davies, 1954), p. 115, there are passages in the novel more understandable to adults than to children, who might be put off by Barrie's elusive prose style. The theme of bad form is absent from the play as are the demise of Mrs. Darling and other elements of the mortality theme that conclude the novel. Barrie did write an additional act showing Wendy grown up and beyond flying, but it was only performed once in 1908. I find the novel more interesting and complex in style and theme. It is also the version sold in children's bookstores as *Peter Pan*, although once having read it one is a little surprised to have found it there.

5. Authors of the additional titles listed are, in order: James F. Bowman, Catherine Traill, Percy St. John, Mayne Reid (with this title in 1858, but first published in 1852), Agnes Strickland, and W.H.G. Kingston. Interesting histories of the Robinsonnade appear in J. Harvey Darton, *Children's Books in England, Five Centuries of Social Life*, 2nd ed. (Cambridge: Cambridge University Press, 1958), pp. 114-20; in Eric Quayle, *The Collector's Book of Boys' Stories* (London: Cassell & Collier Macmillan, 1973); in Harold Francis Watson, *Coasts of Treasure Island, A Study of the Backgrounds and Sources for Robert Louis Stevenson's Romance of the Sea* (San Antonio, Texas: Naylor, 1969). Stevenson lists some specific sources for *Treasure Island* in "My First Book" (1894), *Stevenson's Works*, VI, pp. xxv-

xxxiv: the parrot comes from *Robinson Crusoe* (1719); the pirates from Defoe's *Pyrates* (1724, under the pseudonym of Charles Johnson); Billy Bones and the first chapters from Washington Irving's *Tales of a Traveller* (1824); the stockade from Marryat's *Masterman Ready* (1841-1842); the skeleton pointer from Poe (probably the *Gold Bug* [1843]); the Dead Man's Chest from Kingsley's *At Last, A Christmas in the West Indies* (1871).

6. Quayle, p. 62; Darton, p. 318; "R.L.S.," in *Margaret Ogilvy* (1896), *Barrie's Works*, VIII, p. 85.

7. "Gossip," *Stevenson's Works*, XIII, pp. 141, 134; Marryat (London: Dent, 1896), pp. 5-6.

8. Samuel Bracebridge Hemyng, *Among the Pirates and on the Island of Palms*, Harkaway Series, V (London: Hogarth House, n.d.), pp. 120, 119.

9. Ann Bowman, *Boy Voyagers* (1859).

10. "Gossip," *Stevenson's Works*, XIII, pp. 140-42.

11. "Gossip," *Stevenson's Works*, XIII, p. 132.

12. The parallel between Ben Gunn and Robinson Crusoe has often been noticed. Gunn seems to caricature Crusoe, with his piety and filial devotion dating from his residence on the island. This passage almost suggests the tongue in the cheek, though as most critics agree, *Treasure Island* is straightforward and without irony in its overall impact. Robert Kiely says it has the ingenuousness of Blake's "Songs of Innocence" or Wordsworth's "We Are Seven,"in (*Robert Louis Stevenson and the Fiction of Adventure* (Cambridge, Mass.: Harvard Univ. Press, 1964), p. 80. Richard Aldington makes a similar observation; [see n. 22]. Also [see n. 22] on the minimal moral depth of *Treasure Island*.

13. On the pirate tradition as it influenced Stevenson see Watson, also John Robert Moore, "Defoe, Stevenson, and the Pirates," *ELH*, 10 (1943), 35-60.

14. Byron, "The Corsair," *Complete Poetical Works of Lord Byron*, Students Cambridge ed. (Boston: Houghton Mifflin, 1933), pp. 337-66; canto and stanza references appear in parentheses in the text.

15. Hemyng, pp. 119-120; Ballantyne, *The Coral Island, A Tale of the Pacific Ocean*, illus. Daziel (London: T. Nelson, 1874), p. 255; Marryat, *The Pirate and the Three Cutters* (London: Seeley, n.d.), p. 51. Watson notes that Stevenson hated Marryat's *Pirate* but counts it as an influence since it made so strong an impression (p. 172).

16. Ballantyne, p. 260.

17. "Fenimore Cooper's Literary Offences," *The Complete Humorous Sketches and Tales of Mark Twain*, ed. Charles Neider, illus. Mark Twain (Garden City, New York: Hanover House, 1961), pp. 633-34.

18. Janet Dunbar, *J. M. Barrie, The Man Behind the Image* (Boston: Houghton Mifflin, 1970), p. 165. Peter Davies was the youngest of the three Davies brothers with whom Barrie played out many of the adventures that go into *Peter Pan* at Black Lake near his Surrey home in the summer of 1901. These adventures were photographed by Barrie, who then made them up into a manuscript book, virtually without text, called "The Boy Castaways of Black Lake Island" and attributed to the editorship of the small Peter. After their parents' death, Barrie took all five Davies boys under his wing.

19. Of course a hardy literary tradition often shows itself impervious to its *coup de grace*, as notably, in Arthur Ransome's *Swallows and Amazons* (1931) and Scott O'Dell's *Island of the Blue Dolphins* (1960). In my view William Golding's *Lord of the Flies* (1954) is more original than these, a continuation that is also a new departure.

20. "R.L.S.," in *Margaret Ogilvy, Barrie's Works*, VIII, pp. 94-95 (Stevenson as "spirit of boyhood" and as Jim Hawkins). Refuters of the Stevenson-as-boy theory are: David Daiche, *Robert Louis Stevenson* (Norwalk, Conn.: New Directions, 1947); Kiely, *Stevenson and the Fiction of Adventure*; and Edwin Eigner, *Robert Louis Stevenson and Romantic Tradition* (Princeton, N. J.: Princeton University Press, 1965). Eigner hardly talks about *Treasure Island*, which is odd in a book treating the romance tradition in prose fiction. He seems to lend Stevenson respectability by ignoring the boys' book romance, which is largely what Stevenson understands and praises as romance in his "Gossip," even though he had been more critical of pure adventure stories without moral resonance eight years earlier in "Victor Hugo's Romances" (1874 *Works of Robert Louis Stevenson* [New York: Bigelow and Smith, 1906]. X, pp. 13-35). *R.L.S. To J.M. Barrie, A Vailima Portrait*, introd. Bradford Booth (San Francisco: Book Club of California, 1962), p. 3.

21. "Robert Louis Stevenson," in *An Edinburgh Eleven* (1889), *Barrie's Works*, VIII, p. 249. Lady Cynthia Asquith, his secretary and close friend, is one of the few to deny a boyish streak in Barrie (she says she doubts he ever was a boy [Dunbar, p. 307]). There was a time when he was congratulated for keeping his child's heart, as in a 1905 review in *Outlook*, where he is named the successor of Stevenson in this respect (Dunbar, pp. 176-177). But Beerbohm (1905 review, rprt. in *Around Theaters* [New York: Simon and Schuster, 1959], pp. 357-361), and Skinner (*American Imago*, 14 [1957], 111-142) represent the trend toward devaluing his presumed childishness. Martin Grotjahn, in "Defenses Against Creative Anxiety in the Life and Work of James Barrie"—a commentary on Skinner's article (*American Imago*, 14 [1957], 143-148), carries Skinner's psychoanalysis to its damaging conclusion—that Barrie's immaturity led to bad writing. Harry M. Geduld says much the same in *Sir James Barrie* (New York: Twayne, 1971). Barrie's letter to Miss Masson. December 1922, *Letters of J. M. Barrie*, ed. Viola Meynell (New York: Scribners, 1947), p. 251; "Robert Louis Stevenson," *Barrie's Works*, VIII, 254, 257.

22. Aldington, *Portrait of a Rebel, The Life and Work of Robert Louis Stevenson* (London: Evans Brothers, 1957), p. 143; G. S. Fraser, "Afterword." *Treasure Island* (New York: Signet, 1965), p. 213. There is some disagreement as to the moral depth of *Treasure Island*. In *Stevenson and the Art of Fiction* (New York: privately printed, 1951), pp. 9-10. Daiches finds interesting moral ambiguity in Long John Silver; Kiely, pp. 42-80, discounts such profundities and talks about the classicism, formalism, abstraction of Stevenson's early work, which approaches pure ritual or design, he says. Daiches (*Robert Louis Stevenson*, p. 34) and Kiely (p. 71) agree, however, that *Treasure Island* shows no serious concern with the issue of mortality.

23. Dunbar, p. 362; "Robert Louis Stevenson," *Barrie's Works*, VIII, 256, 254.

24. Geduld, "Preface, *Barrie's Works*, X, 145; Lurie, "The Boy Who Couldn't Grow Up," *New York Review of Books*, XXII (February 6, 1975), 11-15.

25. See n. 4.

22

E. Nesbit's Well Hall, 1915-1921

A Memoir

JOAN EVANS DE ALONSO

God gives us memory so that we may have roses in December.
—*Sir James Barrie*

More than fifty years have elapsed since we lived at Well Hall, Eltham, with E. Nesbit, in the unforgettable atmosphere of that household and its surroundings. It had already seen its heyday, and since the death of her husband, Hubert Bland, the financial pinch had been acutely felt. Old friends found it more difficult to visit, and it was war time. My mother, separated from my father, went to Well Hall to help E. Nesbit (Mrs. Bland to all of us, and later Mrs. Tucker when she remarried) run an elaborate and very modern poultry farm. My mother had had some training in the latest techniques. The old stables and back yard at Well Hall were duly set up for that purpose. To help the household finances, E. Nesbit was already selling garden produce to munitions workers at the nearby Woolwich Arsenal and to the Government as provisions for the two local hospitals.

It was arranged that my mother would join the enterprise as soon as my sister and I went away to boarding school in Huntingdonshire in the fall of 1915. During our school vacations, we children, my two brothers, Geoffrey and Ronald, my sister, Margrey, and I were to be P.G.'s (Paying Guests) at Well Hall. Hopefully we would be good companions (and we were) for E. Nesbit's adopted son, John, and for her granddaughter, Pandora.

John was the natural son of her husband, Hubert Bland, and his secretary, Miss Hoatson, commonly known as Mouse. Mouse was still living at Well Hall when we first went there, and remained I think until E. Nesbit remarried in 1917. This diminutive, vivacious, and competent little woman, with her big brown eyes and mop of grey hair, was, when we arrived, the pivot of all the functional and complicated household finances at Well Hall.

The poultry farm, despite modern know-how, failed almost before it began. There was a shortage and rationing of chicken feed, and the hens, oblivious to the artificial lighting, refused to produce the projected two eggs every twenty-four hours. Furthermore, the water rats living in the moat killed off the hens at an alarming rate, and this soon ended the ill-fated enterprise. After that, mother did wartime work at a local munitions factory and we all made our home at Well Hall.

As I write, many long-forgotten incidents come to mind. In moments of psychological insecurity, childhood memories often bring unsuspected resources of personality. Many are the times I have savored the recollection of our first arrival at Well Hall.

It was at the beginning of the Christmas holiday in December, 1915. Mother met us girls at Liverpool Street Station and shuttled us across London to take a train down to Blackheath where we had to change for the Well Hall station. My brothers, each at a different Public School in the south of England, made it on their own. We all arrived without luggage and therefore with no ration coupons, an occurrence whose continued repetition was to become an endless annoyance. On the way, mother told us something about Well Hall and E. Nesbit. We had read some of her books. She also spoke to us about other people who were living at Well Hall, and especially about John Bland. In 1915 John was a day boy at St. Paul's School in London. He was a real loner and often very sullen, but for us he became another brother. He and Geoffrey grew to be the most intimate of friends. In the early years John would often carry my little sister on his shoulders, give his hand to his niece, Pandora, and tell me to hang on to his coat tails while he took us all over London to see the sights. We were indeed a strange foursome.

That first night we assembled for supper in the dining room, the old Hall, where a long oval table was placed lengthwise in front of a roaring fire. The table looked gay; there was the smell of food and the chatter of voices; everything radiated warmth. But we were bewildered. Grown-ups gathered; there were other P.G.s besides ourselves, and we children, seven to nine strong, as always, congregated at the far end of the table. And then E. Nesbit appeared on the stairway. She was fifty-seven at this time, rather stout, and dressed in flowing sort of dress not unlike today's Caftan, with a kind of longish oriental coat. She wore Turkish slippers and quantities of jangling bangles—she always wore those—reaching almost up to her elbows. Her face was small, her voice warm and soft. Her wispy hair was parted in the middle and knotted in a kind of bun at the back. She wore large spectacles and carried under her arm a box—she was seldom without it—in which was a tin of tobacco, cigarette paper, and a long quill cigarette holder.

She seemed to take us for granted, although she had never seen us before. I don't remember any introductions, but when the meal was served we most certainly were not ignored. One of the great things about life at Well Hall was that we were so much a part of it. We listened to real, palpitating conversations, and we gave our opinions as definitely as the rest. What a contrast to the very strict and conventional boarding school where we spent nine months of the year! Looking back, it seems to me that we lived far, far ahead of our time.

After dinner that night, as he was so often wont to do, Mrs. Bland suggested to John that he carry up some logs and light a fire in the drawing room, which was on the second floor. As he somewhat sulkily carried the basket of logs up the stairs, he dropped one. So far he hadn't said a word to any of us. He had just glared at us. I picked up the log and threw it at him. Furiously, he dumped down the basket and proceeded to chase me. We all became involved in the scuffle, and the ice was broken forever.

I don't remember what we played that night, but nearly always there was something exciting after dinner, in which all ages participated on equal terms, no matter who was visiting. For many old friends, Fabianists and budding poets and playwrights and other writers still came to visit Mrs. Bland. Bernard Shaw and H.G. Wells made frequent appearances at first, but as the war drew on and the old Fabian Group became less closely knit we saw them and the others less often. Whoever came, in any case, might join us in charades (very complicated, often, and inspired by our hostess), dumb-crambo, or rhyming games. Nouns and Adjectives was a great favorite to get everybody started. "The pot was beginning with G: the pot was Golden," Mrs. Bland would say, throwing a little ball to somebody, and then the person to whom the ball was thrown had to add another G-adjective, and so it went on. She excelled at rhyming games, patience, and chess, and she loved to play whist. A game that we played too often to suit me was "Devil in the Dark," a glorified form of hide and seek, in which one of the hiders had been marked in some way different from the others. One had to touch the person being found and feel his head to find out if he were the Devil. I was always terrified and hated it.

The time we spent at Well Hall had extraordinary impact on our lives. Here it was that we learned about the world, grew up, saw our boys become men and go to war, come home on leave, sometimes wounded, or not return at all. Around us we witnessed the destruction of the air-raids, and from the garden wall we watched the arrival of hospital trains at the little local station. We visited and entertained the wounded; we experienced the horrors, destruction, and deprivations of war. We saw the old house gradually become more decrepit, but we also watched a melancholy Mrs. Bland emerge from the shadow of her three years of widowhood into the security and support of her courtship and marriage with the Blands' old socialist friend, Mr. T. T. Tucker, the Skipper. We participated in good adult conversation at meals and in the imaginative activities that pervaded the household. We ran wild in what appeared to be limitless space on the very outskirts of London.

What a training ground for life! What wonderful times we had there, where the order of the day—of our daily life—was shadowed, prodded, and shared by E. Nesbit's warm, enveloping personality. We grew up feeling the financial pinch, which was everywhere, but somehow the lack of money didn't really matter. Thrift and ingenuity were a cult: meanness was abhorred. People, laughter, games, fun, good conversation—there was plenty of all these. And however small and unimportant one was, if he had something worthwhile to say, he was always listened to and encouraged to express himself. Wartime food and rationing, the chanciness of meals, the emphasis on enjoyment, and the challenge of the unexpected: what better preparation for life in the twentieth century?

The spacious old eighteenth-century house we lived in, built over some much older flagstones, has been long since demolished. The site is now a park with a bandstand; when I last saw it the plans were for a children's library to be built upon the grounds, in memory of E. Nesbit. The flagstones, some dated 1586, are still there where the Hall stood in front of the little arched bridge—in earlier times undoubtedly a drawbridge—that joins the Moat Garden to the main grounds. In the sixteenth century this property belonged to the Roper Estate. Margaret Roper was Sir Thomas More's daughter, and legend has it that when he was beheaded in the Tower and his head placed on a spike by the river, Margaret rowed up the Thames, stole her father's head, brought it home, and buried it in the Moat Garden.

Well Hall as we knew it was said to have been built by George III. His watchmaker had lived in the lower part and one of the monarch's ex-mistresses was kept in seclusion on the top floor, where E. Nesbit was later to have her study and bedroom. The poor lady whiled away the time by playing the spinet. It was she who haunted the house, who sighed so loudly on the stairway. I heard her once and shivered.

Wings had been added to the main house, so that the ground floor sprawled out on both sides of the central Hall, the dining room in our day. This Hall had five doors. The main front entrance was seldom opened—the cold blast from outside was too much. A sign read, "The Front Door Is The Back Door," that is, the rear entrance from the Moat Garden side. This entrance gave onto a long passageway, flanked on each side by the bedrooms, that ran into the Hall. Besides the five doors, the Hall had the enormous well of the stairway, and the stairway which ended in the Hall. The walls were well over three feet thick, and there was but one large paned-glass window. During the air raids, we gathered in the Hall to play the most exciting games of "Demon"—a sort of group patience—by light of a flickering candle.

We were absolutely forbidden to go down to the moat level alone, unless of course we were in the punt. Beyond the crescent in front of the house ran the Eltham-Woolwich road, and a cottage stood at each side of the entrance. At first my mother lived in the cottage on the right, but as the war continued, she moved into the main house. All this had been demolished, but on the far side of the moat the old Tudor barn still stands, with a perfect example of an original Tudor fireplace.

Our life during the summer was mostly spent on the moat. The boys, some years older than we girls, would tie us up and shove us off in the old punt with no paddle. But Pandora, my sister, and I soon became experts at rocking ourselves to places of help. On ropes knotted to the old trees that shaded the moat we would swing out and try to kick the far barn wall. We read under the shade of these trees, argued, and played badminton and other games.

Few other restrictions were placed on us, but many a warning or reminder was posted in rhyme and signed by Mrs. Bland with her initials, E. B., formed into a fourleaved clover. A good example is the poem, "The Order of the Bath":

> We know Hygeia's votary refrains
> From throwing matches down the drain,
> Yet some there be who must be better taught,
> Don't use Hygeia's temple as they ought.
> They leave the fountains dripping, bang the door,
> And pour libations on the temple floor,
> Not in the vessel which her Grace provides
> For votaries to scour their foul outsides.
> Who, in the madness of life's low pursuits,
> Invades the temple in his muddy boots?
> And, with the impiety the gods abhor,
> Rubs off the mud upon the temple floor
> (And even on the temple's mat once whiter
> Than snow—the impious, sacrilegious blighter!)
> Who shuts the windows, that the steam may fall
> In tears and slowly sap the temple wall?
> Who strews old shoes about the bather's path?

Who leaves the soapy water in the bath?
Miscreants, repent! And sin this year no more!
With reverent heart approach the bathroom door;
Thus shall Hygeia's blessing still attend
Upon you till one-nine-two-one shall end.

And though we were left free and wild to amuse and fend for ourselves, we were expected to appear for meals. The sound of the first gong meant "Wash-up." At the clang of the second, five minutes later, we were looked for at the table, neat, clean, and civil, at the evening meal in clean clothes, and no squabbling allowed!

Food rationing required that we each have or own colored jar with our ration of sugar, and the same for butter or margarine. A certain amount was taken from each ration every week for cooking purposes. No swapping was allowed until Thursday; then the bargaining began. Cooking, whenever possible, was done in a hay-box cooker. This was a large insulated box with two round, deep holes. The food, after having been brought to a boil in special long, round casseroles, went into the box between preheated iron discs; the lid was sealed tightly, and the casseroles left to cook for hours.

How the whole domestic running of the household was managed, I just don't know. Help came and left; the maids' sitting room became another bedroom, occupied by another P.G. I do remember a boy of about eleven, a cook's son, called Pelham, walking backwards and falling into a large crock of hot marmalade. His knickers were scraped and the marmalade, made with everybody's precious sugar, was reboiled and served. After that, when the marmalade was passed around at breakfast, one said politely, "Have some Pelham!"

In spite of the wartime shortages, E. Nesbit, who loved to prepare delightful surprises, would organize fancy dress dances for us, always using what was on hand. That was half the fun. She would spend hours on the most minute detail, showing more enthusiasm than any youngster. Some evenings she would sit down at the piano and play songs. "Rolling down the Medway" was a great favorite, and we would all sing lustily. Often the carpet would be rolled back for dancing. At other times she would play old sailor ditties to please Mr. Tucker.

Sometimes days would pass without our seeing her. She would be up all night writing, trying to meet some deadline. It was then that she could be ill-humored, though not for long. John would say, "Look out, Mother is casting a gloom." And was she ever! She could be as cantankerous as her own cantankerous Psammead, but in all fairness it was seldom. When *we* started to quarrel, she would produce this magnificent advice: "Try to say nothing. Once you begin you don't know how to stop."

E. Nesbit had many whims. She adored flattery and loved to shock people. But though we often regarded her with awe and bewilderment, she inspired our love and affection. She liked to be embraced, and embraced us often and called us "dear," which I relished, since it was something my own family never did. She smoked like a trooper. She suffered from bronchitis and asthma and so did I. Many times when we were both ill I would be invited to sit in her room and listen to her stories, help in making a dress or mending a sheet, or I would be handed a large magnifying glass and told to see if I could find a pig in some old engraving or print of Shakespeare. She was an enthusiastic Baconian.

Many memories surge up: the hours I spent playing with pieces of the Magic City, scattered and abandoned in the attic; the ritual of washing up the teacups with Mrs. Bland in the dining room in a wooden bowl—a very feminine undertaking and a high privilege—; weeping with her as we saw the first Zeppelin that came down in flames and watched the black human shapes fall from the burning wreck; the unexploded bomb the boys found in the garden that had to be detonated; the piece of shrapnel she found on the pillow beside my sister's head when she came to wake us up because there was an air raid, and my sister in her blue bloomers walking along the high Moat-Garden wall, picking up the red bricks and throwing them down angrily at my brothers in the punt on the moat below. The wall still stands; the bricks are still missing. So much living surrounded us, and so much destruction and death: the comings and goings of so many people long since forgotten.

E. Nesbit's greatest gift to us children was that she, this very talented and busy woman, was generous—generous with herself, her time, her pleasures, her friends, her flowers, her fun. She seemed to have time for us all, to need us, to enjoy us. This little poem, written to console us three young girls when the boys went back up to college—the war was over then—may help to give some idea of the freshness with which she handled and charmed many situations:

> *Jan. 19th, 1920. The Boys Go Up to Cambridge.*
> Darlings, Margery, Avril and Joan!
> Now the boys have left us alone
> We will not grieve and make rainy weather
> But put on our hats and go out together.
>
> We will not grieve about Fortune's malice
> But hurry away to the picture Palace
> Where the jolliest pictures are shown

Darlings Avril, Margery, and Joan.

We will not cry for our lost boy Cambs
But go and return by Electric Trams.
That tram conductor shall not hear a groan
Darlings Margery, Avril and Joan.

And then perhaps—I don't know—we'll see—
We *might* go down to the Ferry for tea.
A jollier idea could hardly be known
Darlings, Avril, Margery and Joan.

And we did go down to the Ferry for tea, where the Skipper, dear Mr. Tucker, served his Mate, as he often called her, and the three of us with a wonderful tea.

23

An Epic in Arcadia

The Pastoral World of *The Wind in the Willows*

GERALDINE D. POSS

Throughout Kenneth Grahame's two collections of short stories, *The Golden Age* and *Dream Days*, his narrator writes fondly of the romantic characters that he, his brothers, and his sisters read about during their childhood. The children liked to choose roles and act out the Arthurian romances, and on the particular day described below, Harold, the youngest boy, seized the occasion of his oldest brother's absence to be Sir Lancelot. Charlotte insisted on being Tristram, and the narrator, who was more inclined that day to dream than to act, accepted a subordinate role without protest:

> "I don't care," I said: "I'll be anything. I'll be Sir Kay. Come on!"
> Then once more in this country's story the mail-clad knights paced through the greenwood shaw, questing adventure, redressing wrong; and bandits, five to one, broke and fled discomfited to their caves. Once again, were damsels rescued, dragons disembowelled, and giants, in every corner of the orchard, deprived of their already superfluous number of heads.... The varying fortune of the day swung doubtful!—now on this side, now on that; till at last Lancelot, grim and great, thrusting through the press, unhorsed Sir Tristram (an easy task), and bestrode her, threatening doom; while the Cornish knight, forgetting hard-won fame of old, cried piteously, "You're hurting me, I tell you! and you're tearing my frock!"[1]

The nostalgia, mock-heroism, and affection expressed in this passage are typical of Grahame's attitude toward romance. He equates the innocence of the children with its ideal world and, to the extent that both are irretrievable, the equation is valid. But he is also aware that the worlds of Homer and Malory are fallen; heroes need villains in order to demonstrate their valor. And he knows that it is only through the uncritical eyes of childhood that the heroic world can truly seem Utopian. For Grahame, the innocent, green world of Arcadia is by far the more appealing, and from time to time, quite casually, in the short stories, he allows us a glimpse of it as it was perceived by the uncomprehending child. Though the Arcadian vision remains intermittent and basically undeveloped in the stories, we can find in them the elements—both positive and negative—that would eventually lead Grahame to fashion the sweet epic in Arcadia that exists in *The Wind in the Willows*.

"The Roman Road," another story in *The Golden Age*, outlines the Arcadian alternative at its most poignant and melancholy. The narrator opens by relating how on a day "when things were very black within" (p. 156) he took a walk along a road which he felt might truly, as the proverb promised, lead to Rome. He meets an artist who, by some coincidence, claims to spend half his year there, and the little boy begins asking questions about the city. As the conversation develops, it becomes evident that the place they are discussing is a creation of fantasy only, and that its inhabitants are those people who have for some reason had to leave the world of poor, working mortals:

> "Well, there's Lancelot," I went on. "The book says he died, but it never seemed to read right, somehow. He just went away, like Arthur. And Crusoe, when he got tired of wearing clothes and being respectable. And all the nice men in the stories who don't marry the Princess, 'cos only one man ever gets married in a book, you know. They'll be there!"
>
> "And the men who never come off," he said, "who try like the rest, but get knocked out, or somehow miss,—or break down or get bowled over in the *mêlée*,—and get no Princess, nor even a second-class kingdom,—some of them'll be there, I hope?" (pp. 165-66)

The world which they envision is one which simply ignores death, women, and pressure to achieve. Rejecting the idea of his death, the little boy includes Lancelot, but it is clearly with the others, the gentle folk who never made it as heroes, that the adult narrator has the greatest affinity. And perhaps such types struck a respondent chord in that hero-worshipping little boy too, who so easily bypassed Arthur and Gawain to slip into the subsidiary role of Sir Kay. If we hear a wistful note here, about not getting the princess and fighting the dragons, we sense relief too, for there is something foolish and even vaguely repellent to the writer in all that activity, and he can imagine a much more satisfactory world, without the "alarums and excursions." His "reluctant dragon," a sensible spokesman for pacifism, elsewhere explains to the earnest and perplexed St. George why he will not participate in a contest:

> "Believe me, St. George," [he says]. "There's nobody in the world I'd sooner oblige than you and this young gentleman here. But the whole thing's nonsense, and conventionality, and popular thick-headedness. There's absolutely nothing to fight about from beginning to end. And anyhow I'm not going to, so that settles it!"[2]

What the dragon seeks, and what finally moves him to agree to fight and succumb on the third charge, is a chance to socialize with the villagers, narrow-minded though they may be, and to find a sympathetic audience for his poetry.

If only one man can win the princess, it seems implicit in the little boy's statement that he did not expect—nor perhaps want—to be that man. The narrator, and by inference Grahame, reveals his ambivalence about women throughout his essays, in the distaste he evinces for the typical female behavior of his older sister Selina and for the tendencies he occasionally notes in his younger sister Charlotte to follow in her footsteps—even though the little girl was still smart enough in *The Golden Age* to want to be Tristram rather than Iseult. In "The Finding of the Princess," another essay in that volume, Grahame approaches the issue with his characteristic charm and indirectness, reflecting upon the subject with perhaps as much light as he was willing to give it.

A boy is walking alone through a wood which leads to a garden. All his literary experience tells him that it is in such places that princesses are found, and notwithstanding his disdain for his sisters, he approaches hopefully:

> Conditions declared her presence patently as trumpets; without this centre such surrounding could not exist.... There, if any-where, she should be enshrined. Instinct, and some knowledge of the habits of princesses, triumphed; for (indeed) there She was! In no tranced repose, however, but laughingly, struggling to dis-engage her hand from the grasp of a grown-up man who occupied the marble bench with her. (pp. 56-57)

The man asks amiably where he "sprang from"; he replies that he "came up stream" in search of the princess, and then adds: " 'But she's wide awake, so I suppose somebody kissed her.' This very natural deduction moved the grown-up man to laughter; but the Princess, turning red and jumping up, declared that it was time for lunch" (p. 58). Indulging his own whimsy, the young man dubs him "water baby," and invites him to stay for the meal. Thus, the little boy is able to sustain his fantasy through the afternoon. When he finally leaves the couple, at their gentle suggestion, the man gives him two half-crowns, "for the other water babies," and the princess gives him a kiss. The story ends as the child drifts into a pleasant sleep, filled with dreams of this kiss. But the narrator notes that at the time he was actually more affected by the man's generosity, which he described (no pun, I think, intended) as a "crowning mark of friendship" (p. 60). This is understandable: a gift not for oneself but for one's friends is a gesture of regard and affection much easier to accept gracefully than an inevitably embarrassing kiss. But the judgment also suggests that the magic the child had tried so hard to attach to his real princess ultimately failed him. She was not as satisfying as the dream into which he finally incorporated her. From the very start the scene was wrong; the princess was awake, and maybe just a bit too awkward and embarrassed herself. How much more beautiful it would have been had she been asleep.

Heroism, heterosexual love, and death—all are approached gingerly, with occasional humor and gentle irony, in the stories of the 1890s. But a decade later, in *The Wind in the Willows*, Grahame finally develops a golden age of his own imagining rather than Malory's, and the ambivalence is, in his own way, resolved.[3] The ideal world that blossoms in his novel is like the world at the end of the Roman Road. It is an unpressured world of good-natured fellows who eschew nonsensical fighting. And as for the princess, no one need worry about competing for her, or living with her once she has awakened, for she is simply not there. What remains is an Arcadian world bounded by a lovely river, a Wild Wood that really threatens no evil, and a Wide World that one need never bother about at all. Through his book Grahame weaves the gentler trappings of epic, dividing it into a classical twelve chapters, but omitting from the work all aspects of the heroic life that might cause strife and pain and eventually death.

The book opens, in the epic manner, with a statement of theme: it is to be about the "spirit of divine discontent and longing," a spirit so strong in spring that it reaches to the "dark and lowly little house" of the domestic Mole, luring him out in search of some gentle adventure.[4] Later this same spirit draws him back home, if only for a visit, and this we recognize as the epic pattern in little: the journey out and the journey back. As in picture books, it is diminutive and relatively safe, because it is a journey within an innocent pastoral milieu. At his most heroic, the childlike Mole must make his necessary passage to the Wild Wood, and the Rat must strap on his guns to follow him, but this too quickly leads to warmth and comfort and piles of buttered toast. The Rat is there to protect the Mole, the Badger to protect them both, and the ubiquitous Friend and Helper ultimately to protect them all.

With his creation of the Friend and Helper, Grahame has neatly seized control of the gods, scaling another epic problem down to comfortable size. In "The Olympians," prefaced to *The Golden Age*, he had characterized adults by their power to affect lives with their foolishness and petulance, to blame children for the wrong offenses, and to ignore those pleasures that beckoned so obviously to the young. The Homeric gods stood in a similar relation to men, exacting vengeance, playing favorites, and generating continual concern about sacrifice, devotion, and protocol. Such Olympians, whether as adults or gods, have been eliminated from *The Wind in the Willows*. The animals in Grahame's ideal world are truly innocent, and so they are spared the anguish that questioning, knowledge, and the inevitable desire to influence their fate would produce. What they have, instead, is the benign, all but unsexed figure of Pan, who sits at the center of the book, but demands no recognition and no offerings. And unlike the Olympian gods, who were always leaving awesome and intimidating signs of their presence—whether by dazzling men with their beauty, or by metamorphosing into birds at the ends of their earthly visits—Pan bestows the gift of forgetfulness, asking no thanks for his benevolence. Dimly, in the seventh chapter, the Rat can hear this song: "*Lest the awe should dwell—And turn your frolic to fret—You shall look on my power at the helping hour—But then you shall forget*" (p. 132). And as he and the Mole move closer, the Rat says finally: "This time, at last, it is the real, the unmistakable thing, simple—passionate—perfect" (p. 132). But he cannot repeat it and shortly falls asleep, as the song fades into the gentle reed talk produced by the wind in the willows.

Grahame, who could never find a lady to match the sleeping princess of romance, and who was evidently unhappy in his own marriage,[5] wisely disposed of these instruments of the gods as one more safeguard against unhappiness. Occasionally, in his descriptive passages, his prose will carry him past the limits of his chaste, bachelor's paradise, and he will celebrate the sexual aspect of the natural cycles: "June at last was here. One member of the company was still awaited; the shepherd-boy for the nymphs to woo, the knight for whom the ladies waited at the window, the prince that was to kiss the sleeping summer back to life and love" (p. 42). But the passion he alludes to metaphorically is utterly missing (or, as for the Rat, forgotten) in his animal world.

Laurence Lerner describes the two ways in which Arcadias can traditionally accommodate sex. The first is to offer fulfillment of desire; the second to eliminate desire all together.[6] But if, in the latter case, the characters must make a conscious effort to conquer or deny desire that they actually feel, then they are experiencing the rigors of asceticism and moving toward heroism again. The most natural path to a happy, asexual world is the path back to childhood, and Lerner translates a passage from Virgil's *Eclogues* which recalls this innocent state:

> When you were small I saw you (I was then your guide) with your mother, picking the dewy apples in our orchard. I had just entered the year after my eleventh year; already I could touch the delicate branches from the ground. I saw you and, ah, was lost: this wicked treachery of love caught me.

The world that Virgil regards with such sophisticated nostalgia is like the world of Grahame's child-men, who, despite their enjoyment of the manly and epic pleasures of hearth and home and a story well told, will never enter the year after their eleventh year. They may be threatened by the social upstarts from the Wild Wood,[8] but they will never have their Arcadia destroyed by the passion or treachery of love.

Yet even without the help of gods and women, the comic Toad manages to create a hell for himself. The most active character in this pastoral paradise, and the only actual wanderer, Toad is also the most shallow of the lot. Perhaps this is not completely ironic, for it reflects the single-minded intensity of purpose that the hero—or at any rate the man of action—needs in order to complete his task. And if Toad's only task is to heed that spirit of divine discontent and longing presumably wherever it takes him, Grahame nevertheless indicates that it should not be taking him where it is. His pursuit of activity and novelty for its own sake is not ennobling and heroic as Toad fancies, but rather a mischanneling of a natural instinct. The other animals may travel less, but they seem to be experiencing much more. Grahame has obvious affection for Toad (Green suggests that he represents the submerged bohemian in Grahame himself),[9] yet he is still demonstrating in Toad the problems of an unexamined life devoted to acquisition and external adventure in a world that is retreating further and further from nature.

Green writes that "most of Toad's adventures bear a certain ludicrous resemblance to Ulysses' exploits in the *Odyssey*; and the resemblance becomes detailed and explicit in the last chapter, which parodies the hero's return and the slaying of the suitors."[10] In general, however, *The Wind in the Willows* parallels epic in a way that is more reverential than parody is. Grahame is simply being eclectic about what he can include in his own ideal world. If Toad's adventures mimic those of Odysseus, the joke is almost always on Toad. He incorporates the hero's idiosyncracies, but he is all style, without the center of strength and intelligence of Odysseus, and without the hero's true capacity for anguish.

First and most obvious, Toad shares Odysseus' delight in singing his own praises. After he seizes the same motor car for the second time, he composes a small paean of praise to his resourcefulness:

> The motor-car went Poop-poop-poop,
>   As it raced along the road.
> Who was it steered it into a pond?
> Ingenious Mr. Toad! (p. 196)

Seconds later he realizes he is being pursued and shifts: "O my!... What an *ass* I am" (p. 197). While Odysseus taunts Polyphemus with the fact that it was he, "Odysseus, Sacker of Cities,"[11] who had blinded him, and never thinks to blame himself for the seven years on Calypso's island that the boast costs him, we are nevertheless aware of his compensating qualities. Without such arrogance, he would not be a sacker of cities, and had he not planned his escape from the Cyclops' cave, he and his men would have died. Had Toad, on the other hand, shown a little restraint, he might simply have spared himself and his friends a lot of trouble.

Toad's second seizure of the car followed what might have been a twenty-year jail term, rounded off by a magistrate of medieval speech patterns and Olympian irrationality ("fifteen years for the cheek" [p. 114]). It would have been an epic term, had he served it, the same length of time Odysseus spent away from home before Athene secured Zeus' permission to free him from Calypso. Toad's escape is likewise arranged through the efforts of a woman, the gaoler's daughter, who, like Athene (and perhaps Nausicaa?), appeals to her father for mercy and plans on her own to let him slip out, disguising his aristocratic toad's body in the clothing of a washerwoman, as Odysseus was disguised and withered, upon his return to Ithaca, to look like an old warrior.

Throughout *The Odyssey*, Odysseus longs for the pleasures of home, for his wife, and for the son he left in infancy. The longing tinges all his voyages with urgency and sadness, and the ambivalence lends depth to the character and the story. But for Toad there is never ambivalence; his exaggerated swings from joy to remorse seem due to an inability to accommodate two contrary states of feeling simultaneously. He loves his friends, but once he has left them, and until he gets into trouble, he forgets them completely. And neither is he nostalgic for his home. Instead, what seems to stir him is pride of ownership. His description to the gaoler's daughter—"Toad Hall ... is an eligible self-contained gentleman's residence, very unique; dating in part from the fourteenth century, but replete with every modern convenience" (p. 138)—is, as the lady says, more in the nature of a classified advertisement than an affectionate remembrance, and she replies perceptively: "Tell me something *real* about it" (p. 138).

Even the excitement of travel that he relates to the Mole and the Rat seems false on his lips. He speaks of "the open road, the dusty highway.... Here to-day, up and off to somewhere else to-morrow! Travel, change, interest, excitement! The whole world before you, and a horizon that's always changing" (p. 28), and the statement may faithfully record Grahame's own enthusiasm for travel.

As dramatic change does not necessarily imply growth or excitement in *The Wind in the Willows*, permanence does not imply boredom or stagnation. Enjoyment of the life on the river bank merely involves Thoreau's ability to hear a different drummer, one who is quieter, requiring greater patience and sensitivity from the listener. That pattern of pastoralism, the Mole, is not dead to the calls around him. "We others," Grahame writes (pp. 80-81),

> who have long lost the more subtle of the physical senses, have not even proper terms to express an animal's intercommunications with his surroundings, living or otherwise, and have only the word "smell," for instance, to include the whole range of delicate thrills which murmur in the nose of the animal night and day, summoning, warning, inciting, repelling. It was one of these mysterious fairy calls from out of the void that suddenly reached Mole in the darkness making him tingle through and through.... He stopped dead in his tracks, his nose searching hither and thither in its efforts to recapture the fine filament, the telegraphic current, that had so strongly moved him. A moment, and he had caught it again; and with it this time came recollection in fullest flood.
>
> Home!

Athene produced a mist which so obscured the shores of Ithaca that Odysseus did not know he had finally returned. No one could have so befuddled the faithful Mole, who was not to be diverted, and desensitized, by journeys: "For others the asperities, the stubborn endurance, or the clash of actual conflict, that went with Nature in the rough; he must be wise, must keep to the pleasant places in which his lines were laid and which held adventure enough, in their way, to last for a lifetime" (p. 76).

That the Mole recognizes other modes of existence and makes this conscious decision to limit himself is in keeping with pastoral tradition. Reflecting on the genre, Patrick Cullen observes:

> Arcadian pastoral can and does satirize the artifices and corruptions of the nonpastoral world ... but there is, implicitly or explicitly, a counterpoising awareness of the limitations of pastoral values and

with that a greater sense of the multivalence of experience, a sense of the potential legitimacy of urban and heroic modes.[12]

This "potential legitimacy" is not realized in the Toad, who is satirized for his recklessness (" 'Smashes, or machines?' asked the Rat. 'O, well, after all, it's the same thing—with Toad' " [p. 63]). In the chapter entitled "Wayfarers All," however, Grahame does suggest what these other modes of existence might be. Disturbed at the autumn departure of his friends who are following the longing to go south, the Rat must face the call of adventure himself, and while the migration of the birds may be all instinct, the case of the Sea Rat cannot be so clearly explained. Grahame allows his River Rat to be enchanted by the words and the way of life of the other animal, without suggesting where instinct ends and conscious will begins. Is the River Rat tied to the river, as the birds are seasonally to the north and south? Or does the Rat's allegiance to the river spring from habit that can be changed? When the chapter is over and the Rat's seizure past, our relief for him is mingled with a sense of the validity of other styles of life, even though for the Rat and the Mole, Grahame has reaffirmed the value of pastoral, with "adventure enough, in [its] way, to last for a lifetime" (p. 76).

It is often stated that, with the possible exception of "The Reluctant Dragon," the essays and short stories that Grahame wrote in the 1890s are not children's literature. Deciding on which shelf to place *The Wind in the Willows* is more difficult. There do not seem to be many children today who share Alistair Grahame's prodigious verbal faculties (he was once called "a baby who had swallowed a dictionary"[13]), and most of the encouragement about introducing the novel to children may be found in books that are as idealistic and nostalgic as Grahame's work itself. The reasons for the difficulties children have with the book may go beyond the occasional near-archaic words and the complex metaphors. Perhaps it is the sophisticated intelligence that informs *The Wind in the Willows* that is hardest for the child to appreciate. It is the same spirit, the longing for a golden age, that infused his short stories, and although the obtrusive elegance of the narrative voice has receded, the ironies remain. Part of the pleasure of reading an Arcadia lies in the perception both of its limited but highly artful simplicity and of its ever-budding but never fully blossoming allegory. To a great extent such sophisticated perception exists for adults in all children's literature. The writer selects and guides his naive reader, manipulating facts, breaking harsh truths gently, attempting, however unconsciously, to instill an appreciation of those values that he holds most dear. But the ideal reader remains, or should remain, the child, who will take it all quite seriously, and innocently allow the writer silently to pull the strings. The ideal reader of *The Wind in the Willows*, however, knows as much as the writer. He not only understands "how jolly it was to be the only idle dog among all these busy citizens" (p. 3) and comprehends the metaphor of "Nature's Grand Hotel" (p. 154), but more important, knows, with Virgil, how it feels to be no longer too young to reach the branches, and has some sense of the "spirit of divine discontent and longing" from which the work springs.

Notes

1. "Alarums and Excursions," *The Golden Age* (New York and London: John Lane, 1902), pp. 38-39. Subsequent page references are to this edition and will appear in the text.

2. "The Reluctant Dragon," *Dream Days* (Garden City, N.Y.: Garden City Pub. Co., 1898), p. 220.

3. Peter Green writes of the period preceding the composition of *The Wind in the Willows*: "[Grahame] progressively stifled his conscious urge towards personal anarchy and artistic individualism; he came to terms with his successful career in the City; and close on top of this he made an emotionally disastrous marriage. The inevitable result was that—as in the cases of Lear and Carroll—his imaginative, creative impulses were driven down deep into his subconscious mind. His son Alistair provided the focal point for their transmutation and eventual release.... Repressed, unhappy, driven in on himself, badly bruised by contact with adult passion, Grahame turned ... to the world of symbol and myth. In so doing he released the full strength of his genius" (*Kenneth Grahame: A Study of His Life, Work and Times* [London: John Murray, 1959], p. 265).

4. *The Wind in the Willows*, illus. Ernest Shepherd, intro. Frances Clarke Sayers (New York: Scribners, 1908, 1959), p. 1. Subsequent references are to this edition and will appear in the text.

5. See Green, pp. 196-238, and note 3 above.

6. *The Uses of Nostalgia: Studies in Pastoral Poetry* (New York: Schoecken, 1972), pp. 86-87.

7. Lerner, p. 86. The passage is from *Eclogue* VIII, ll. 38-42.

8. Green writes: "The Wild Wooders, stoats, weasels, and the rest, are clearly identified in Grahame's mind with the stunted, malevolent proletariat of contemporary upper-middle-class caricature" (p. 246).

9. Green believes that "Toad ... is a sublimation of all [Grahame's] unrecognized desires, and is harried by all the forces which Grahame himself found particularly terrifying" (p. 251).

10. Green, p. 260.

11. *The Odyssey*, p. 153

12. *Spenser, Marvell and the Renaissance Pastoral* (Cambridge: Harvard University Press, 1970), p. 3.

13. Quoted in Green, p. 237.

24

Narnia

The Author, the Critics, and the Tale

WALTER HOOPER

Before the recent revival of fairy tales got fully under way, C.S. Lewis's seven Chronicles of Narnia were treated a little like "hand-me-down" clothes which are passed down from big to little children and are immediately given up when the little ones outgrow them. Now that people are returning to the old distinction between stories which can only be read by children and those which can be enjoyed by people of all ages, the Narnian books occupy a position on something like a "Jacob's Ladder" and are continually being passed up and down from young to old, from old to young, depending on which member of the family discovers them first. Of the million copies of the Chronicles sold in England and the United States last year, about half were bought by college students.

Professor Tolkien's *Hobbit* and *Lord of the Rings* grew out of the stories he told his children, but Lewis, who was a bachelor for most of his life and knew little about children, wrote fairy tales simply because he liked them himself and because he found them the best art-form for what he had to say. As scholars of the past, both men knew that the association of fairy tales and fantasy with children is very recent and accidental. Fairy tales gravitated to the nursery when they became unfashionable with adults. It surely marks an important recovery that they are coming back—indeed *are* back—into fashion with whoever likes them of whatever age.

Asked how he came to write the first Chronicle of Narnia—*The Lion, the Witch and the Wardrobe*—Lewis said: "All my seven Narnian books, and my three science fiction books, began with seeing pictures in my head. At first they were not a story, just pictures. The *Lion* all began with a picture of a Faun carrying an umbrella and parcels in a snowy wood. This picture had been in my mind since I was about sixteen. Then one day,

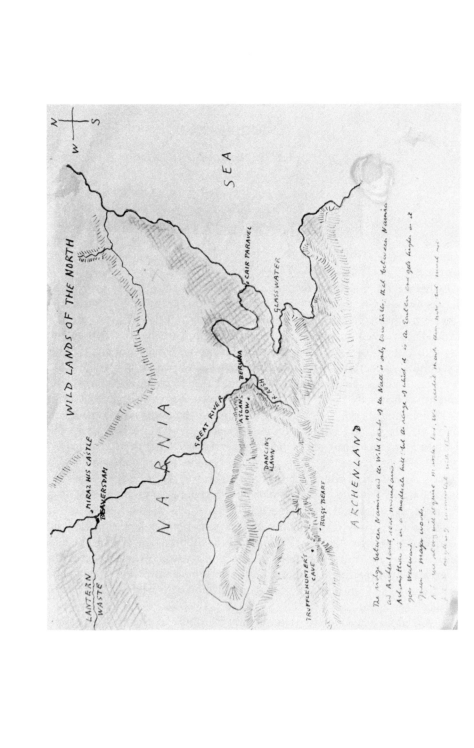

when I was about forty, I said to myself: 'Let's try to make a story about it.' "[1]

Though Lewis had probably forgotten it, there is some evidence which would seem to indicate that the initial impetus behind his Narnian stories came from real children.

In the autumn of 1939 four schoolgirls were evacuated from London to Lewis's home on the outskirts of Oxford. It was his adopted "mother," Mrs. Moore, who mainly looked after the evacuees, but Lewis shared the responsibility of entertaining the young visitors. On the back of another book he was writing at the time, I found what I believe to be the germinal passage of the first story of Narnia—*The Lion, The Witch and the Wardrobe*. It says: "This book is about four children whose names were Ann, Martin, Rose and Peter. But it is most about Peter who was the youngest. They all had to go away from London suddenly because of the Air Raids, and because Father, who was in the army, had gone to the War and Mother was doing some kind of war work. They were sent to stay with a relation of Mother's who was a very old Professor who lived by himself in the country."

I've been told by a neighbor who used to see them across her back fence that the schoolgirls did not remain very long in Oxford, and I've never been able to discover whether Lewis wrote any more of the story at this time. The next we hear of the book is from Chad Walsh who says that, when he visited Lewis in the summer of 1948, he talked "vaguely of completing a children's book which he had begun "in the tradition of E. Nesbit.' "[2] Then, on the 10th of March, 1949, Lewis read the first two chapters of *The Lion, the Witch and the Wardrobe* to his friend, Roger Lancelyn Green, who is the only person to read all seven stories in manuscript. Spurred on by Lancelyn Green's encouragement, *The Lion* was completed by the end of the month. More "pictures" or mental images— which Lewis said were his only means of inspiration—began forming in his head and the next two stories, *Prince Caspian* and *The Voyage of the "Dawn Treader,"* were completed by the end of February, 1950. Before the year was out he had written *The Silver Chair* and *The Horse and His Boy* and made a start on *The Magician's Nephew*. The final installment, *The Last Battle*, was written two years later.

Lewis is generally thought to have been the best-read man of his time. Though this, in itself, would not ensure readable books, the combination of his vast learning, his superior abilities as a prose-stylist, and his rich and vivid imagination have resulted in the Narnian books being first, though not foremost, extremely well-written adventure stories. What has led people to read the stories over and over again—what I'd say is the foremost reason for their success—is, I think, quite simply their "meaning."

Objections to the books are rare, but those that have come make claim that the Narnian battles and wicked characters frighten children and give them nightmares. I believe there is no better answer to these charges than that given by Lewis himself in his defense of fairy tales in his essay "On Three Ways of Writing for Children." While agreeing that we must not do anything (1) "likely to give the child those haunting, disabling, pathological fears against which ordinary courage is helpless," he was strongly opposed to the notion that we must keep out of the child's mind (2) "the knowledge that he is born into a world of death, violence, wounds, adventure, heroism and cowardice, good and evil":

Let there be wicked kings and beheadings, battles and dungeons, giants and dragons, and let villains be soundly killed at the end of the book. Nothing will persuade me that this causes an ordinary child any kind or degree of fear beyond what it wants, and needs, to feel. For, of course, it wants to be a little frightened.[3]

Lewis was much gratified by the extraordinary success of the Narnian books. Of the many fan-letters he received, he seemed most pleased with those from children. Whereas adults usually wanted to know where he got his "ideas," children—not being required to write learned articles—let the stories act on them more directly.

To the many children who pleaded with him to write more stories, Lewis's answer was usually the same as that he gave me: "There are only two times at which you can stop a thing: one is before everyone is tired of it, and the other is after!" Almost all wrote of their love for Aslan, the Creator and ruler of Narnia. Last year an eleven-year-old, Lucy Fryman, from Texas was so anxious to talk to someone who had known Lewis that she addressed the following words to his life-long friend, Owen Barfield:

I have read Mr. Lewis's books. I got so envoveled in them all I did was eat, sleep, and read. I wanted to write to you and tell you I understand the books. I mean about the sy[m]bols and all . . . I know that to me Aslan is God. And all the son's and daughter's of Adam and Eve are God's children. I have my own philosophies about the books. If it is possible I would like to meet you. None of my friends (well some of them) liked the books. I tried to explain to them but they don't understand about symbols. I never really did until I read the books.

I think it'd be inaccurate to say that most readers make the instant connection, as Lucy did, between Aslan and God. Lewis wanted it to happen naturally, or not at all. When another little girl asked what Aslan meant in the last chapter of *The Voyage of the "Dawn Treader,"* when he tells the children that in their world they must learn to know him by "another name," Lewis answered:

> As to Aslan's other name, well, I want you to guess. Has there never been anyone in *this* world who (1) Arrived at the same time as Father Christmas (2) Said he was the Son of the Great Emperor (3) Gave himself up for someone else's fault to be jeered at and killed by wicked people (4) Came to life again (5) Is sometimes spoken of as a Lamb (at the end of the "Dawn Treader")? Don't you really know His name in this world?[4]

Lewis used a capital "H" in the "His" above because Aslan is Christ. In another place he explained the reason for his reticence in saying no more than this: "Why did one find it so hard to feel as one was told he ought to feel about God or about the sufferings of Christ? I thought the chief reason was that one was told one ought to. An obligation to feel can freeze feelings ... But supposing that by casting all these things into an imaginary world, stripping them of their stained-glass and Sunday school associations, one could make them for the first time appear in their real potency? Could one not thus steal past those watchful dragons? I thought one could."

Professor Tolkien once told me that he thought the Christian elements in the Narnian stories too "obvious." But I think this is because he not only knew the Bible better than most of us, but began by knowing what Lewis was "up to." Judging from what I hear, only about half Lewis's readers guess that Aslan is meant to be Christ—and that half is made up about equally of children and adults. I side with Lewis in not wishing to attract the attention of those "watchful dragons," but as the Narnian books are, whether I like it or not, undergoing very detailed analysis, I offer the following comments about what I think the Christian elements in them are. This requires, first of all, clearing up a linguistic difference between Lewis and his readers.

It's about as natural as sneezing for moderns to call something an "allegory" when it has a meaning slightly different from, or other than, the one the author gives it. In this sense you can "allegorize" practically anything. The reason why Lewis and Tolkien claimed that their books are not allegories is that they were using the ancient definition of the term: by allegory they meant the use of something real and tangible to stand for that which is real but intangible: Love can be allegorized, patience can be allegorized, anything *immaterial* can be allegorized or represented by feigned physical objects. But Aslan and Gandalf are already physical objects. To try to represent what Christ would be like in Narnia is to turn one physical object into another (supposed) physical object—and that is not, by Lewis and Tolkien's definition, an allegory.

There are those who consider Satan the "hero" of Milton's *Paradise Lost*, by which they mean, not that he is in any way good, but that he's the best drawn character in the poem. Long before Lewis wrote the Narnian stories, he explained in his *Preface to Paradise Lost* (ch. xiii) why it is so much easier to draw a bad Satan than a good God:

> To make a character worse than oneself it is only necessary to
> release imaginatively from control some of the bad passions which,
> in real life, are always straining at the leash; the Satan, the Iago,
> the Becky Sharp, within each of us, is always there and only too
> ready, the moment the leash is slipped, to come out and have in
> our books that holiday we try to deny them in our lives. But if
> you try to draw a character better than yourself, all you can do is
> to take the best moments you have had and to imagine them
> prolonged and more consistently embodied in action. But the real
> high virtues which we do not possess at all, we cannot depict in a
> purely external fashion. We do not really know what it feels like
> to be a man much better than ourselves.

In talking with Lewis about his almost unbelievable success in picturing the divine Aslan—Who is a million times more interesting than any of his equally convincing bad characters—I found him reluctant to take any credit, pointing out that Aslan pushed His *own* way into the books. Not only has Aslan received the highest praise of anyone or anything in the books, but, perilous compliment though it may sound, I think most readers (of which I am one) have been unable to divorce Aslan from Christ. Though it is a contradiction in terms, some love Him even more than His Original. I'm reminded of a little boy here in Oxford who chopped through the back of his wardrobe and half-way through the bricks of the house to get to Him. Aslan is not a "reinterpretation" of Christ, as I think *Jesus Christ Superstar* is meant to be. He is, as Lewis says, "an invention giving an imaginary answer to the question, "What might Christ become like, if there really were a world like Narnia and He chose to be incarnate and die and rise again in *that* world as He actually has done in ours?' "[6] But some of us, on meeting absolute goodness, discover it to be too strong for us. I remember Lewis reading an article in which the writer referred to Aslan as "smug," and I know this pained him. "Do you think Aslan 'smug'?" he asked. I think I replied that what would sound perfectly ordinary coming from God would sound deranged coming from a mere man. The humanitarians may think *us* unkind for holding clear and definite beliefs, but they can hardly expect the Creator of all worlds to qualify every statement with "so it seems to me" or "in my opinion."

The closest parallel between Aslan and Christ comes in *The Lion, the Witch and the Wardrobe* where Aslan offers His life to save Edmund. This is very similar to Christ's vicarious death on the cross, but if the analogy is pressed too closely it will be discovered that nowhere—not even here—does Lewis provide us with a geometrically perfect equivalent of anything in the Bible or Christian doctrine. Lewis hoped that by seeing Aslan die on the Stone Table we'd not only be better able to grasp the significance of what happened in the actual history of this world, but see that it was a very good thing in itself and in the context Lewis gave it.

Not only is "disguise" part of Lewis's intention, but it is also essential to see that what is in one book or world cannot be the same in another book or world. What "Miss T" eats does not remain as it was but *turns into* "Miss T." The instructions Aslan gives Eustace and Jill on how to discover Prince Rilian is meant, I think, to reinforce the importance of following Christ's commandments. On the other hand, if, while reading *The Silver Chair*, we're thinking only of Christ's instructions to the rich young man recounted in St. Mark 10: 17-21, we'll have missed what we are meant to be attending to in Narnia. It's afterwards, minutes or hours or perhaps even years afterwards, that the two worlds are to be joined in our minds. But even if that juncture *never* takes place, we will have benefited enormously from *The Silver Chair*, for it is part of the success of a great author that the sense of his book not depend on the reader knowing the original source of its ingredients.

Is there any good to be had from source-hunting? My belief is that when teachers come across children who feel they have solved a "puzzle" by discovering that Narnia is the name of a place in Italy, that Aslan is the Turkish word for lion, the teacher should lead him away from the suspect realm of anthropology to true literary pleasures by showing him how one thing becomes a *different* thing in another book. For instance, it's not enough to say that the immediate source of Shakespeare's *Romeo and Juliet* is Arthur Brooke's extremely ugly *Tragical History of Romeus and Juliet*: we need to show him what a completely different use Shakespeare made of the story if we are to help him appreciate the latter's genius.

More than most books, the Narnian tales are specially rich hunting grounds for scholars. In chapter xiii of *The Voyage of the "Dawn Treader"* the children find three Lords of Narnia fast asleep under an enchantment, round a table spread with exotic foods supplied by a beautiful Princess.

On the table is the cruel-looking knife with which the White Witch killed Aslan. The Princess' father, Ramandu, appears but is unable to speak until a bird lays a live coal on his lips. Among the many possible "sources," other than Lewis's own imagination, for these elements are those we all know about. There is Rip Van Winkle; there is the passage in I Kings 17:6 which tells how ravens fed Elijah with "bread and flesh in the morning, and bread and flesh in the evening." The Knife recalls King Pelles' sword which struck the Dolorous Blow. The bird takes us back to Isaiah 6:6: "Then flew one of the seraphims unto me, having a live coal in his hand, which he had taken with the tongs from off the altar: and he laid it upon my mouth." It is inevitable that a man so widely-read as Lewis should have remembered all these things—but they, neither collectively nor individually, are what *his* story is about.

Besides their obvious parallels, the Narnian books are suffused throughout with moral teaching of a quality which I don't believe anyone, whatever his beliefs, could fairly object to. The tales are not, as might be imagined, built around moral themes which were in the author's mind from the beginning, but grew out of the telling and are as much a part of the narrative as scent is to a flower. The morality of Lewis's books goes far deeper and touches on levels of human understanding rarely attempted even by those who write for adults. An especially good example occurs in *The Voyage of the "Dawn Treader"* (ch. x). As Lucy searches the Magician's Book for the spell which will make the Dufflepuds visible, she comes across a spell which will let you know what your friends say about you. Not even wishing to avoid this dangerous thing, Lucy says the magical words and hears her good friend, Marjorie, say very unkind things about her to another person. Later, when Aslan discovers what poor heart-broken Lucy has done, He says, "Spying on people by magic is the same as spying on them in any other way. And you have misjudged your friend. She is weak, but she loves you. She was afraid of the older girl and said what she does not mean." "I don't think I'd ever be able to forget what I heard her say," answers Lucy. "No, you won't," replies Aslan.

Are there many of us who have not found, like Lucy, that such a dangerous course, once taken, forbids return? I've never seen the enormous difference between what our friends *say*, and what they really *think*, about us so unforgettably portrayed.

In *The Last Battle*, which won the Carnegie Medal for the best Children's Book of 1956, and is the most theological of all the books, Lewis uses a stable door as the way out of Narnia. Those familiar with Lewis's beliefs can understand how characteristic it is that he will not allow his readers to camp too long on any of his earthly creations. As we must, in reality, pass on, he will not write "and they lived happily ever after" till it is safe to do so. It is certainly not safe to do so at the beginning of *The Last Battle*, which is, in my opinion, the best-written and the most sublime of all the Narnian stories, the crowning achievement of the whole Narnian creation. Everything else in all the other six stories finds its meaning in relation to this book. Not that one can't enjoy the other stories separately; but, as Lewis would say, you cannot possibly understand the play until you've seen it through to the end. Lewis insists on taking us to the end— and beyond.

If *The Last Battle* is re-read less often than the other fairy tales this is probably because the first eleven chapters, which take place in the old, familiar Narnia, are so extremely painful to read. Almost everything we have come to love is, bit by bit, taken from us. Our sense of loss is made more excruciating because we are allowed—even encouraged—to believe that things will eventually get back to "normal." We feel certain that the King, at least, will not be deceived by Shift's trickery: but he is. When Eustace and Jill arrive we know it will only be a matter of time until all is put right. Yet, despite their willingness to help, there is so little they can do without the help of Aslan. And where, by the way, *is* He? Our hearts warm within us as Jewel the Unicorn recounts the centuries of past happiness in which every day and week in Narnia had been better than the last:

> And as he went on, the picture of all those happy years, all the thousands of them, piled up in Jill's mind till it was rather like looking down from a high hill on to a rich, lovely plain full of woods and waters and cornfields, which spread away and away till it got thin and misty from distance. And she said:
>
> "Oh, I do hope we can soon settle the Ape and get back to those good, ordinary times. And then I hope they'll go on for ever and ever and ever. *Our* world is going to have an end some day. Perhaps this one won't. Oh Jewel—wouldn't it be lovely if Narnia just went on and on—like what you said it has been?"
>
> "Nay, sister," answered Jewel, "all worlds draw to an end; except Aslan's own country."
>
> "Well, at least," said Jill, "I hope the end of this one is millions of millions of millions of years away." (ch. viii)

So do we all. Yet a few minutes later Farsight the Eagle brings word that Cair Paravel, the high seat of all the Kings of Narnia, has been taken by the Calormenes. And, as he lay dying, Roonwit the Centaur asked the King to remember that "all worlds draw to an end and that noble death is a treasure which no one is too poor to buy" (ch. viii).

Lewis's didactic purpose ought to be clear to those who are conversant with orthodox Christianity. He uses his own invented world to illustrate what the Church has been teaching since the beginning, but which is becoming more and more neglected or forgotten. Namely, that this world will come to an end; it was never meant to be our real home—that lies elsewhere; we do not know, we cannot possibly know, when the end will come; and the end will come, not from within, but from without.

Most of the events in *The Last Battle* are based on Our Lord's apocalyptic prophecies recorded in St. Matthew 24, St. Mark 13 and St. Luke 21. The treachery of Shift the Ape was suggested by the Dominical words found in St. Matthew 24:23-24:

> If any man shall say unto you, Lo, here is Christ, or there; believe it not. For there shall arise false Christs, and false prophets, and shall shew great signs and wonders; inasmuch that, if it were possible, they shall deceive the very elect.

The Ape almost—almost—succeeds in deceiving even the most faithful followers of Aslan. First through trickery and, later, when he becomes the tool of Rishda Tarkaan and Ginger the Cat, in propounding his "new theology": the confusion of Aslan and the devil Tash as "Tashlan." As the monkey Shift is a parody of a man, so his "theology" is a parody of the truth. We are prepared for ordinary wickedness in an adventure story, but with the advent of the "new theology' we move into a new and dreadful dimension where ordinary courage seems helpless.

When it seems quite certain that Eustace and Jill will soon die fighting for Narnia, they speculate as to whether, at the moment of their death in Narnia, they will be found dead in England. Frightened by the idea, Jill begins a confession which she breaks off mid-sentence. "What were you going to say?" asks Eustace. She answers:

> I *was* going to say I wished we'd never come. But I don't, I don't, I don't. Even if we *are* killed. I'd rather be killed fighting for Narnia than grow old and stupid at home and perhaps go about in a bath chair and then die in the end just the same.   (ch. ix)

From that point onwards Lewis lets go the full power of his imagination, and we are carried relentlessly forward into what is truly the *last* battle of Narnia, in front of the Stable. There the King, the children, and the remnant of faithful Narnians are either slain or make their way inside. The Stable has become none other than the way into Aslan's Country, and, drawing out this brilliant piece of symbolism, Lewis has Jill say in a moment of selfless appreciation: "In our world too, a Stable once had something inside it that was bigger than our whole world."   (ch. xiii)

What is a little confusing, but which is partly explained in chapters iv and v, and fully cleared up in the last chapter, is that all (except one) of the "friends of Narnia"—Digory Kirke, Polly Plummer, Peter, Edmund and Lucy Pevensie, Eustace Scrubb, and Jill Pole—died together in a railway crash in England. They are reborn in glory and, inside the Stable, Eustace and Jill meet all the others. The exception is Susan Pevensie who, "no longer a friend of Narnia" (ch. xii), has drifted of her own free will into apostasy. Liberal clergymen and other "kind" but mistaken people, preferring the temporary passion of Pity to the eternal action of Pity, have found the absence of Susan a reason for calling Lewis "cruel." But they are well answered in *The Great Divorce* where, explaining why those who have chosen Hell shall not be allowed to veto the joys of Heaven, he says: "Every disease that submits to a cure shall be cured: but we will not call blue yellow to please those who insist on still having jaundice, nor make a midden of the world's garden for the sake of some who cannot abide the smell of roses."[7]

With a terrible beauty that almost makes the heart ache, and which is perhaps only matched by Dante's *Paradiso*, Aslan goes to the Stable door and holds His Last Judgment. Those who are worthy pass in, the others turn away into darkness. Inside, the children watch as Aslan, fulfilling the apocalyptic prophecies of the New Testament, destroys Narnia by water and fire and closes the Stable door upon it for ever.

After this dazzling feat of the imagination, one might reasonably expect that Lewis could not help but let us down in "unwinding" his story. He knew that the merest slip of the pen could have cast a shadow of incredulity over all that went before, and he proceeded very cautiously in opening the children's eyes to where they are. The question was how do you portray heaven? How make it *heavenly*? How "wind" *upwards*?

The answer lay in finding—and then trying to describe—the difference between the earthly and the eternal world. Years before, writing about the difference between allegory and symbolism, he said:

> The allegorist leaves the given—his own passions—to talk of that which is confessedly less real, which is a fiction. The symbolist leaves the given to find that which is more real. To put the difference in another way, for the symbolist it is we who are the allegory. We are the "frigid personifications"; the heavens above us are the "shadowy abstractions"; the world which we mistake for reality is the flat outline of that which elsewhere veritably is in all the round of its unimaginable dimensions.[8]

Symbolism, as described here, was not for Lewis a fanciful bit of intellectualism. He believed that Heaven is the real thing of which earth is an imperfect copy. His problem was not only of finding some way to illustrate this, but to describe the heavenly life in such a way that it would not seem a place of perpetual negations. In his essay "Transposition," he suggests that we think of a mother and son imprisoned in a dungeon. As the child has never seen the outer world, his mother draws pencil sketches to illustrate what fields, rivers, mountains, cities and waves on a beach are like:

> On the whole he gets on tolerably well until, one day, he says something that gives his mother pause. For a minute or two they are at cross-purposes. Finally it dawns on her that he has, all these years, lived under a misconception. "But," she gasps, "you didn't think that the real world was full of lines drawn in lead pencil?" "What?" says the boy. "No pencil-marks there?" And instantly his whole notion of the outer world becomes a blank ... So with us. "We know not what we shall be"; but we may be sure we shall be more, not less, than we were on earth.[9]

Lewis had a knack of making even the most difficult metaphysical concepts understandable and picturing the otherwise unpicturable. In order that his readers will feel as comfortable in the world beyond the Stable door as the children in the book, he brings in homely details such as the fact that Narnian clothes felt as well as looked beautiful and (I'll never forget how much Lewis disliked "dressing up") the even more pleasant fact that "there was no such thing as starch or flannel or elastic to be found from one end of the country to the other" (ch. xii). Then, as the children and many of the animals they have come to love follow Aslan further into the country, their sense of strangeness wears off till it eventually dawns upon them that the reason why everything looks so familiar is because they are seeing for the first time the "real Narnia" of which the old one had only been a "copy." As they rejoice in this discovery, Lord Digory, whom we first met as old Professor Kirke in *The Lion, the Witch and the Wardrobe*, explains the difference between the two, adding "It's all in Plato, all in Plato: bless me, what *do* they teach them at these schools!" He is referring, of course, to Plato's *Phaedo* in which he discusses immortality and the unchanging reality behind the changing forms.

One other little detail, overlooked perhaps by the majority of readers as it is blended so perfectly into the narrative, concerns the manner in which resurrected bodies differ from earthly ones. The children discover that they can scale waterfalls and run faster than an arrow flies. This is meant to be a parallel to the Gospel accounts of Christ's risen body: though still corporeal, He can move through a locked door (St. John 20:19) and ascend bodily into Heaven (St. Mark 16:19).

When the children reach the Mountain of Aslan they are joined by all the heroes of the other six books, Reepicheep the Mouse, Puddleglum the Marsh-wiggle and a host of other old friends. Uneasy that their joy may yet be snatched from them, and that they may be sent back to earth, they turn to Aslan who answers the question in their minds: "Have you not guessed?" He says, "The term is over: the holidays have begun. The dream is ended: this is the morning."

After that we are told that "He no longer looked to them like a lion." Lewis is here referring to the passage in the Athanasian Creed which states that Christ is both God and Man "not by conversion of the Godhead into flesh: but by taking of the Manhood into God." This means that Aslan was transformed into a Man—which Manhood He keeps for all time. "The things that began to happen after that," says Lewis, "were so great and beautiful that I cannot write them"—and, of course, neither can I or anyone else.

There has never been a book written, I fancy, in which the assumptions of the author were not present, implicitly or explicitly. Even the most blameless stories of child-life have at their base beliefs about something or the other. There is no such thing as not believing *anything*. One who does not agree with Christianity must agree with something else. Will it lead to better ends than those pre-figured in Lewis's books? I have read many modern works of literature about which I am forced to say "I admire the workmanship, but deplore the sentiments"; but only of the Narnian Chronicles can I unhesitatingly say, "This is beautiful, and this is right."

Notes

1. C. S. Lewis, "It All Began With a Picture . . ." in *Of Other Worlds: Essays and Stories*, ed. Walter Hooper (London, Geoffrey Bles, 1966), p. 42.

2. Chad Walsh, *C. S. Lewis: Apostle to the Skeptics* (New York, Macmillan 1949), p. 10.

3. "On Three Ways of Writing for Children," in *Of Other Worlds*, p. 31.

4. Quoted in Kathryn Lindskoog, *The Lion of Judah in Never-Never Land* (Grand Rapids, Eerdmans, 1973), p. 16.

5. "Sometimes Fairy Stories May Say Best What's to be Said," in *Of Other Worlds*, p. 37.

6. *Letters of C. S. Lewis*, ed. W. H. Lewis (London, Geoffrey Bles, 1966), p. 283.

7. C.S. Lewis, *The Great Divorce, A Dream* (London, Geoffrey Bles, 1945), p. 112.

8. C. S. Lewis, "Allegory," in *The Allegory of Love; A Study in Medieval Tradition*, (London, Oxford 1936), p. 45.

9. C. S. Lewis, "Transposition," in *They Asked for a Paper* (London, Geoffrey Bles 1962), p. 178.

25

Maurice Sendak and the
Blakean Vision of Childhood

JENNIFER R. WALLER

In his studio, to the right of his desk amid reproductions of the works of Watteau, Goya, and Winslow Homer, Maurice Sendak has a reproduction of one of William Blake's works.[1] In an interview, Sendak describes Blake as "from the first, my great and abiding love ... my teacher in all things."[2] While the influence of George MacDonald, Andrew Caldecott, Attilio Massiono, and the tradition of the American comic book are all much more immediately definable in Sendak's work, the strength of his emotional response to William Blake is undeniable. In the same interview, he asserts Blake to be his favorite artist and goes on to explain that "of course, the *Songs of Innocence* and the *Songs of Experience* tell you all about this: what it is to be a child—not childish, but a child inside your adult self—and how much better a person you are for being such."[3]

It is interesting to compare Sendak's insights into childhood with Blake's and, as well, to compare their responses to the challenge of combining artistic vision and entertainment in a composite medium. For Blake, the state of childhood, with its innocent ignorance of destructive reason and of the processes of adult's self-conscious rationalization and self-justification, represented a time when the human imagination was most potent. Adulthood too often brought the destruction of the powers of the imagination. Blake's reassertion of the power of the imagination was, of course, part of his rebellion against the reasonableness and moderation of eighteenth-and nineteenth-century classicism. Imagination became a "Divine Vision" which allowed the poet to achieve by his own art what the child could do spontaneously—transcend the limitations of the senses and the restrictions of rational categorization. The child of the *Songs of Innocence* seeking to find out "Little Lamb who made thee / Dost thou know who made thee?" perceives an answer not by his powers of reasoning but by the strength of his love. The child's power of perception, enjoyment, and responsiveness represent imagination unfettered by the constricting demands of rationalist philosophy, whether in Lockean reason or established theology. That such childhood perception could be re-created was, in a sense, evidence enough for Blake that the Divine existed in man.

Like Blake, Sendak draws unusual strength from the vision of imagination. Like Blake too, he uses the image of childhood to represent the liberation of his creativity: "An essential part of myself—my dreaming life—still lives in the potent urgent light of childhood."[4] Commenting directly on his own work, he defines the relationship he has with "the kid I was"—an interesting phrase—who did not grow "up into me" but "still exists somewhere in the most graphic, plastic physical way."[5] The presence of this child is indispensable to his work, for as he asserts, "one of my worst fears is losing contact with him."[6] To lose contact with this vision of childhood would be to destroy the substance of Sendak's creative talent—his extraordinary powers of evocative imagination and his sensitivity to the experience of childhood.

Both artists, as illustrators *and* authors, seek to use their composite form to express their vision through structural tension. Often their words may rationalize experience which may be either elaborated, or sometimes contradicted, by the illustrations, which bring out more fully the dreamlike, wordless level of the unconscious. Since Blake was obsessed with the intention of destroying the dualistic world of mind and body, time and space, he saw in the composite medium the possibilities of dramatizing "the interaction of the apparent dualities in experiences."[7] Sendak on the other hand, because he was writing and illustrating children's books, was forced to the realization that a child's book is not simply read or rationally understood: "There's so much more to a book than just the reading; there is a sensuousness. I've seen children touch books, fondle books, smell books."[8]

Any artist working in a composite medium clearly faces special problems. Sendak has developed a style of illustration which can initially be explained by reference to the *Little Bear* books. Here the text and Sendak's illustration are both enclosed within a formal decorative border. Like Blake, Sendak is not merely aiming for some kind of aesthetically satisfying unit. Neither does he want to make the pictures express only the fabric of the text. This would in Sendak's estimation be a "serious pitfall."[9] He hopes to allow "the story to speak for itself, with my picture as a kind of background music—music in the right style and always in tune with the words."[10] Background music such as that which accompanies film, it should be noted, is an essential element of the dramatic structure, making the listener only partially aware of feelings which he may be unwilling or unable to verbalize. Sendak's concern in this way to assimilate divergent art forms into a harmonious unity seems to be becoming more insistent recently as he establishes his reputation in the no-man's land where he is both author and artist. With Sendak's own works, *Where the Wild Things Are* and *In the Night Kitchen*, we can go a step further and put him in an explicitly Blakean context.

> My mother groaned! My father wept.
> Into the dangerous world I leapt:
> Helpless, naked, piping loud;
> Like a fiend hid in a cloud.
> Struggling in my father's hands:
> Striving against my swadling bands;
> Bound and weary I thought best
> To sulk upon my mother's breast.
> —*Works*, p. 28

Some of the same is apparent in *Where the Wild Things Are*. Max's rebellion and frustration at his punishment spread over four pages and are described in the text:

> That very night Max's room a forest grew / and grew— / and grew until his ceiling hung with vines and the walls became the world all around / and an ocean tumbled by with a private boat for Max and he sailed off through night and day.

As the bedroom is transformed into the land "where the wild things are," the phrases become longer and more unwieldly until the reader must gasp for breath. Each stage in the transition is marked by the physical act of turning a page, and by the time the rumpus commences the visual images have taken over entirely from the words. The illustrations, which initially remained neatly contained within a white border on one side of the centerfold, have now swamped the page. The tensions between the competing mediums of prose and picture illustrate the transformation from Max's initial reasoned reaction, described in words, to his wild frenzy and cathartic rage, which can only be illustrated in wordless pictures. Inside the space of one children's picture book, the illustrations have conquered the page leaving the child in the midst of Experience like Blake's child in "The Garden of Love":

> So I turn'd to the Garden of Love
> That so many sweet Flowers bore,
> And I saw it was filled with graves,
> And tombstones where flowers should be:

And priests in black gowns, were walking their rounds,
And binding with briars my joys and desires.
—*Works*, p. 26

Where the Wild Things Are, surely one of the best children's books of our time, presents a responsiveness to childhood strikingly akin to Blake's in which childhood is not a world of idyllic escapism but of combined vulnerability and creativity. One of Blake's most important contributions to the development of nineteenth-century Romantisicm was the recognition of the experience of childhood as the subject and inspiration of serious poetry. The child was no longer just the passive recipient of moral commonplaces, though Blake did not neglect this notion. His small emblem book *The Gates of Paradise*, written and illustrated for children, was a powerful and pessimistic exemplum of the vanity of human existence. But the thrust of his work was to express, for the first time in English literature, spontaneous experiences of childhood and assertions of the independence and integrity of childhood experience.

The *Songs of Innocence*, in particular, asserts that childhood is a time of freedom from the constricting demands that lie behind the adult's acceptance of established theology and philosophy. Freed of these demands, even the child in "The Chimney Sweeper" is open, sensitive, and responsive to human delight and sorrow. It was not a totally idyllic world, for the world of innocence is full of the portents of experience. The predominant tone of the poems is still one of vulnerability, weeping, and lamentation. This awareness of the ambivalence of childhood experience separates Blake's responses to the child from later Romantic exploitations of the symbol of childhood. Blake's child, like Wordworth's, possesses an intuitive power of responding and knowing. But Blake does not contemplate the state of childhood nostalgically. Wordsworth looks at childhood through the eyes of an adult awakening to his lost innocence and attempting to recapture it simply because he is adult and aware of his lost security. Blake, rather, leaps into a state of childhood and re-creates the moment when pain and vulnerability mingle with joy, perception, and lack of cynicism. Blake's child is not observed coming from heaven "trailing clouds of glory"; rather he *is* that glory for a brief and vulnerable moment. We see feelingly through his liberated responsiveness.

Generations of post-Romantic children's writers have wallowed in their own sense of nostalgia for their younger selves, so that childhood is usually portrayed as a time of innocence and only fleeting pain. But for Blake, and I would argue, Sendak, the approach is different. Sendak's evocation of childhood separates him from most contemporary children's writers in much the same way as Blake's creation of childhood separated him from Wordsworth's contemplation of the state. This is not to deny that Sendak is in the Romantic tradition. He is extremely conscious that elements of subjective biographical experience and responsiveness are the substance of his art. His description of the genesis of his books—"if something strikes me and I get excited, then I want it to be a book"[11]— sounds like a vaguely expressed Wordsworthian "overflow of powerful feelings." But in describing the impact of childhood experience on his work, he makes an important distinction between the act of remembering childhood or "pretending that I'm a child" and the action of a "creative artist who also gets freer and freer with each book and opens up more and more."[12] Perhaps most significantly, he destroys the connection between himself as adult and the child when he speculates that "the kid I was never grew up into me."[13] Thus, like Blake, he does not use the child to comment upon himself as the adult. The connection implicit in Wordsworth's phrase, "The child is father of the man," does not exist for Sendak in the context of his imaginative creation.[14] Like Blake, he seems to be asserting that "Imagination has nothing to do with Memory," rather it is "Divine Vision."[15] Thus he attempts to shear off the partisan preoccupations which invade our own memories of childhood now that we are adult—our nostalgia, our obsessions with the lost opportunities and pastimes of childhood.

His assault on our more conventional responses to childhood is revealing. Some reviewers agonized over the disturbing evocations of *Where the Wild Things Are* or the unveiling of a small boy's penis in *In the Night Kitchen*. Psychologists and librarians have reacted with their own understanding of childhood—or rather their own need to believe that some part of human existence can be, and therefore should be, protected from pain, fear, and the menace of chaos. For such readers, Max in *Where the Wild Things Are* may be a disturbing creation; his imagination makes him as vulnerable as the playful children in the pastures of Innocence. His world of mischievous make-believe is so fragile that his mother's anger can shatter it and thrust him into the expanding world of his own rage and fear, the world of experience. In this state he creates from within himself demons which are really reflections of his own aggression. Eventually these menaces will be overcome and controlled and the child will return to bed and thus to what may be read as analogous to Blake's state of further or mature innocence, where the lamb and the tiger are reconciled. The book's ending is not merely a happy conclusion. There is a real sense of "look we have come through" —as Sendak has explained, he risked his own imagination in writing the tale: "When I write and draw I'm experiencing what the child in the book is going through. I was as relieved to get back from Max's journey as he was. Or rather, I like to think I got back."[16]

Like Blake, Sendak has taken seriously the horror and the largely helpless frustration of childhood that have to be sublimated into fantasies. Wordsworth's child meditates and broods on the beauty and challenge of nature. Self-consciously he appears to be preparing himself for the time when he will be a man. Blake's children are laughing, playing, weeping, and above all asking questions or arguing with others: "Little Lamb who made thee ... ?"; "Father, father, where are you going?"; "Can I see another's woe ... ?" (*Works*, pp. 8, 11, 17). One of the most striking characteristics about Sendak's recurring prototypal figure of Max in each of his forms—human or canine—is his assertiveness and his astonishing curiosity. Kenny in *Kenny's Window* dares loneliness and despair on his mission to find answers for his questions: "What is an only goat?"; "Can you fix a broken promise?"; "What is a Very Narrow Escape?". Maybe he would even dare to ask: "Tyger, did he who made the Lamb make thee?" (*Works*, p. 25). Moreover, like the questioner in *Innocence and Experience*, Kenny sometimes receives only half-answers or answers which are truer to feeling than they are to logic.

Generations of critics have argued about the nature of Blake's states of Innocence and Experience. Certainly in the *Songs of Experience*, cynicism and self-consciousness creep into the imagined world making previous situations suddenly seem unendurable and tragic. The change is not one from happiness to sadness, for sadness has already been present in *Innocence*. Rather, the world of Urizen—of definition and order—has destroyed freedom and sensitivity. When children are observed at play, jealous nostalgia invades the "Nurse's Song":

> When the voices of children, are heard on the green
> And whisprings are in the dale:
> The days of my youth rise fresh in my mind.
> My face turns green and pale.
>
> Then come home my children, the sun is gone down
> And the dews of the night arise
> Your spring & your day, are wasted in play
> And your winter and night in disguise.
>
> -*Works*, p. 23

Defending himself against the charge that he frightens our little ones, Sendak describes what he sees as the experience of childhood in terms which significantly parallel Blake's creation of joy and love, of curiosity and knowledge, intermingled with vulnerability and pain. Children are not, he claims, "drab, but they're not innocent of experience either. Too many parents and too many writers of children's books don't respect the fact that kids know a great deal of pleasure, but often they look defenceless too. Being defenceless is a primary element of childhood."[17]

Sendak's approach to childhood is as unsentimental as Blake's. Like Blake, he regards the material of his childhood experience as the substance of his imaginative powers. His childhood world is invaded by fears which may be unendurable if perceived wholly by an adult but which may eventually be controlled by the courage of a child's imagination.

An examination of *In the Night Kitchen* may illustrate his Blakean view of childhood a little further. The dream world presented is a bewildering one, and tumbling through it is Mickey, full of rage and frustration at his exclusion from the adult world. While lying in his bedroom, his rage wells up and his shout swamps the page. Instantly his adventures begin as he tumbles into dreamland, shedding his clothes as he passes the chandelier. Suddenly he appears as round and chubby, and somehow his naked body emphasizes his vulnerability. Just why he is so helpless becomes apparent on the next page when the bakers, whose eyes are closed and sightless, loom up obviously intending to bake Mickey (the blind forces of Urizen?). Throughout the tale, those closed eyes of the bakers and Mickey's own dreaming eyes seem to reinforce the absence of communication between the opposing characters. The bakers' activities swamp the next few pages; their self-satisfied grins dominate the pages. Eventually Mickey is able to again take control of the action and his bewildering environment by the power of his own imagination. The pictures become smaller as he creates an escape plan from the dough, suggesting quick, purposeful action. But when he is threatened by nonexistence, the bakers again loom up across the page as figures in a nightmare.

Mickey secures himself inside a milk bottle, floating like a baby in the womb. From here Mickey is able to provide the bakers with their milk, and he is free to leave—falling out of the dream in rather the same bewildering fashion that he fell into it. In sleep looking back on the experience, the "oh" of terror becomes the "ho" of recognized victory, then the "hum" of weariness and finally the "yum" of reaping his imaginative reward. On the final page he becomes, in his own mind at least, the victorious provisioner of our needs. But the battle has been an arduous one. Mickey's courage, and finally the superior powers of his imagination as he conjures up his methods of escape, have allowed him to foil the menaces that surround him. But they have been very extreme. He has been surrounded by menacing portents like jars that are labeled "Baby Syrup" and "Infant Food" with pictures of plaintive children on the outside. The terror of the experience seems to be aggravated by Mickey's failure to communicate with these smug self-satisfied adults. Mickey must always act independently in order to protect himself. The fat gnomes bear little resemblance to real adults. But then, perhaps, the child's perception of an adult has similarly little relation to the adult's perception of himself.

Like Blake's children, Sendak's Mickey lives in a separate world of ingenuity, sensitivity, and sometimes delight. He is often vulnerable, subjected to fear and pain, but his courage and his persistent imagination finally defeat the self-obsessed adult world. For all the terrors Mickey encounters, the book remains amusing and ingenious; just as the world of Innocence, for all its portents of sorrow, is one of peace and love. Sendak's trust in the ability of the childhood imagination to ultimately accommodate the terrors of experience is obvious.

Sendak's books, unlike many contemporary works for children, are not therapeutic in intent. They do not explain to the child how to imagine, what to imagine, how to reinterpret the adult world. They simply attempt to reflect and evoke the child's imaginative experience. Perhaps for this reason, children quickly identify with the protagonists and can easily act out plays about *Where the Wild Things Are* or what it is like to be Max or Mickey or Hector. Like Blake, Sendak has preferred to leap into the middle of the experience of childhood rather than to contemplate it from a nostalgic viewpoint. To place Sendak alongside Blake in the manner I have sketched in this paper is necessarily to ignore many of the evident influences upon his work. But it does, I believe, illuminate a central part of his genius. When we compare their visions of childhood in particular, we understand something of how Sendak's Max is a totally believable and fascinating child in his own right, in a way in which probably no other book child is. It demonstrates how, despite the brevity of the text in most of his books, so many complicated human experiences and emotions are evoked. It shows also that it is not simply technical superiority and slick promotion that make Sendak the most popular children's writer-illustrator of the 1960s and 1970s. Rather, it is the singular depth of perception of the nature of childhood experience which he possesses. In a very real sense he has emancipated the children's picture book. He has demonstrated that it may actually be about children, not just about loveable steam shovels or cute dogs or shapes—or even about the children we as adults want to remember or imagine. He presents the child as the Human Force Divine, in a very real Blakean sense.

Notes

1. N. Hentoff, "Among the wild things," in *Only Connect*, ed. S. Egoff et. al. (Oxford: Oxford University Press, 1969), p. 327. Quotations from Blake are

taken from *The Poetry and Prose of William Blake*, ed. David V. Erdman (New York: Doubleday, 1970). References to the "Songs of Innocence and Experience" are incorporated in the text and referred to as *Works*.

2. "On Receiving the Hans Christian Andersen Illustrator's Medal," *Top of the News*, XXVI (1970), 368, Hereafter cited as "Andersen."

3. "Questions to an Artist Who is Also an Author: a conversation between Maurice Sendak and Virginia Haviland." *US Lib. of Cong. Quart. J.*, XXVIII (1971), 273.

4. "Andersen," p. 366.

5. Hentoff, p. 329.

6. *Ibid.*

7. W. J. T. Mitchell, "Blake's Composite Art," in *Blake's Visionary Forms Dramatic*, ed. by David Erdman and J. E. Grant (Princeton, N.J.: Princeton University Press, 1970), p. 62.

8. "Questions to an Artist," p. 264.

9. Hentoff, p. 339.

10. *Ibid.*

11. "Questions to an Artist," p. 266.

12. *Ibid.*, p. 268.

13. Hentoff, p. 329.

14. *W. Wordsworth: Poetry and Prose*, ed. W.M. Merchant (London: Hart-Davis 1955), p. 551.

15. "Annotations to Wordsworth's *Poems*," *Works*, p. 655.

16. Hentoff, p. 344.

17. *Ibid.*, p. 329.

26

Harriet the Spy

Milestone, Masterpiece?

VIRGINIA L. WOLF

Many years after the publication of Louise Fitzhugh's *Harriet the Spy*, there remains considerable uneasiness about the novel's status as literature. Ms. Fitzhugh, who was also the author of a sequel, *The Long Secret* (Harper, 1965), and the co-author with Sandra Scoppettone of *Suzuki Beane* (Doubleday, 1961) and *Bang, Bang, You're Dead* (Harper, 1969), died on November 19, 1974. On the publication of HARRIET, she was called "one of the brightest talents of 1964"[1] Several short reviews praised the novel for its vigor and originality.[2] On the other hand, in the most extensive review which the book received, Ruth Hill Viguers objected strongly to its "disagreeable people and situations" and questioned its "realism" and its suitability for children.[3]

Today, now that many books are even more overt and harsh in their criticism of contemporary society, such objections are less common.[4] To my knowledge, critics have only briefly and rarely mentioned the novel in recent years. The only prize it has ever received is the Sequoyah Award in 1967, given by the children of Oklahoma. It has been a perennial bestseller for both Harper and Dell. It would seem that the novel survives principally because children are devoted to it. *The Arbuthnot Anthology* does recognize the novel as a milestone of children's literature, praising it as "contemporaneous" and implying that it is a forerunner of those more recent novels valuable for their immediate social relevance.[5] However, since no book ever survives for very long on the basis of its contemporaneousness, such praise is at best a dubious honor.

The novel can be read as social criticism. It is, on one level, an illuminating portrait of contemporary, urban, American life. Harriet's parents are so caught up in their own lives that they do not get to know their own daughter until she is eleven years old. The Robinsons sit in stony silence when alone together and come alive only when they have a chance to display their latest acquisition to a visitor. The Dei Santi family's preoccupation with their store prevents their understanding of one of their sons. The rich divorcee Agatha Plummer retreats to her bed in order to get attention. Harrison Withers lives alone in two rooms with his bird cages and his twenty some cats, trying to outwit the Health Department. The image which arises is one of a fast-paced, materialistic, complex society in which individuals are isolated in their own private worlds.

This isolation results in a failure of communication and consequently in a scarcity of meaningful human relationships. It results in a misunderstanding of unique individuals such as Harrison Withers and Harriet while it encourages conformity. Harriet's world is full of people who have no real understanding of their own special interests or abilities. This is especially evident of her classmates. Pinky Whitehead is a nonentity. Marion Hawthorne and Rachel Hennessey merely ape their mothers. In Harriet's words, "THEY ARE JUST BATS. HALF OF THEM DON'T EVEN HAVE A PROFESSION."[6] Living by means of pretense, the people of Harriet's world are afraid to hear or to seek the truth.

To read the novel as social criticism, however, is to see it in only one dimension. To read it as simply a socially relevant message is to ignore its structure. In its form, the novel is reminiscent of many contemporary adult novels which are constructed on the premise that reality is inevitably a matter of individual perception.[7] In such novels, our experience of the fictive world is structured by the point of view from which the novel is told. Perceiving, thinking, and feeling as one character does, we learn more about him or her than we do about the world which he or she describes. In other words, limiting us to Harriet's point of view, *Harriet the Spy* is fundamentally a thorough characterization of Harriet.[8] The enveloping point of view is, for the most part, third person, telling us what Harriet feels and thinks but emphasizing what she does, sees, and hears. The notebook entries, which are in the first person, record her actual language and reveal the content and thinking process of her mind. Each point of view enriches the other. The notebook entries reveal the limitations of Harriet's mind as a vehicle for understanding her world, and that which we see over her shoulder, as it were, fleshes out our understanding of the nature and sources of these limitations, allowing us to perceive both her and her world more fully than she does.

The previous description of contemporary society is not Harriet's. We obtain it by synthesizing bits and pieces of what we see by means of Harriet. Furthermore, this portrait of her world allows us insight into Harriet which she only gradually and then only intuitively possesses. We are allowed to see the extent to which this world has shaped and inhibited her. Harriet, too, is virtually isolated from intimacy with other people. This explains her need for window-peeping and writing in her notebooks. Given her environment, these activities are her only opportunities for self-discovery and growth. Imaginatively and ingeniously, she attempts to break out of her isolation, as a spy.

Harriet is, of course, unconscious of this way in which her environment has influenced her. As her notebook entries reveal, she understands herself on a much more superficial level. Ole Golly, her nurse, has given her faith in herself and an enthusiasm for knowing life and for finding her own way:

OLE GOLLY SAYS THERE IS AS MANY WAYS TO LIVE AS THERE ARE PEOPLE ON THE EARTH AND I SHOULDN'T GO ROUND WITH BLINDERS BUT SHOULD SEE EVERY WAY I CAN. THEN I'LL KNOW WHAT WAY I WANT TO LIVE AND NOT JUST LIVE LIKE MY FAMILY. (p. 32)

With naive self-confidence and extraordinary energy, Harriet attempts to follow this advice. Finding her sources of information limited, she sets up her spy route. So often puzzled by what she observes, she communicates her opinions and questions to a notebook, frequently with a notation such as "THINK ABOUT THAT" (p. 141). Her notebook entries reveal, on the one hand, that she is engaged in self-discovery, learning what she likes and dislikes in the process of honestly stating her responses to what she sees. On the other hand, they are a record of mind unfettered by sympathy and almost totally self-absorbed. Seen through Harriet, the world is no more than a spy-route, no more than a place and an opportunity for amusement and knowledge. Furthermore, in this role, Harriet is no more than a spy. She is an observer rather than a participant. While she is exposed to many different life styles, her experience is only vicarious. She can learn to be honest with herself, but she cannot learn to share. She can learn to evaluate but only to a lesser degree to empathize.

The key to the limitations of Harriet's quest for knowledge occurs very early in the novel with Ole Golly's quotation of a passage from Dostoievsky:

Love all God's creation, the whole and every grain of sand in it. Love every leaf, every ray of God's light. Love the animals, love the plants, love everything. If you love everything, you will perceive the divine mystery in things. Once you perceive it, you will begin to comprehend it better every day. And you will

come at last to love the whole world with an all-embracing love.
(pp. 22,24).

Harriet translates this in terms of her own egocentric experience of the
world: " 'I want to know everything, everything,' screeched Harriet suddenly, lying back and bouncing up and down on the bed. 'Everything in
the world, everything, everything' " (p. 24).

The novel portrays the process whereby Harriet begins to learn to
love. Her experience with life for eleven years has been almost totally self-
centered; it has been a process of imbibing rather than of giving. It is not
until she loses Ole Golly, her notebook, and finally her friends that she
is forced to give a little. Isolated and misunderstood, she is directly confronted with her need for people and by the demand to conform. At first,
she meets this demand head on, refusing to give an inch. She forces her
parents to find a way of understanding her, and she finally relents only
after Ole Golly's letter arrives. By the end of the novel, we must feel that
Harriet has moved closer to the human community and that she has done
so by accepting that "OLE GOLLY IS RIGHT. SOMETIMES YOU
HAVE TO LIE" (p. 297).

Many adults have been horrified by this piece of advice, yet quite
simply and straight-forwardly it states a fact of existence with which all
children must come to terms. Negative criticism, especially from a child,
usually evokes hostility, and children therefore learn to repress their disagreement and dislike. Unfortunately, in the process of doing so, many,
out of fear or guilt, lose touch with these feelings. Having done so, their
critical abilities and their trust in their own perceptions are, to varying
degrees, lost. They learn to conform, to accept the other person's perception. They become the boring and bored Marion Hawthornes and
Robinsons of this world. The beauty of Ole Golly's advice is that it does
not question Harriet's truth. It allows her to retain her own individual
identity.

Harriet's ability to empathize is still not fully developed at the end
of the novel. She is still to some extent locked in her own world. But she
has grown. She has learned how to be an onion; she has written a story
about Harrison Withers; and in the closing scene of the novel, she is able
to imagine what it is like to be Sport and Janie. "She made herself walk
in Sport's shoes, feeling the holes in his socks rub against his ankles. She
pretended she had an itchy nose when Janie put one abstracted hand up
to scratch. She felt what it would feel like to have freckles and yellow hair
like Janie, then funny ears and skinny shoulders like Sport" (p. 297).

The novel gives us the experience of Harriet's inner growth. Ultimately, then, it is psychological realism. Realizing this, we should be able

to understand why the charge that the novel lacks realism is false or, better, irrelevant.[9] The novel does not attempt to portray reality fully or journalistically. It is rooted in Harriet's experience, and that is a limited experience. If, then, characters seem like caricatures or types, this is justified. We can only experience them when and as Harriet does. The merits of this limited point of view result from the distortion it causes.

In addition to characterizing Harriet, this structural device is the source of the novel's criticism of contemporary urban American society. I do not mean to imply that Harriet is merely Ms. Fitzhugh's mouthpiece. As we have seen, Harriet is often incapable of understanding those whom she observes. Her judgments are simply her emotional reactions to particular individuals. It is not what Harriet says which is the source of our understanding. It is Harriet's quest, her attempt to observe as many ways of life as she can for the sake of finding her own way. Experiencing life with Harriet, we are repeatedly engaged in evaluating a vast range of people in terms of Harriet's likes and dislikes. This process sets up a pattern for us with Harriet as *our* standard of measurement. The sharp contrast between Harriet and her world implicitly criticizes the sterility and conformity which she encounters. Harriet's personality illustrates that happiness and creativity are the results of the freedom to be and to find oneself. Having had such freedom, Harriet is an individual.

To be sure, the novel does not exalt the American ideal of individuality as some kind of panacea. We are aware of the distorted perspective. Harriet is insensitive. Her invasion of others' privacy demonstrates the danger of extreme individualism as does the pain her friends feel on reading what she has written of them in her notebook. We feel the limits of this ideal most fully in Harriet's suffering after she loses Ole Golly, her friends, and her notebook. Her need for love and understanding is overwhelming, and her isolation is deadening. For the first time, she becomes bored with her own mind.

At this point, Harriet is helpless. She cannot see that she has done anything wrong and responds to her friends' abuse with a total lack of understanding: "I HAVE A FEELING THAT EVERYONE IN THIS SCHOOL IS INSANE" (p. 192). Her descriptions of her friends in her notebook are, from her point of view, merely the truth, written down for her own use and not for the sake of hurting them. Understanding Harriet, we can share her conviction that her friends are wrong. But we can also see vividly that the simple truth is not enough, that Harriet is trapped by her inability to understand other people's feelings. Without love, there is no way out of this situation. Someone has to give.

It becomes clear that *Harriet the Spy* is at its deepest level a celebration and an exploration of the nature and the development of love. Ole Golly's quotation from Dostoievsky is central to our understanding. In its portrait of Harriet, the novel allows us to see that self-love is rooted in self-discovery; love of others, in self-love; and knowledge of others, in love. Harriet's quest for self-discovery is the first stage. This is transcended and the second stage begun when she fully comprehends her need for understanding from others. Next comes her discovery that she can maintain her own sense of the truth (her integrity) without being insensitive to others. This allows her to give, and having given, she moves on to the final stage, a growing awareness of others. By the end of the novel, Harriet has learned "THAT SOME PEOPLE ARE ONE WAY AND SOME PEOPLE ARE ANOTHER AND THAT'S THAT" (p. 277). Less articulate than Dostoievsky, this is nevertheless Harriet's restatement of the heart of Ole Golly's quotation: "if you love everything, you will perceive the divine mystery in things" (p. 24).

We have not exhausted the novel's implications. These are rich and multiple. But this discussion suggests that the novel is more than the overt, simplistic social criticism of so many of the recent realistic novels for children. *Harriet the Spy* is not a message book. It is first and foremost an experience. On the primary level, we are immersed in Harriet and, by means of her, her world. The fusion of Harriet and her world is the source of the novel's richness. This structural device sets up a pattern of comparison and contrast which, on the symbolic level, achieves theme. In T. S. Eliot's words, we are given an "objective correlative," in Ezra Pound's, a "vortex." We are confronted with vivid, unforgettable images: that of a child looking into a series of rooms and those of a series of rooms in which people play out their private dramas, virtually unaware of the rest of the world. With the spy route superimposed on the spy, we get a dialectic radiating throughout the novel with one image reflecting, qualifying or opposing another.

Obviously, I believe that *Harriet the Spy* will survive. Harriet and her adventures are memorable. Like all good literature, the novel transcends the particular, evoking the inner spirit of a character and her world to explore eternal questions about love and happiness and truth. Significantly, the novel is not a fantasy like so many children's masterpieces. Perhaps this is revelatory of the mid-twentieth century. In any case, it is fortuitous for children's literature. Louise Fitzhugh has proven that contemporary, realistic fiction of psychological and philosophical depth is a viable possibility for children. *Harriet the Spy* is a milestone and a masterpiece of children's literature—perhaps *the* masterpiece of the mid-twentieth century.

Notes

1. Margaret F. O'Connell, "The Pick of the Racks," *The New York Times Book Review*, November 1967, p. 54.

2. For example, see *The Bulletin of the Center for Children's Books*, XVIII (1964), 53-54; *Library Journal*, LXXXIX (1964), 64; and *The New York Times Book Review*, February 25, 1968, p. 18.

3. "On Spies and Applesauce and Such," *The Hornbook*, XLI (1965), 74-75.

4. Nevertheless, in my part of the country (the midwest), such objections have been and continue to be the basis for censorship of the novel. It has been periodically removed from the shelves of school libraries, as recently as the spring of 1974, because adults have complained that children are imitating or might imitate Harriet's window-peeping.

5. May Hill Arbuthnot, Dorothy Broderick, Shelton L. Root, Jr., Mark Taylor, and Evelyn L. Wenzel, eds. (3rd ed.; Glenview, Illinois: Scott, Foresman, 1971), p. 1078.

6. (New York: Dell, 1964), p. 278; hereafter, references to this work will be cited parenthetically.

7. For example, Nabokov's *Pnin* or Barth's *The Floating Opera*; both highly complex novels play with distortions arising out of a single point of view.

8. See my article, "The Root and Measure of Realism," *Wilson Library Bulletin*, XLIV (1969), 409-15, for a more detailed study of Harriet's personality.

9. Sheila Egoff attempts to deal with this charge in "Precepts and Pleasures: Changing Emphasis in the Writing and Criticism of Children's Literature" in *Only Connect: Readings on Children's Literature*, ed. Sheila Egoff, G. T. Stubbs, and L.F.A. Ashley (Toronto: Oxford University Press, 1969), pp. 439-40; basically I agree with Ms. Egoff's opinion that the novel's realism is that of inner reality, but I do not agree that the author's approach "is best described as 'naturalistic' rather than 'realistic' " (p. 439).

Index

A Apple Pie. See Greenaway, Kate
Aesop, 2, 78–79, 132, 148–54
Alcott, Louisa May, ix, 2, 48, 191–
200; *Little Women*, 78, 191–200
Alger, Horatio, 48
Alice in Wonderland. See Carroll,
Lewis
Alonso, Joan Evans de, 229
American Tract Society, 84
Andersen, Hans Christian, 84, 138,
189; *Little Fir Tree*, 84; *Little
Match Girl*, 84; *Snow Queen*, 189;
Steadfast Tin Soldier, 84
Arbuthnot, (May Hill), x, xi, 265
Architects of Yiddishism. See Gold-
smith, Emanuel
At the Back of the North Wind. See
MacDonald, George
Auden, W. H., 85, 171
Authentic existence, 68
Avianus, 150

Babar. See Brunhoff, Jean de
Bacon, Sir Francis, 151–52
Ballantyne, R. M., 216
Barbauld, Mrs. (Letitia Aikin), 188
Barrie, Sir James M., 2, 81, 224–25;
Peter Pan, 3, 50, 215–26
Baum, L. Frank, 11, 19, 21, 23, 28,
30; *Land of Oz*, 22; *Ozma of Oz*,
19–20, 23, 28; *Road to Oz*, 22,
29; *Wizard of Oz*, 11, 28, 30–31,
49, 158
Beagle, Peter: *The Last Unicorn*, 49
Belfast. *See* Rope-skipping

Belgium. *See* Rope-skipping
Benjamin Bunny. See Potter, Beatrix
Black Beauty (Anna Sewell), 61
Blake, Kathleen, 215
Blake, William, 189, 260–61, 263–66;
"Garden of Love," 262; *Gates of
Paradise*, 263; "Nurse's Song,"
265; *Songs of Experience*, 260;
Songs of Innocence, 189, 260–63
Book Named the Governor. See Elyot,
Sir Thomas
Book of Games. See Greenaway, Kate
Brother Blue. *See* Hill, Dr. Hugh
Morgan
Browne, Frances, 202
Browning, Robert, 95, 188; *Pied
Piper*, 2, 92–98, 188
Brunhoff, Jean de: *Babar*, 23–25, 28,
30–31
Bunyan, John, 173; *Pilgrim's Progress*,
46, 78, 192
Burnett, Frances Hodgson, ix, 2, 47,
201–12; *Little Lord Fauntleroy*,
47, 201–12; *Little Princess*, 201,
204–6, 212; *One I Knew Best of
All*, 201; *Secret Garden*, 3, 47,
201, 204
Burroughs, Edgar Rice, 47
Butler, Francelia, 72, 113

Caldecott, Randolph, 187
Caldwell, Anne: *Origins of Psychopharmacology from CPZ to LSD*,
153
Carroll, Lewis (pseud. for Rev.

Charles Lutwidge Dodgson), ix, 2, 27, 47, 48, 85; *Alice in Wonderland*, 36, 49, 61, 80–81, 158
Caxton, William, 76, 150
Cech, John, 2, 125–46
Charlotte's Web. See White, E. B.
Chaucer, 150
Chesterton, G(ilbert) K(eith), 76, 160; "The Ethics of Elfland," 76
Children's Literature, 55–56, 58–59
Cid, The, 77
Cinderella, 203, 210–11
Cole, Sheila R., 80
Collodi, *See* Lorenzini, Carlo
Cooper, James Fenimore, 46
Coral Island. See Ballantyne, R. M.
Crews, Frederick C.: *Pooh Perplex*, 32
Croxall, Samuel, 152
Cruikshank, George, 183
Cutler, May, 1

Dame Wiggin of Lee and Her Seven Wonderful Cats. See Greenaway, Kate
Dealings with the Fairies. See MacDonald, George
DeAngulo, Jaime, 73
Death, 2, 67, 72–90
Defoe, Daniel, 46–47; *Robinson Crusoe*, 46–47, 215; Robinsonnade, 215
Dodgson, Rev. Charles Lutwidge. *See* Carroll, Lewis
Dominican Republic. *See* Rope-skipping
Dr. Doolittle. See Lofting, Hugh

Early American Children's Books. *See* Rosenbach, A. S. W. Catalog
Eliot, George, 31, 194
Eliot, T. S., 2, 99–112; "Bustopher Jones: The Cat About Town," 108; "Growltiger's Last Stand," 102; "Gus, The Theatre Cat," 107; 'Macavity: The Mystery Cat," 104–6; "Mr. Mistoffelees," 106; "Mungojerrie and Rumpel-steazer," 99; "Of the Awefull Battle of the Pekes and the Pollicles . . . ," 109; "Old Gumbie Cat," 100; *Old Possum's Book of Practical Cats*, 99–112; "Rum Tum Tugger," 100; "Skimble-shanks: The Railway Cat," 108; "Song of the Jellicles," 110
Elyot, Sir Thomas: *Book Named the Governor*, 151
England. *See* rope-skipping

Fabian group. *See* Nesbit, E.
Faerie Queene. See Spenser, Edmund
Fifty Works of English and American Literature We Could Do Without, 81
"Firebird," (Stravinsky), 76
Fitzhugh, Louise: *Harriet the Spy*, 2, 269–74
France. *See* Rope-skipping
France, Marie de, 150

Gagnon, Laurence, 1, 66–71
Gates of Paradise. See Blake, William
Georgics. See Virgil
German Popular Stories, 183
Germany. *See* Rope-skipping
Ginger and Pickles. See Potter, Beatrix
Goethe, Johann Wolfgang, 95
Goldilocks, 46
Goldsmith, Emanuel, 51
Goodrich, S(amuel) G. (pseud. Peter Parley), 47
Gower, John, 150
Grahame, Kenneth, 2, 207, 237–246; Alistair (son), 245; *Dream Days*, 237; *Golden Age*, 207, 237–38, 241; *Golden Key*, 2, 85–86; *Wind in the Willows*, 237–46
Granny's Wonderful Chair. See Browne, Frances
Gray, Effie. *See* Ruskin, John
Greece. *See* Rope-skipping
Greenaway, Kate, ix, 182–89; *A Apple Pie*, 187; *Book of Games*, 186; *Dame Wiggins of Lee and Her Seven Wonderful Cats*, 187; *Little Ann*, 186; *Marigold Garden*, 186; *Under the Window*, 184
Grimm brothers, 28, 64, 74, 95, 182–83
Gruelle, Johnny, 11–18; birth of, 12; as cartoonist, 12; marriage of, 13; daughter (Marcella), 13; *Raggedy Andy*, 14; *Raggedy Ann*, 1, 2, 11–17; *Raggedy Ann and Andy and*

the Camel with the Wrinkled Knees, 16; Raggedy Ann and the Paper Dragon, 17
Gulliver's Travels (Swift, Jonathan), 46

Happy Prince. See Wilde, Oscar
Harriet the Spy. See Fitzhugh, Louise
Hearn, Michael Patrick, 182
Heidegger, Martin, 66, 86
Heisig, Father James W., 2, 155
Hill, Dr. Hugh Morgan (Brother Blue), 2, 125–146; Ruth (wife), 141; King Lear, 126, 132; "Miss Wunderlich," 131–32; "Muddy Duddy," 142–44; "O Martin, O King," 133; "Once I Had a Brother," 129–30; Othello, 132, 139; "Ugly Duckling, Soul Brother Number One . . . ," 130–31
Hillman, James, 1, 7
Hispaniola, 220
Hobbit. See Tolkien, J. R. R.
Hodge, Marion C., 2, 99
Hollander, Ann, 191
Hooper, Rev. Walter, 247
Huckleberry Finn. See Twain, Mark
Hughes, Arthur, 171
Huizinga, 141
Hungary. See Rope-skipping
Hymns in Prose for Children. See Barbauld, Mrs. (Letitia Aikin)

Inauthentic existence, 69
In the Night Kitchen. See Sendak, Maurice
Italy. See Rope-skipping

Jacobs, Joseph, 149
Jacobs, Leland B.: Foreword, ix–xi
Janeway, James, Token for Children . . . Joyful Deaths of Several Young Children, 83
Japan. See Rope-skipping
Jemima Puddle-duck. See Potter, Beatrix
Johnny Town-mouse. See Potter, Beatrix
Joyce, James: Ulysses, 106
Jung (Karl), 8
"Juniper Tree," 74

Kay, Helen, 123
Kenny's Window. See Sendak, Maurice
King Alfred, 150
King of the Golden River. See Ruskin, John
Kingsley, Charles: Water-Babies, 78
Koppes, Phyllis Bixler, 201

La Fontaine, Jean de, 150
Lang, Andrew: Fairy Books, 75–76
Lanier, Sidney: Boy's King Arthur, 76
La Touche, Rose. See Ruskin, John
Lear, Edward, 80
Leatherstocking Tales. See Cooper, James Fenimore
L'Estrange, Sir Roger, 79, 149, 151–52
Lewis, C. S., 2, 63, 72, 85, 87, 171, 247–59; "On Three Ways of Writing for Chidren," 250; Narnia Chronicles, 2, 87, 247–59, including: Horse and His Boy, 249; Last Battle, 87, 249, 254, 256; Lion, the Witch, and the Wardrobe, 247, 249, 252, 258; Magician's Nephew, 249; Prince Caspian, 249; Silver Chair, 249, 253; Voyage of the Dawn Treader, 249, 252, 253–54
Life and Death. See Zim, Herbert and Sonia Bleeker
Light Princess. See MacDonald, George
Little Ann. See Greenaway, Kate
Little Fir Tree. See Andersen, Hans Christian
"Little girl that had no tongue." See MacDonald, George
Little Lord Fauntleroy. See Burnett, Frances Hodgson
Little Match Girl. See Andersen, Hans Christian
Little Pig Robinson. See Potter, Beatrix
Little Prince. See St. Exupéry, Antoine de
Little Princess. See Burnett, Frances Hodgson
Little Women. See Alcott, Louisa May
Locke, John, 79, 151, 261
Lofting, Hugh: Dr. Doolittle, 62
Lokator, 97

Lord of the Rings. See Tolkien, J. R. R.

Lorenzini, Carlo (pseud. Collodi): career of, 156–57; *Pinocchio*, 2, 155–70

Lurie, Alison, 225

Luxembourg. *See* Rope-skipping

Lydgate, (John), 150

Macbeth, 132

MacDonald, George, 2, 85, 171, 260; *At the Back of the North Wind*, 2, 85, 171–72, 184; *Dealings with the Fairies*, 171; "Giant's Heart," 173; *Light Princess*, 173; "little girl that had no tongue," 173–81; *Princess and Curdie*, 171; *Princess and the Goblin*, 2, 171; *Wise Woman*, 171

Macready, William C., Jr., 93

Marigold Garden. See Greenaway, Kate

Marryat, Frederick, 216; *Masterman Ready*, 47, 216

Mary Poppins. See Travers, P. L.

Masterman Ready. See Marryat, Frederick

Milne, A. A., 25–39, 63; *Autobiography*, 33–37; *House at Pooh Corner*, 38; *Winnie-the-Pooh*, 2, 25–28

Miner, Robert G., Jr., 148

Moore, Anne Carroll, ix, x

Morte d'Arthur, 76

Motif-Index of Folk Literature. See Thompson, Stith

Nakhman, Rabbi, 252

Narnia Chronicles. See Lewis, C. S.

Nesbit, E., ix, 2, 3, 61, 229–36, 249; Bland, Hubert (first husband), 229; Tucker, T. T. (second husband), 234–36; Fabian Group, 231; Well Hall (home), 2, 229–36; Miss Hoatson, 229; Wells, H. G., 231; *Phoenix and the Carpet*, 3; *Railway Children*, 3; Shaw, George Bernard, 231

Newbery, John, 72, 187

New York Times Book Review. See Cole, Sheila R.

New Zealand. *See* Rope-skipping

Nightingale and the Rose. See Wilde, Oscar

Odyssey, 242–43

Old Possum's Book of Practical Cats. See Eliot, T. S.

One I Knew Best of All. See Burnett, Frances Hodgson

Othello. See Hill, Dr. Hugh Morgan

Parley, Peter. *See* Goodrich, S(amuel) G.

Peter Pan. See Barrie, Sir James M.

Peter Rabbit. See Potter, Beatrix

Phaedrus, 150

Phalereus, Demetrius, 150

Phoenix and the Carpet. See Nesbit, E.

Picasso's World of Children. See Kay, Helen

Pie and the Patty-Pan. See Potter, Beatrix

Pied Piper. See Browning, Robert

Pilgrim's Progress, 46, 78, 192

Pinocchio. See Lorenzini, Carlo

Plato, 258

Pooh Perplex. See Crews, Frederick C.

Poss, Geraldine D. 237

Potter, Beatrix, 28, 39–44, 61; *Benjamin Bunny*, 43; *Ginger and Pickles*, 39; *Jemima Puddleduck*, 43; *Johnny Town-mouse*, 41–42; *Peter Rabbit*, 41–42; *Pie and the Patty-Pan*, 42; *Little Pig Robinson*, 40; *Roly Poly Pudding*, 42; *Squirrel Nutkin*, 41; *Tailor of Gloucester*, 43; *Tale of Mr. Tod*, 39–41; *Tale of Pigling Bland*, 40–41; *Tale of the Flopsy Bunnies*, 39–41; *Two Bad Mice*, 42

Princess and Curdie. See MacDonald, George

Princess and the Goblin. See MacDonald, George

Punch and Judy, 78

Puppets, 2

Pyle, Howard, 14, 77

Queenan, Bernard, 2, 92

Raggedy Andy. See Gruelle, Johnny

Raggedy Ann. See Gruelle, Johnny

Raggedy Ann and Andy and the Camel with the Wrinkled Knees. See Gruelle, Johnny

Raggedy Ann and the Paper Dragon. See Gruelle, Johnny

Raikes, Robert, 72

Railway Children. See Nesbit, E.

Richardson, Samuel, 153

Robin Hood, 77

Robinson Crusoe. See Defoe, Daniel

Roland, 77

Roly Poly Pudding. See Potter, Beatrix

Rope-skipping, 113–24; Belfast, 113–15, 118–20, 122; Belgium, 117; Dominican Republic, 122; England, 120; France, 115–18, 120–21; Germany, 117–18; Greece, 116, 122–23; Hungary, 120; Italy, 116, 121; Japan, 121; Luxembourg, 123–24; Scotland, 115; Spain, 120; Sweden, 120; Yugoslavia, 115; United States, 114, 117, 119, 120–21

Rosenbach, A. S. W. Catalog, 83

Rousseau, J(ean) J(acques), 47, 207. *Emile*, 47

Rumpelstiltzkin, 65

Ruskin, John, 3, 85, 182–89; Effie (wife), 183; La Touche, Rose, 183, 189; *King of the Golden River*, 183, 187

Sadler, Glenn Edward, 2, 171

Sale, Roger, 1, 19–31

Sandford and Merton (Thomas Day), 47

St. Exupéry, Antoine de, 86; *Little Prince*, 2, 66–68, 86

Secret Garden. See Burnett, Frances Hodgson

Seelye, John, 46

Selfish Giant. See Wilde, Oscar

Sendak, Maurice, 2, 49, 63, 260–67; *In the Night Kitchen*, 262, 264, 266; *Kenny's Window*, 265; *Where the Wild Things Are*, 262–64, 267

Scotland. *See* Rope-skipping

Shakespeare, 31

Shaw, Bernard. *See* Nesbit, E.

Sicroff, Seth, 39

Sidney, Sir Philip, 151–52

Singer, Isaac Bashevis, 51–57

Snow Queen. See Andersen, Hans Christian

Socrates, 149

Songs of Experience. See Blake, William

Songs of Innocence. See Blake, William

Southey, Robert: "Goldilocks," 46

Spain. *See* Rope-skipping

Spenser, Edmund, 31; *Faerie Queene*, 208

Squirrel Nutkin. See Potter, Beatrix

Stevenson, Robert Louis, 2, 215–16, 223; *Treasure Island*, 215, 217–18, 224, 226

Stowe, Harriet Beecher: *Uncle Tom's Cabin*, 84

Strewel Peter, 61

Sunday school literature, 72–73, 83

Sweden. *See* Rope-skipping

Swiss Family Robinson. See Wyss, Johann David

Symbolism, 53, 54, 257

Tailor of Gloucester. See Potter, Beatrix

Tale of Mr. Tod. See Potter, Beatrix

Tale of Pigling Bland. See Potter, Beatrix

Tale of the Flopsy Bunnies. See Potter Beatrix

Tarzan of the Apes. See Burroughs, Edgar Rice

Their Island Home.... See Verne, Jules

Thompson, Stith: *Motif-Index of Folk Literature*, 73

Thoreau, Henry David, 208

Token for Children ... Joyful Deaths of Several Young Children. See Janeway, James

Tolkien, J. R. R., 2, 49, 63, 84–85, 87, 247, 251–52; *Hobbit*, 84, 247; *Lord of the Rings*, 49, 247

Tom Sawyer. See Twain, Mark

Travers, P. L., 1, 58–65; *Mary Poppins*, 1, 58–60, 64

Treasure Island. See Stevenson, Robert Louis

Triumphant Deaths of Pious Children, 83

Tundra Books. *See* Cutler, May

Twain, Mark, 84, 207; *Huckleberry*

Finn, 46, 50, 207; *Tom Sawyer*, 84, 207
Two Bad Mice. See Potter, Beatrix

Ulysses. See Joyce, James
Uncle Tom's Cabin. See Stowe, Harriet Beecher
Under the Window. See Greenaway, Kate
United States. *See* Rope-skipping

Verne, Jules, ix, 216; *Their Island Home* . . . , 216
Virgil, 208, 210, 246; *Georgics*, 210

Waller, Jennifer R., 260
Wanley, Nathaniel: *Wonders of the Little World*, 93
Water-Babies. See Kingsley, Charles
Wells, H. G. *See* Nesbit, E.
White, Alison, 80
White, E. B., 66, 85; *Charlotte's Web*, 66–67, 69–71, 85

Wilde, Oscar, 47, 81–83; *Happy Prince*, 47, 82; *Selfish Giant*, 82; *Nightingale and the Rose*, 82–83
Wilder, Laura Ingalls, 63
Williams, Martin, 11
Wind in the Willows. See Grahame, Kenneth
Winnie-the-Pooh. See Milne, A. A.
Winters, Yvor: *Defense of Reason*, 102
Wise Woman. See MacDonald, George
Wizard of Oz. See Baum, L. Frank
Wolf, Virginia L., 269
Wonders of the Little World. See Wanley, Nathaniel
Wordsworth, William, 207–9, 263–64
Wyss, Johann David, 47, 216; *Swiss Family Robinson*, 216

Yugoslavia. *See* Rope-skipping

Zim, Herbert and Sonia Bleeker: *Life and Death*, 79